DISMEMBERMENTS

DISMEMBERMENTS

Perspectives in Forensic Anthropology and Legal Medicine

Edited by

ANN H. ROSS

Department of Biological Sciences, North Carolina State University, Raleigh, NC, United States

EUGÉNIA CUNHA

National Institute of legal Medicine and Forensic Sciences, Lisbon, Portugal
Centre for Functional Ecology, Department of Life Sciences, University of Coimbra, Coimbra, Portugal

ELSEVIER

ACADEMIC PRESS
An imprint of Elsevier

Academic Press is an imprint of Elsevier
125 London Wall, London EC2Y 5AS, United Kingdom
525 B Street, Suite 1650, San Diego, CA 92101, United States
50 Hampshire Street, 5th Floor, Cambridge, MA 02139, United States
The Boulevard, Langford Lane, Kidlington, Oxford OX5 1GB, United Kingdom

Notices
Knowledge and best practice in this field are constantly changing. As new research and experience broaden our
understanding, changes in research methods, professional practices, or medical treatment may become necessary.

Practitioners and researchers must always rely on their own experience and knowledge in evaluating and using
any information, methods, compounds, or experiments described herein. In using such information or methods
they should be mindful of their own safety and the safety of others, including parties for whom they have a
professional responsibility.

To the fullest extent of the law, neither the Publisher nor the authors, contributors, or editors, assume any liability
for any injury and/or damage to persons or property as a matter of products liability, negligence or otherwise, or
from any use or operation of any methods, products, instructions, or ideas contained in the material herein.

British Library Cataloguing-in-Publication Data
A catalogue record for this book is available from the British Library

Library of Congress Cataloging-in-Publication Data
A catalog record for this book is available from the Library of Congress

ISBN: 978-0-12-811912-9

For Information on all Academic Press publications
visit our website at https://www.elsevier.com/books-and-journals

Working together
to grow libraries in
developing countries

www.elsevier.com • www.bookaid.org

Publisher: Stacy Masucci
Acquisition Editor: Elizabeth Brown
Editorial Project Manager: Tracy I. Tufaga
Production Project Manager: Vijayaraj Purushothaman
Cover Designer: Miles Hitchen

Typeset by MPS Limited, Chennai, India

Dedication

We dedicate this book to the victims in hopes that this work will assist practitioners with case resolution that will bring closure to the victims' families.

"Justice delayed is justice denied" —Sir William E. Gladstone

Contents

12. The Pattern of Violence and Aggression

ANN H. ROSS, ASHLEY HUMPHRIES
AND EUGENIA CUNHA

List of Contributors

Bradley J. Adams Office of Chief Medical Examiner, New York City, NY, United States

Alberto Amadasi LABANOF (Laboratory of forensic anthropology and odontology), Department of Biomedical Science for Health, University of Milan, Milan, Italy

Corinne N. Ambrosi Office of Chief Medical Examiner, New York City, NY, United States; Department of Forensic Medicine, New York University School of Medicine, New York City, NY, United States

Jen G. Atkins Laboratory for Human Craniofacial and Skeletal Identification (HuCS-ID Lab), School of Biomedical Sciences, The University of Queensland, Brisbane, QLD, Australia; Gross Anatomy Facility, School of Biomedical Sciences, The University of Queensland, Brisbane, QLD, Australia

Desiré Brits Human Variation and Identification Research Unit (HVIRU), School of Anatomical Sciences, University of the Witwatersrand, Johannesburg, South Africa

Jodi M. Caple Laboratory for Human Craniofacial and Skeletal Identification (HuCS-ID Lab), School of Biomedical Sciences, The University of Queensland, Brisbane, QLD, Australia; Gross Anatomy Facility, School of Biomedical Sciences, The University of Queensland, Brisbane, QLD, Australia

Annalisa Cappella LABANOF (Laboratory of forensic anthropology and odontology), Department of Biomedical Science for Health, University of Milan, Milan, Italy

Cristina Cattaneo LABANOF (Laboratory of forensic anthropology and odontology), Department of Biomedical Science for Health, University of Milan, Milan, Italy

Eugénia Cunha National Institute of Legal Medicine and Forensic Sciences, Lisbon, Portugal; Centre for Functional Ecology, Department of Life Sciences, University of Coimbra, Coimbra, Portugal

Tania Delabarde Forensic Institute of Paris, Paris, France

Aluisio Trindade Filho Civil Police Department of the Federal District, Brasilia, Brazil; Brazilian Association of Forensic Anthropology (ABRAF), Brasilia, Brazil

Wes Fisk Gross Anatomy Facility, School of Biomedical Sciences, The University of Queensland, Brisbane, QLD, Australia

Andrea Gentilomo Institute of Legal Medicine, University of Milan, Milan, Italy

Amanda R. Hale Department of Biological Sciences, North Carolina State University, Raleigh, NC, United States

Ashley Humphries Department of Biological Sciences, North Carolina State University, Raleigh, NC, United States

José Vicente Pachar Lucio Forensic Pathology, Medico Legal Institute of Panama, Republic of Panama

Bertrand Ludes Forensic Institute of Paris, Paris, France; Faculty of Medicine, University Paris-Descartes, Paris, France

Jeffrey J. Lynch Laboratory for Human Craniofacial and Skeletal Identification (HuCS-ID Lab), School of Biomedical Sciences, The University of Queensland, Brisbane, QLD, Australia

Marcos Paulo Salles Machado Brazilian Association of Forensic Anthropology (ABRAF), Brasilia, Brazil; Civil Police Department of Rio de Janeiro, Rio de Janeiro, Brazil

Debora Mazzarelli LABANOF (Laboratory of forensic anthropology and odontology), Department of Biomedical Science for Health, University of Milan, Milan, Italy

Brandon Meikle Laboratory for Human Craniofacial and Skeletal Identification (HuCS-ID Lab), School of Biomedical Sciences, The University of Queensland, Brisbane, QLD, Australia

Caterina Oneto LABANOF (Laboratory of forensic anthropology and odontology), Department of Biomedical Science for Health, University of Milan, Milan, Italy

Deborah Radisch North Carolina Office of the Chief Medical Examiner, Raleigh, NC, United States

Christopher W. Rainwater Office of Chief Medical Examiner, New York City, NY, United States; Department of Anthropology, Center for the Study of Human Origins, New York University, New York City, NY, United States; New York Consortium in Evolutionary Primatology, New York City, NY, United States

Hadaluz Osorio Restrepo Research Group in Forensic Sciences, National Institute of Legal Medicine and Forensic Sciences, Bogotá D.C., Colombia

Ann H. Ross Department of Biological Sciences, North Carolina State University, Raleigh, NC, United States

César Sanabria-Medina Biomedical Sciences Research Group, School of Medicine, Universidad Antonio Nariño, Bogotá D.C., Colombia; National Group of Forensic Pathology, National Institute of Legal Medicine and Forensic Sciences, Bogotá D.C., Colombia; Research Group in Forensic Sciences, National Institute of Legal Medicine and Forensic Sciences, Bogotá D.C., Colombia

Carl N. Stephan Laboratory for Human Craniofacial and Skeletal Identification (HuCS-ID Lab), School of Biomedical Sciences, The University of Queensland, Brisbane, QLD, Australia

Maryna Steyn Human Variation and Identification Research Unit (HVIRU), School of Anatomical Sciences, University of the Witwatersrand, Johannesburg, South Africa

Criminal Dismemberments: A Discussion of Their Multidisciplinary Nature and Guide to Best Practice

Eugénia Cunha[1,2], Amanda R. Hale[3] and Ann H. Ross[3]

[1]National Institute of Legal Medicine and Forensic Sciences, Lisbon, Portugal [2]Centre for Functional Ecology, Department of Life Sciences, University of Coimbra, Coimbra, Portugal
[3]Department of Biological Sciences, North Carolina State University, Raleigh, NC, United States

Almost a decade after the National Academy of Sciences' published report, many forensic sciences are continuing to strive for best practice guidelines regarding the myriad of cases encountered globally. One particularly challenging area concerns criminal dismemberments and their relationship to motive and manner of death, both of which are vital to case resolution. One important fact that is evident throughout this text is that criminal dismemberments require a multidisciplinary approach to accurately ascertain the motivation and patterning that can aid practitioners in providing evidence to the authorities. Another emerging aspect is the crucial role forensic anthropologists can play in determining best practices for these types of cases. Thus, this volume was written to explore how practitioners currently approach these types of cases and to examine geographic or culturally specific patterns of dismemberment.

Twenty-eight years after Symes' (1992) introduction of dismemberments to forensic anthropological examination, we felt the need to provide and update the current methods utilized in various forensic laboratories globally and begin the discussion of guidelines for best practice. In conjunction, this book presents a concentrated overview to galvanize more relevant scientific investigations moving forward. In an era where forensic evidence must meet the demands of court admissibility, standardization is essential. From a more global standpoint, practitioners should also feel a duty to provide the most accurate assessments possible and use new cases to expand upon existing knowledge.

Notwithstanding the new, substantial book by Black and colleagues (2017), covering criminal dismemberments, we felt a more global perspective was still needed for two reasons. First, despite considerable research and literature on mutilation of the human body, there was a gap concerning the role of the forensic anthropologist in solving these cases. Second, the motivation of criminal dismemberment cannot be fully understood without a conscious understanding of its cultural role. Thus, the purpose of this volume was to have representation from various geographic regions including Europe, Africa, Australia, and the Americas. We are aware that this is not representative of the "world," but it is a broad view nonetheless. In the absence of a truly "global" presentation, we were able to amass two main groups among the geographic regions—those that represent more violent countries, such as South Africa, Brazil, Colombia, and much of Central America while the remaining five nations are representative of differentially driven and less frequent violence.

SOUTH AMERICA

In Chapter 2, Dismemberment of Victims in Colombia: A Perspective From Practice, Sanabria-Medina and Osorio Restrepo present a historical review of body mutilation and discuss criminal dismemberments in light of the Colombian armed conflict from 1980 to 2005 and its continued practice by "organized criminal gangs." They assert that while some authors declare dismemberment to be a rare occurrence, during the last three decades, Colombia has witnessed such unprecedented frequencies that physical spaces for diverse forms of mutilation are common. The discussion of the armed conflict dismemberments includes *terror technologies* and *terror as spectacle*. This illustrates the difference between individual psychoses involved in body mutilation and that of war crimes. Dismemberment by chainsaw was touted in witness recounts, but the bodies examined thus far have revealed no evidence of chainsaw marks—rather, high frequencies of sharp and blunt-force trauma have emerged, which are more consistent with machetes. More recent violence has been at the hands of paramilitary successor groups that have displaced thousands of Colombian residences and have established *casas de pique* that are specially designed to dismember victims. Since many methods of body mutilation have been discovered/recounted, the authors detail cut throat, decapitation, dismemberment, and quartering. They portend that correct interpretation of bone trauma allows for a more thorough reconstruction of the death. To assist investigators, the authors detail the proper interpretation and documentation of bone injuries. Considering the legal implications of torture versus disposal, a thorough understanding of the differences is paramount.

In Chapter 3, Dismemberment in Brazil: From Early Colonization to Present Days, Trindade Filho and Machado present both historical and contemporary cases from Brazil. Brazil represents one of the most violent countries in the world with frequent dismemberments reported. The authors assert that the reasons for dismemberment in Brazil can be religious or cultural in nature, intent of punishment and intimidation by the State, or a demonstration of power by criminal elements. In other forms, dismemberment has been performed to facilitate transport and concealment. The country has a long documented history of dismemberment recorded by the colonial Portuguese by indigenous populations and archaeological evidence suggests the even longer history of this practice. They present two historical cases that epitomize this practice: the dismemberment of separatist Tiradentes and more recently the Lampião gang in 1938. The authors then discuss the current statistics of dismemberment for some main cities, and then present five cases where different motivations for dismemberment were discerned.

CENTRAL AMERICA

In Chapter 4, Postmortem Criminal Mutilation in Panama, Pachar presents the most common types of criminal dismemberments observed in the Panamanian region. They also propose regional protocols for the approach and study of these cases. Cases where whole bodies were present were demographically young males with known gang affiliations. All showed signatures of homicide as manner of death. Throughout this chapter, Pachar discusses the use of dismemberment as a discursive, symbolic element within known narco-trafficking rings. This suggests that intentional homicide followed by mutilation and dismemberment is meant to communicate symbolically within the local communities. He suggests the addition of *mixed* and *indeterminate* dismemberment types to the classification system since fragmentation can serve more than one purpose simultaneously. They propose the development of interinstitutional standards could serve the medicolegal community more readily where local and regional authorities are still fragmentary in violent regions.

SOUTH AFRICA

In Chapter 5, Dismemberment in South Africa: Case Studies, Steyn and Brits present four unsolved cases, a common occurrence in South Africa. They present both traditional criminal dismemberments that are motivated by the need to transport or dispose of the body as well as hinder identifications. However, South Africa also encounters a widely practiced cultural purpose for dismemberment. "Muti" or medicine murders that are associated with traditional belief systems to harvest human body parts for medicinal treatment. While this practice is illegal, many traditional healers still make muti available either through the actual murder of individuals or sourcing remains from the dead and the living. This chapter places dismemberment in a wider perspective than those usually ordained. While the cases presented suggest that traditional motivations for dismemberment are found in South Africa, traditional belief systems contribute to much of this practice. Thus, the authors present a perspective that requires contextual information for case resolution. Unfortunately, the political and economic climate do not currently allow for much information that can aid in the identification of the victim(s) and perpetrator(s).

EUROPE

In Chapter 6, A Dismemberment Case From Portugal: How a Dozen Bones Can Tell the Story, Eugénia Cunha presents a case study involving the recovery of a partial skeleton

(6% of the remains) showing cut marks consistent with dismemberment. The case centers on a classic anthropological approach to unidentified remains and the more recent inclusion of trauma assessment. Careful attention to detail was required to differentiate marks made by scavengers and intentional marks made by the perpetrator(s). Following positive identification of the victim, uniform and linear cut marks were observed that were consistent with a form of sharp force trauma. Following current literature, the cut marks are interpreted to be consistent with sawing and scanning electron microscope (SEM) analysis was employed for a more detailed view. Careful examination of the pattern also allowed inference on body position and timing of injuries.

In Chapter 7, The Potential of Histological Analysis in Dismemberment Cases, Delabarde and Ludes explore the potential of histological analyses of bone and soft tissue around penetrating injuries. First, penetrating injuries are examined for the presence of exogenous particles. They outline the common procedures for bone histology with a focus on evaluating trauma. In addition, they discuss histochemical methods that aid in the detection of mineral components, such as iron, aluminum, lead, and copper. They present three cases from France.

Case 1 exhibited lower limb dismemberment consistent with postmortem removal. Using both stereomicroscopy and a variety of staining techniques, ferric residue was identified in the trabecular bone, lignin particles were demonstrated in the wound, and blue particles thought to be tool residue were present. During case resolution, it was discovered that the victim had been hidden below wooden pallets prior to dismemberment, and the implement recovered at the scene was a handsaw with both iron and blue paint components. Cases 2 and 3 are both criminal decapitation and the same analyses were able to confirm contextual crime scene findings even though both victims were in different states of presentation. In addition, iron sources resulting from hemorrhage and those from exogenous metal particles may be able to be distinguished increasing the value of these methods for case resolution.

In Chapter 8, Dismemberment and Toolmark Analysis on Bone: A Microscopic Analysis of the Walls of Cut Marks, Cattaneo and colleagues acknowledge the insufficiency of current research to the analysis of cut marks. However, they assert that the analysis itself can be fruitful for defining the class characteristics of the blade employed and can enable both forensic pathologists and anthropologists to discern class of weapon in some cases. They present a challenging case that involved the use of different tools during dismemberment, and they were left with insufficient information from the literature. Thus, the authors performed case-driven research to ascertain injury details to aid judicial authorities. Since autopsy findings were unable to provide information on the tools that caused the blunt injuries and dismemberment, anthropological analyses were undertaken. Anthropological analysis involved isolation of the injuries for microscopic analysis including scanning electron microscopy with energy dispersive X-ray spectroscopy (SEM-EDX) to detect possible metallic residues left by the blunt object. Dismemberment analysis included both macro- and microscopic investigation with steromicroscopy and SEM-EDX. The goal was twofold: (1) to provide a morphological and metric description and (2) highlight a chemical pattern that may indicate the presence of metallic residues that may be consistent with the presumed knives recovered. Following the protocol outlined, the team found all dismembered and sharp force injuries to be linked to each of the recovered weapons. Their careful and thorough approach emphasizes the multifaceted nature of these cases.

AUSTRALIA

In Chapter 9, Skeletal Evidence of Sharp-Force Disarticulation and Tissue Flensing in 54 Cases Exhibiting Approximately 4200 Bone Strike Injuries, Stephan and colleagues present a unique context for dismemberment, with 54 cases of historic medical teaching skeletons exhibiting extensive dismemberment practice. In conjunction, they present a new injury class, "edge-shear." This chapter is informative in terms of sources of large-scale exemplar injuries that can be used for educational purposes. The skeletal teaching collection at the University of Queensland is comprised of multiple individuals from the Calcutta Bone Trade with numerous markers of dismemberment by semiskilled individuals.

UNITED STATES OF AMERICA

In Chapter 10, Intentional Body Dismemberment Following Nonhomicidal Deaths: A Retrospective Study of Body Packer Cases in New York City, Adams and Rainwater detail two dismemberment cases that were deemed accidental. These cases involved two Hispanic individuals who were "body packers," or an individual who ingests packets of illicit drugs for the purpose of smuggling. The purpose of this chapter is to present a situation where dismemberment was employed for transport, disposal, or concealment purposes, but the manner of death was accidental. No clear pattern was discerned except that most cases did not involve transection of the torso or abdomen. Understanding the context of dismemberment is vital to interpreting manner of death.

In Chapter 11, Toolmark Identification on Bone: Best Practice, Ross and Radisch propose best practices for tool mark identification illustrated by three cases using digital microscopy. Namely, they detail the identification protocols used in tool mark comparisons in dismemberment and disarticulation cases from a forensic anthropological perspective. Or more accurately, what forensic anthropological analyses can reveal about dismemberment and disarticulation cases from initial findings through prosecution. In cases where there is not a suspected implement, only the class of tool can be assessed, whereas when there is a comparative tool from the crime scene to be compared, it is possible via microscopic methods to achieve correspondence. The authors recommend performing test marks with the suspected tool on the same type of skeletal element to account for cortical and trabecular bone composition. Because of the inherent subjectivity, Ross and Radisch recommend avoiding definitive statements such as this tool made this mark and to follow a series of sequential questions outlined in the chapter. This chapter is the first step in developing a specific protocol for tool mark examination on bone from a forensic anthropological perspective. The goal of this chapter is to provide guidelines to build best practice standards for tool mark examination as standardizing laboratory procedures should always be a central concern.

In Chapter 12, The Pattern of Violence and Aggression, Ross and colleagues present a summary of cross-cultural patterning in dismemberment cases and how these patterns can direct future research programs. This chapter illustrates the similarities and differences among countries employing a meta-analysis from published data. They illustrate the failure of current research to highlight trends found globally. This chapter recommends a systematic reporting of dismemberment and mutilation cases that can further aid in the development of best practice guidelines.

This volume clearly illustrates the necessity of hard tissue experts for the accurate identification of criminal dismemberment. As hard tissue experts, in cases where criminal dismemberment is suspected, a forensic anthropologist can be vital to case resolution. This book presents 11 chapters derived from several countries globally to offer both a geographic and cultural perspective to the motive and patterning of criminal dismemberments. It is our hope that this volume can provide practitioners with the information necessary to provide standards for the assessment of suspected injuries related to dismemberment and interpretation of perpetrator motivation.

Dismemberment of Victims in Colombia: A Perspective From Practice

César Sanabria-Medina[1,2,3] *and Hadaluz Osorio Restrepo*[3]

[1]Biomedical Sciences Research Group, School of Medicine, Universidad Antonio Nariño, Bogotá D.C., Colombia [2]National Group of Forensic Pathology, National Institute of Legal Medicine and Forensic Sciences, Bogotá D.C., Colombia [3]Research Group in Forensic Sciences, National Institute of Legal Medicine and Forensic Sciences, Bogotá D.C., Colombia

INTRODUCTION

Dismemberment is the result of a series of movements leading to separate one or more body parts (head or limbs) of a human body. Despite the fact that this action may also occur in the context of medical—surgical acts and as a consequence of different accidents and diseases, it is commonly associated with the perpetration of a criminal conduct whose main motivations are (1) to facilitate the transportation of the corpse, (2) to achieve its concealment, (3) to hinder the identification of the body (Symes, 1992; Symes et al., 2002), and (4) to prevent the authority from obtaining evidence that would serve to incriminate the perpetrator.

This chapter discusses different topics concerning the analysis, interpretation, and documentation of cases of dismembered bodies that are examined multidisciplinarily during the medicolegal autopsy, emphasizing the role of forensic anthropology, which is the discipline that among others, does the analysis and interpretation of bone trauma. In addition, the chapter presents information reported about this criminal practice in Colombia, which reached high levels during the internal armed conflict between 1980 and 2005. In 2012 the practice of dismemberment increased due to the actions of "organized criminal gangs" or BACRIM who adopted this practice reaching levels of concern, to the point of creating the so-called *casas de pique* or chop houses, which are physical spaces where victims are taken to be tortured, dismembered, and assassinated.

Dismemberments
DOI: https://doi.org/10.1016/B978-0-12-811912-9.00002-2

Furthermore, this chapter addresses the etymological discussion of some technical terms that are commonly used during the process of necropsy of bodies that present some type of intentional mutilation, such as cut throat, decapitation, dismemberment, and quartering.

BRIEF HISTORICAL ASPECTS OF DISMEMBERMENT, DECAPITATION, AND CUT THROAT

Throughout the history of civilizations and in virtually all continents, there are reported cases of victims who were dismembered, decapitated, or chopped. Perhaps the oldest cases of beheadings and cut throat are reported in the religious literature—although the literature does not establish a difference between the two terms. For example the Judeo-Christian Bible, mainly the Old Testament, indicates that representative characters, such as St. Paul and St. John the Baptist, as well as not so famous characters, such as Holofernes, Assyrian General of King Nebuchadnezzar (1125–1103 BC), were killed by this practice.

In the 16th century in Europe, Anne Boleyn and Catherine Howard, queens of England for short periods (1533–1536 and 1540–1542) were sentenced to beheading while they were the wives of Henry VIII. Towards the end of the 18th century the use of guillotine was frequent during the French Revolution and subsequent periods, where many illustrious and common citizens were sentenced to die in this manner.

Dismemberment was also incorporated as a war strategy in some pre-Hispanic societies. One example is mentioned by Andrushko et al. (2010), who reported its use in prehistoric central California, approximately 5000 years ago, from the early period (3000–500 BC) up to the late period (AD 900–1700). Authors report findings in the excavations including dismemberments and possession of instruments made of human bones used as trophies, which constituted an important part of war practices in tribes of central California.

In pre-Columbian Central America situations of dismemberment have also been reported, as it is the case of the *mexicas*, who after sacrificing their victims proceeded to their dismemberment, either for anthropophagical practices framed in ritual contexts, or with more "practical ends" as to build awls, spoons, and musical instruments (González, 1985).

In Colombia, during the wars of independence from Spain, there was a case of dismemberment that still remains in the collective memory of Colombian society, as the victim was a leader of the independence activities. It is the case of the process pursued against José Antonio Galán, captured and killed by the Spanish army in 1781. Following his decapitation and dismemberment, the army issued an order to send the dismembered body parts to different populations for its public exhibition (Acevedo, 2011).

In the historical context of dismemberments and decapitations it has been frequent the presence of at least one of the following three variables: (1) often, the victim occupied a leadership role either social, religious, or military; (2) the aim of the act was to punish some contravention committed by the victim; and (3) to produce terror in the population by the exhibition of the dismembered parts of the body to send a message of what could happen to whomever tried to go against the regime or tried to follow a criminal conduct.

The list of beheaded, cut throat, or dismembered peoples throughout history is very extensive and a good number of the well-known cases share the three mentioned variables. Dismemberment was a generally punitive practice pursued by governments, which granted it a legal character. Currently, no civilized society contemplates this practice in its legal ordering and it is considered a punishable conduct associated to homicide and torture.

In the context of contemporary criminality, there are a great number of cases reported either by the mass media or the scientific literature (see Konopka et al., 1991; Rajs et al., 1998; Ehrlich et al., 2000; Quatrehomme, 2007; Delabarde and Ludes, 2010; Porta et al., 2016, among others). For example, the summary executions via the decapitation or cut throat of victims performed by armed extremist organizations, such as ISIS and al-Qaeda are very well known in the world due to these groups' use of mass media, especially the internet, to broadcast their crimes.

Nowadays, dismemberment can be classified into the following contexts: (1) those associated to war crimes, (2) those associated to homicides by common or organized crime, and (3) those associated to homicides with psychiatric motivations.

DISMEMBERMENT IN COLOMBIA

Some authors indicate that dismemberment is rare and uncommon in forensic medicine (Di Nunno et al., 2006; Morcillo-Méndez and Campos, 2012; Porta et al., 2016). In spite of this, dismemberment is definitely not a "relatively rare method" in Colombia particularly in the last three decades, a period in which paramilitary groups used it frequently within their war practices, as well as new armed actors associated to organized crime who arose in the last 6 years, for example, the BACRIM or "organized criminal gangs." These actors have also implemented this macabre practice with unprecedented frequencies at the national and possibly international levels, with the aggravating circumstance of having created the so-called *casas de pique*, which are physical spaces where criminals take their victims to apply diverse types of torture and subsequent beheading, cut throat, dismemberment, or quartering, which ends with the death of the victims.

DISMEMBERMENT ATTRIBUTED TO PARAMILITARIES

The paramilitaries were actors who participated in the internal armed conflict between the early 1980s and late 2005. That year, a peace treaty was signed between them and the Colombian Government through the implementation of Law 975 of 2005, known as the "Justice and Peace Law."

Initially, the main objective of paramilitary groups was to fight guerrilla groups, however, and as often happens in almost all internal armed conflicts, large numbers of civilians became victims. As a result of the information provided by some paramilitaries who demobilized following Law 975 of 2005, authorities were able to locate large numbers of clandestine graves containing bodies or body parts of people killed by these actors. Additionally, after confessions of paramilitaries, society learned about the diversity of torture techniques, sexual violence, dismemberment practices, and other cruel and inhuman treatments applied by these groups. With the statements of paramilitaries following their disarmament it was also possible to acknowledge the existence of the "schools of death" in which perpetrators were trained to improve different dismemberment techniques, among other practices described later in this chapter (Quevedo-Hidalgo, 2008).

The modus operandi of guerrilla groups and paramilitaries began to differentiate from each other with the passage of time. The guerrillas, especially the Revolutionary Armed Forces of Colombia (FARC) and the National Liberation Army (ELN), began to increase the massive kidnaping of civilians, military personnel, and politicians; additionally, they carried out harassment acts against the civilian populations through terrorist attacks with bombs and gas pipettes. Guerrillas also perpetrated violent takeovers of entire municipalities and police stations, as well as attacks on electrical network stations, and destruction of public infrastructure, such as hospitals, health units, schools, etc. Another characteristic of Colombian guerrilla groups is their location: usually, the heads of the organizations are located in camps in the jungles, while an extensive network of urban militias extend in the peripheral centers of large cities (Arias-Quintero et al., 2011).

The paramilitaries were characterized by instilling terror in the civilian population through massacres, selective killings, forced disappearance of persons, torture, forced displacement, concealment of bodies of their victims in clandestine graves, and the rape of women, among other practices. Within their practices others include the public scorn of the victims, the use of hot iron to be introduced inside the victims' body, the application of salt in open wounds, hammering of the fingers, pulling out of the fingernails, suffocation with waterjets, and the use of tools like machetes and chainsaws to dismember or quarter victims (Memoria Histórica, 2008).

Returning to the topic of the "schools of death," the Colombian newspaper *El Tiempo*, in its special report "Colombia seeks 10,000 dead" (Sierra, 2007), presented the case of Francisco Villalba, a demobilized paramilitary and author of *La Masacre del Aro*, a massacre perpetrated in the municipality of Ituango, Department of Antioquia, who declared to justice how he was trained to dismember people:

> In the midst of 1994, I was sent to a course [...] where the training field was located [...] The victims were elderly people who were taken alive and tied in trucks [...] The instructor said to us: "You stand here and so-and-so stands there. This person should convey security to the one who's quartering... [...] The instructions ordered us to take their arms off, as well as the head, and to quarter them up alive. [Victims] came crying asking one to not kill them, saying that they had family. (Sierra, 2007)

Villalba describes the process: "People were being cut off from the chest to the stomach to remove the guts (viscera). Legs, arms, and head were then removed. Everything was done with a machete or a knife. The remaining organs (remnants of viscera), were pulled out with the hands. Us, who were in training, would take out the intestines." The bodies were then taken to mass graves, where it is calculated that more than 400 people were buried (Sierra, 2007).

In these "schools," practices were carried out with all kinds of tools: machetes, knives, and also chainsaws. As mentioned in the first report of the Group of Historical Memory of the CNRR (National Commission of Reparation and Reconciliation) (2008), the use of the chainsaw and the training on how to use it to perform the quartering of living persons are part of the *terror technologies* employed by paramilitaries in Colombia to instill fear in the communities using *terror as spectacle.*

So far, there are no official statistics about the number of victims dismembered by the paramilitary forces. However, official figures shown here refer to the number of bodies found in clandestine graves attributed to these groups between 2005[1] and 2017 (Fig. 2.1), which allow an approximate calculation on the frequency of such criminal conduct.

As illustrated in Fig. 2.1, the number of graves found during this process is 5276, in which 6744 bodies were found. The difference between these two numbers indicates that at least 1468 bodies (many of them with dismemberment signs) were found in collective graves, which hypothetical allows us to infer that the number of bodies dismembered by paramilitary groups could not be inferior to 1468. In fact, it must exceed this figure if we consider, for example, the report by the National Center of Historic Memory (CNMH) for only three Colombian departments, which states that *"identified mutilations are compatible with those of other 222 dismembered corpses that have been exhumed in the departments of Caquetá, Huila and Putumayo..."* (National Center of Historical Memory CNMH, 2014).

Additionally, the CNMH (2013) reported that between 1981 and 2012, 588 cases of deaths have been documented in the context of massacres or selective murders in which acts of cruelty took place and involved violent practices, such as cut throat, quartering, beheading, evisceration, castration, impalement, and burning with chemicals and blow-torches. Some of these practices were performed with chainsaw and machete. Of these acts of cruelty, 63% were attributed to paramilitary groups, 21.4% to unidentified armed groups, 9.7% to members of the public force, 5.1% to guerrillas, and 0.7% to paramilitary groups and security forces in joint actions.

Although the scenario about the figures of dismembered bodies is quite uncertain, more ambiguous is the number of bodies that are pending to be found, recovered, and examined in the context of medicolegal necropsies, because as mentioned by Sanabria-Medina and Osorio (2015), it seems that a large number of victims need yet to be recovered, and these numbers must be added to the aforementioned figures. According to different mass media sources, the total number of assassinated people is far from the 5909 bodies found so far, and certainly approaches numbers between 22,000 and 35,000 victims (Caracol Radio, 2012). The search for victims still continues despite the fact that many cases may have an uncertain end, since many bodies were thrown in the rivers, given to crocodiles (El Mundo Internacional, 2011; Verdad Abierta, 2011), or were incinerated in clandestine crematoriums (El Espectador, 2009).

DISMEMBERMENT WITH CHAINSAW

The use of the chainsaw in the Colombian armed conflict is first evidenced in the massacre that took place in the municipality of Trujillo, in the North of Valle del Cauca

[1]2005 is the year in which paramilitary groups ceased their belligerent actions due to an agreement with the Colombian government. Likewise, it is the year when forensic archeology techniques were applied in the search for clandestine graves and the recovery of bodies by authorities. The search continues to this day.

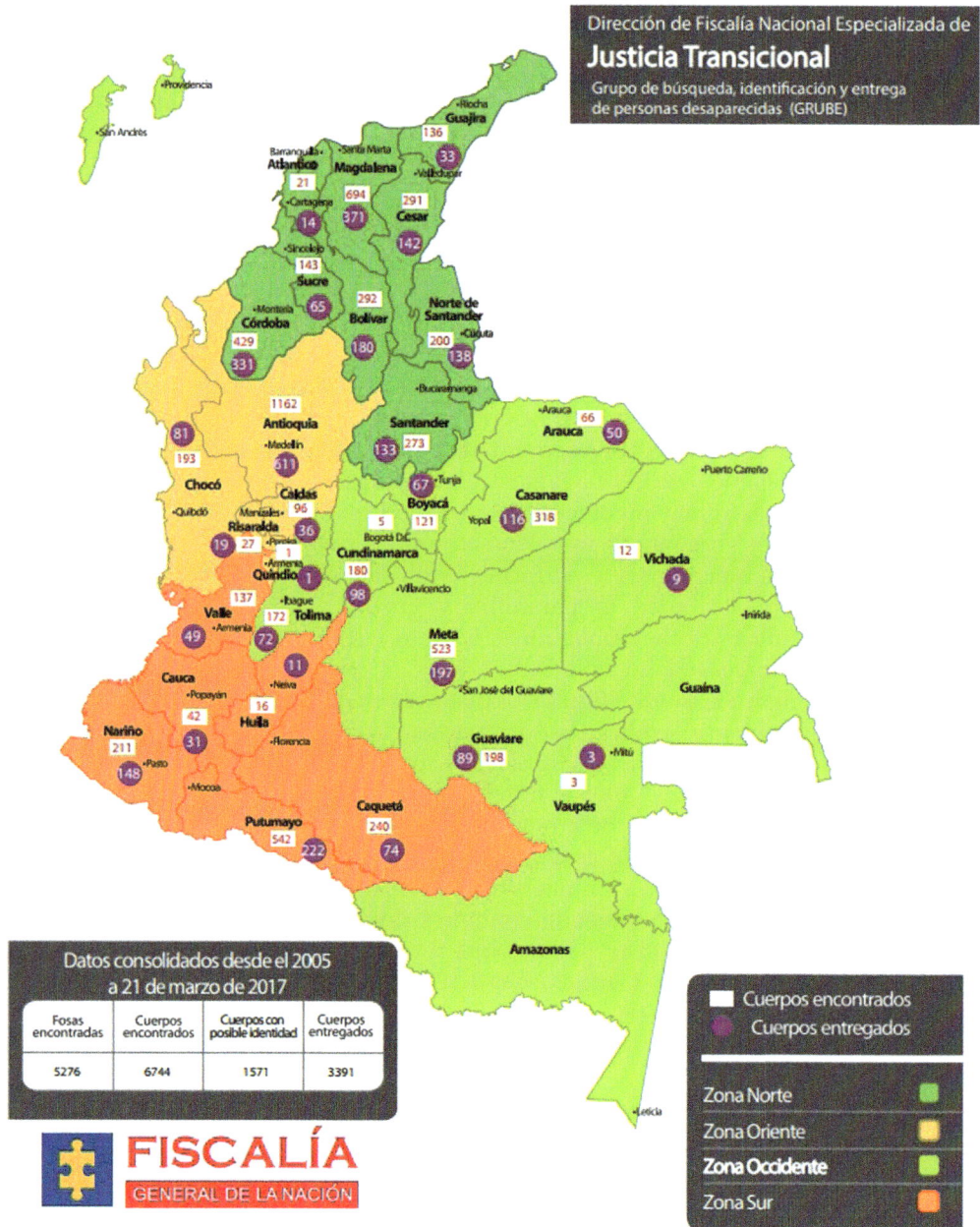

FIGURE 2.1   Geographical distribution of clandestine mass graves attributed to Colombian paramilitary groups. Source: From http://www.fiscalia.gov.co/jyp/wp-content/uploads/2017/03/mapa-de-colombia-2017-03-21-2.pdf. Consultation held March 22, 2017.

department. Between 1988 and 1994 this population suffered collective massacres, selective homicides, forced disappearances, as well as forced displacement of thousands of its residents (Arias-Quintero et al., 2011). The events that occurred between March 31 and April 1, 1990, in Trujillo are known as forced disappearances of "La Sonora," where 11 people were arrested, 1 was released, and the remaining 10 were subjected to torture. The report published by the Group of Historic Memory notes: "lastly, a chainsaw was used to dismember them alive and let them bleed. Heads and trunks were deposited in different sacks and then thrown into the waters of the Cauca River" (Grupo de Memoria Histórica, CNRR, 2008: 54).

Some of the cases of dismemberment with the use of chainsaw from which information is known due to journalistic investigations and confessions by demobilized paramilitaries were those executed by José David Velandia, also known as "Steven the quarterer." Velandia was characterized for including in his everyday conversations with close friends and other paramilitaries stories about the way in which he killed his victims: "First I place the chain saw on their neck and once they are lying on the floor I cut their arms and legs" (Sierra, 2007).

Another case in which the chainsaw was used to cause terror amongst civilian populations, was that of the Naya massacre, at the boundary between the departments of Valle del Cauca and Cauca, in the south of Colombia. Indigenous and black communities of farmers and fishermen mainly populate these regions. Around Easter 2001 a group of men from the *Bloque Calima* (Calima block) of the United Self-defense Forces of Colombia (AUC), under the command of José Éver Veloza, alias "HH," began the most bloody paramilitary incursion of the troubled history of the region. Although the Office of the Attorney General has recognized 30 assassinations, peasants of the region state that more than 100 victims resulted from the Naya massacre at the hands of around 400 paramilitary soldiers. A woman who managed to survive with her two children heard how the paramilitaries destroyed the restaurant and began the massacre: "*...I heard chainsaw noises,*" she said (Verdad Abierta, 2009).

One aspect that has caught the attention of Colombian medical examiners and forensic anthropologists who have had the opportunity to examine cases of dismembered corpses whose death is attributed to paramilitary groups is that despite the large number of accounts by former paramilitaries about the use of the chainsaw, the dismembered bodies recovered so far have presented no signs of such tool. Contrarily, in the vast majority we have found a high frequency of signs by sharp and blunt force mechanisms, mainly by the use of machetes. As an exception to this finding, the CNMH (2016) states in one of their investigations on the Colombian armed conflict that "*... on September 3rd, 2003, the bodies of the three Fonseca brothers were found inside the pit; [all] dismembered and burned with quicklime (...) Protocols emitted by Legal Medicine indicated that the weapons used were sharp and piercing* <u>*and a chainsaw was used for their dismemberment*</u>."

"NEW PARAMILITARIES" AND THE *CASAS DE PIQUE*: THE NEW SCENARIOS OF DISMEMBERMENTS IN COLOMBIA

As mentioned before in this chapter, paramilitary groups existed "officially" until 2005. However, various mass media sources have documented how some of these ex-combatants returned to their criminal activities through "successor paramilitary groups," among which are the so-called organized criminal gangs or BACRIM, the Autodefensas Gaitanistas and the Clan of the Gulf, among others.

These groups have a solid military apparatus, which includes a large number of combatants as well as weaponry. In addition, they have occupied territories that used to be controlled by paramilitaries and guerrillas. Intelligence actions by the government have established that there are strong ties between these "successor groups" and drug trafficking. This factor turns them into organized delinquency, which is not considered, or at least not officially, part of the internal armed conflict. The modus operandi of these groups is similar to the paramilitaries, that is, they are attributed cases of forced disappearance, forced displacement, torture, and homicides.

"Successor groups" have successfully colonized part of the rural territories previously occupied by the guerrillas and the former paramilitaries with the aim of gaining territorial control for drug trafficking. These groups have reached big cities like Medellín, in the department of Antioquia, and Buenaventura, in the department of Valle, in the southwest of Colombia.

Perhaps because of its privileged geographic location next to the Pacific Ocean, the city of Buenaventura is one of the most affected by the actions of these groups as it is highly strategic for national and international drug trafficking related activities. This city and its surroundings have seen the forced disappearance of many of its inhabitants, added to the macabre practice of torture, dismemberment, and other cruel and inhuman treatments.

The population of Buenaventura has historically suffered aberrant abuses perpetrated by members of left-wing guerrillas, paramilitary groups, and their successors. A former head of the United Self-defense Forces of Colombia (AUC) would have indicated to the Office of the Attorney General that his men killed more than 1000 people in Buenaventura between 2000 and 2015. The Revolutionary Armed Forces of Colombia (FARC) have committed murders, among other very serious crimes. The violence from all factions has led to widespread forced displacement: since 2000, an average of approximately 10,000 residents of Buenaventura, have fled from their homes each year, according to official figures (Human Rights Watch, 2014).

The paramilitary successor groups are responsible for the disappearance of a large number—possibly hundreds—of residents of Buenaventura over the past years. These groups quarter their victims and throw their remains to the bay or the mangroves that extend in its borders, or bury them in clandestine graves, according to residents' and officials' testimonies. Residents allege that *casas de pique* exist in several neighborhoods where groups dismember their victims. Several residents with whom Human Rights Watch spoke indicated that they have listened to people who screamed and begged for mercy while they were being dismembered alive. In March 2014, after judicial investigators found blood stains in two alleged *casas de pique* in the city, the police indicated that they identified several places where victims would have been dismembered alive before their remains were thrown into the sea (Human Rights Watch, 2014).

Between 2012 and 2014, dismembered human remains from at least 10 people were found in Buenaventura, many of whom appeared in the beaches and shores of the city as well as surrounding areas, as indicated by official testimonies and media articles. These macabre findings point to the existence of an apparently routine practice by "successor groups," which consists of dismembering people after forcibly disappearing them (Human Rights Watch, 2014).

The phenomenon of the so-called *casas de pique* has not been exclusive to the city of Buenaventura. In 2016, as part of the raids made by the authorities to a neighborhood in Bogotá known as "the Bronx" and recognized by the presence of activities related to drug trafficking, several houses were found with spots of blood in their floors and walls. Genetic profiling of this biological substance revealed that the blood belonged to different people.

ANALYSIS OF BONE TRAUMA ASSOCIATED TO CUT THROAT, DECAPITATION/BEHEADING, DISMEMBERMENT, AND QUARTERING

It is important that the forensic examiner (pathologist, medical examiner, or forensic anthropologist) is sure about the meaning of the terms *decapitation* or *beheaded*, *cut throat*, *dismemberment* and *quartering*, because even though all these can be done with the same tool and can coexist in the same body, the final result marks the difference between each of them:

Cut Throat

Cut throat is a cut on the anterior region of the neck; usually dissects anterior muscles, and can eventually touch the hyoid bone, the pharynx, the larynx, the esophagus, and a good part of the set of veins and arteries, without sectioning the cervical spine. The *head stays attached to the body by the spine*.

Decapitation or Beheaded

Decapitation or beheaded implies the cut throat described above plus the complete sectioning or cutting of the spine, which can occur by simple separation of the body parts through sharp force mechanism or blunt force mechanism with a sharp-edged tool. There might also be decapitation in other violent contexts such as traffic accidents, in which the cervical spine can be sectioned by tearing or crushing.

Dismemberment

Dismemberment refers to the separation of the upper or lower limbs using a sharp force mechanism or blunt force mechanism with a sharp-edged tool. It can also occur in other violent contexts by means of tearing or crushing.

Quartering

Quartering differs from the three previous terms in the sense that it is the "separation" of anatomical segments of any part of the body by sharp force or blunt force mechanism with a sharp-edged tool, or the combination of both, as it will be illustrated in the case presented in this chapter. The quartering may occur in other violent contexts, usually accidental, although in these cases the term per se is not used, as it is commonly associated to a criminal activity.

A correct analysis and interpretation of bone trauma enables the reconstruction of the events surrounding death as well as the search for evidence to establish circumstances of death.

Literature about dismemberment is rare and is often limited to case reports. The only systematic studies on this subject have been conducted by Symes et al. (1995) and Dirkmaat et al. (2008), whose observations on tool marks on bone are currently the main sources of information for forensic anthropologists (Porta et al., 2016).

Bone injuries by sharp force and blunt force mechanisms, which are often found in cases of dismemberment and decapitation, have been the object of scientific research, mainly in the field of forensic anthropology (Reichs, 1998; Humprey and Hutchinson, 2001; Di Nunno et al. 2006; Kimmerle and Baraybar, 2008; Symes et al., 2012; Porta et al., 2016), especially in experimental studies (Walker and Long, 1977; Symes et al., 1998, 2005; Arias-Quintero et al., 2011). Also, the improvements of the methodologies and protocols for the documentation of trauma by sharp force mechanism (Pijoan and Pastrana, 1987; Lewis, 2008; Marciniak, 2009) have broadened the perception, analysis, and forensic interpretation of this type of trauma. These studies have improved their results due to the systematic modernization of devices of analysis traditionally used to examine and document this type of alteration (microscopy, stereomicroscopy, digitization of cameras, among others), which allow the researcher to see what the human eye cannot.

BONE INJURIES BY SHARP FORCE AND BLUNT FORCE MECHANISM WITH SHARP-EDGED TOOL OR CORTO-CONTUNDENTE

Like other types of traumas, the analysis and interpretation of sharp force and blunt force trauma with a sharp-edged tool on bone is mainly based on the differential evaluation of the morphology of the bone defects and the associated fracture patterns. It is important to consider that these may vary according to the intrinsic biomechanical factors of the injured bone (type of structure involved, bone density, anatomic location injured, among others) and extrinsic factors, such as the type of tool used, how it was used, and the angle at which it hit the bone, among others (Guerrero, 2016).

Sharp force and blunt force trauma with a sharp-edged tool can lead to bone defects that will take the form of incisions, punctures, or cuts (Reichs, 1998; Kimmerle and Baraybar, 2008; Symes et al., 2012). The characteristic feature that any sharp-edged tool leaves on the bone has been named *kerf* in the literature. The *kerffloors* are defined as the point where the progress of the blade ends (Humprey and Hutchinson, 2001).

A hallmark of bone trauma by sharp force mechanism is that it is caused with a sharp-edged tool. Although a large number of objects can have these characteristics, Kimmerle and Baraybar (2008) propose two broad categories for their classification, which are particularly based on the size and weight of the item. These are: *short or long* and *light or heavy.*

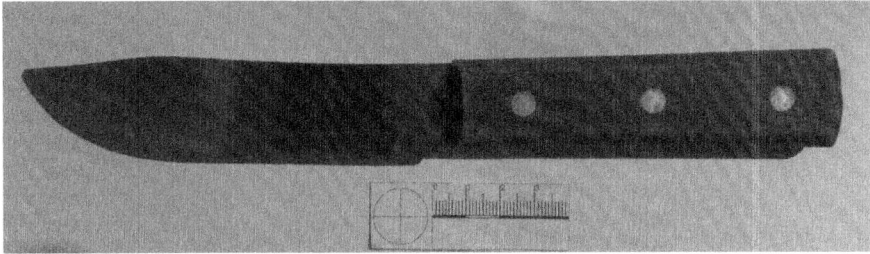

FIGURE 2.2   Kitchen knife. Note its main characteristics: (1) blunt upper edge, (2) sharp lower edge, (3) tipped termination. Source: *César Sanabria-Medina, National Group of Forensic Pathology, INMLCF, Bogotá D.C., Colombia; INMLCF, Bogotá D.C., Colombia.*

For example, all types of knives and other tools that can be used with one hand and whose main function is to cut or saw, which will mainly depend on the blade characteristics, are classified as *short* and *light* objects. Christensen et al. (2014) indicate that within this classification, knives can be cataloged under two general types, depending on the shape of the blade: *serrated* or *not serrated*. Functionally, these objects are not used as energy efficient vectors, that is, the force will mainly come from the weight of the aggressor and not the *momentum* generated by the oscillating movements of the tool (Kimmerle and Baraybar, 2008). Its main purpose is to cut through relatively soft materials.

Sharp and piercing tools usually have tipped terminated blades that are penetrating and sharp (Figs. 2.2 and 2.3) and an opposing thicker and unsharpened edge, which resembles a "V" on its transverse view (Reichs, 1998). Depending on how these tools are used, they usually generate bone alterations like incisions, punctures, and indentations. If the used blade was serrated (Figs. 2.4 and 2.5), it might produce identifiable striations in the wall of the cut, which is useful to determine its class characteristics (Guerrero, 2016) (Figs. 2.9–2.11).

Other tools that can be classified under the category of short and light are saws. Although at present these elements are fabricated under diverse specifications of sizes and shapes, as well as manual or mechanical, by definition a saw is simply a toothed or a serrated blade (Symes et al., 2012) (Figs. 2.4 and 2.5). In functional terms, saws are designed to cut into hard material, which is possible by the action of pulling, pushing, or turning the blade, manually or mechanically, generating the sliding and constant compression of its teeth on a surface. Generally, the arrangement of the teeth on the blade will prevent it from bending while in use. Thus, it will create a defect of greater width than the blade itself, and the transverse view of bone defects will resemble a "U" (Gibelli et al., 2012). On bone, saws typically cut the material by compression and subsequent removal of the tissue located in front of the blade's teeth, in the direction in which the blade is moving (Symes et al., 2012). A detailed analysis of the bone defects generated by the saw reveals important information about its class, which includes the type of blade, its thickness, shape, type, and spatial distribution of its teeth as well as the direction of the cut (Christensen et al., 2014).

In addition to the aforementioned classification, there are also long and heavy tools that include machete, axes, and swords, among others. These types of elements will allow to cut or chop a certain material using mainly the energy generated by its balancing in the

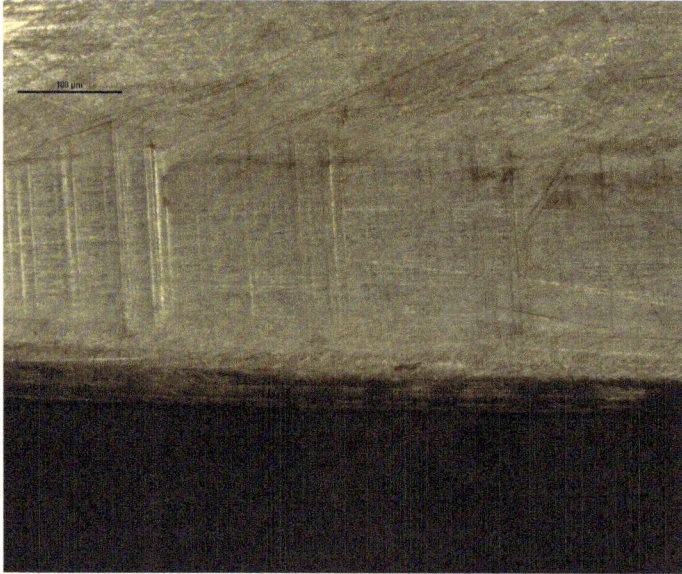

FIGURE 2.3   Detail of the lower lateral aspect of the common kitchen knife blade. Note the vertically oriented striations on the sharp edge of the blade. Source: *Juan Manuel Guerrero R., National Group of Forensic Pathology, INMLCF, Bogotá D.C., Colombia. Taken from Sanabria-Medina, C. (Ed.), 2016. Patología y antropología forense de la muerte: la investigación científico-judicial de la muerte y la tortura, desde las fosas clandestinas, hasta la audiencia pública, pp. 569–636. Forensic Publisher, Bogotá D.C.*

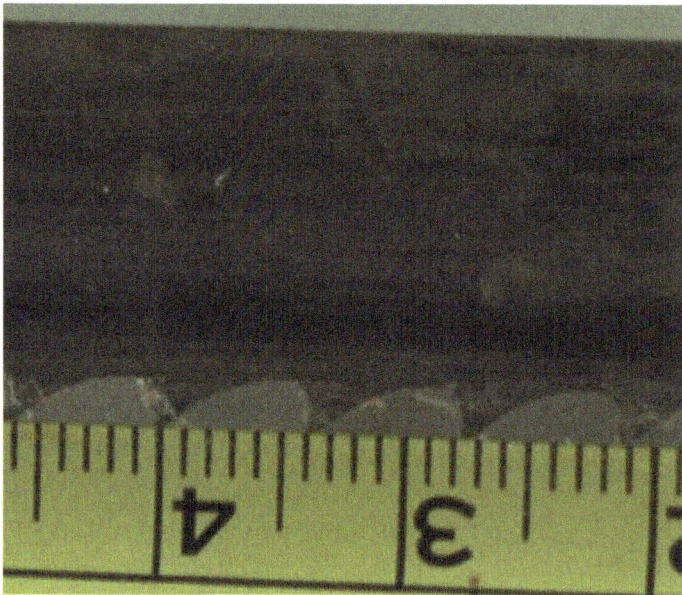

FIGURE 2.4   Detail of the inferior aspect of an endless saw blade (serrated tool). Source: *Taken with permission from Arias-Quintero, J.D., López-Tobón, Y.V., Pérez, T.P.D., 2011. Estudio experimental de marcas de corte en hueso producidas por dos agentes mecánicos: motosierra y sierra sinfín. Monografía de grado para optar al título de Antropólogo. Universidad de Antioquia, Facultad de Ciencias Sociales y Humanas, Departamento de Antropología, Medellín, Colombia.*

air or its *momentum*. According to this, bone defects generated by these elements usually consist of incisions or slicings that partially or completely segment the structure. Bone injured by these tools usually presents fragmentation(s) and/or associated fractures in the areas adjacent to the cut (Guerrero, 2016).

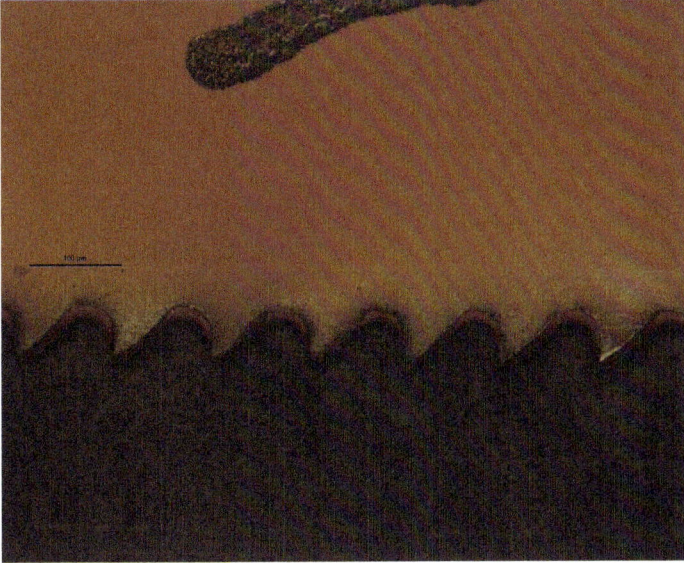

FIGURE 2.5 Detail of the lower lateral aspect of the blade of a hand saw (serrated tool). Source: *Juan Manuel Guerrero R., National Group of Forensic Pathology, INMLCF, Bogotá D.C., Colombia. Taken from Sanabria-Medina, C. (Ed.), 2016. Patología y antropología forense de la muerte: la investigación científico-judicial de la muerte y la tortura, desde las fosas clandestinas, hasta la audiencia pública, pp. 569–636. Forensic Publisher, Bogotá D.C.*

CLASSIFICATION OF SHARP FORCE WOUNDS

Bone defects generated by sharp force mechanisms will depend significantly on extrinsic factors, such as the type of tool used, its angle of impact on the bone, the aggressor's strength, as well as on intrinsic factors that respond to the biomechanical properties of the affected bone structure. Thus, there may be multiple systems to classify this type of trauma. Işcan and Steyn (2013) propose three simplified categories that are mainly based on the characteristics of bone alterations and the mechanics employed to generate the injury: (1) piercing and/or stabbing injuries, (2) incised injuries, (3) sharp or blunt force injuries generated with a sharp-edged tool, which are ultimately the typical lesions that are usually found in cases of decapitation and dismemberment, which are summarized by Guerrero (2016). Other specific types of sharp force trauma classifications can be found in Kimmerle and Baraybar (2008).

Piercing or Stabbing Wounds

These injuries typically occur when the tip of the tool impacts perpendicularly on the outer surface of a bone structure by a penetrating movement, creating defects that might reflect the shape, length, thickness, and approximate depth of the tool used. These types of trauma can be classified as sharp or cleft defects (Işcan and Steyn, 2013). Piercing and/or stabbing injuries are essentially blunt force trauma generated with a sharp element that has a tip (Symes et al. 2002). For example, a knife puncturing the skeletal tissue will show a conical or "V" shape on its transverse aspect, with smooth and sharp edges and vertical striations on its walls (Figs. 2.6 and 2.7). Generally, the skeletal alterations resulting from these tools are deeper rather than wider; the width of the defect will be the same as the blade,

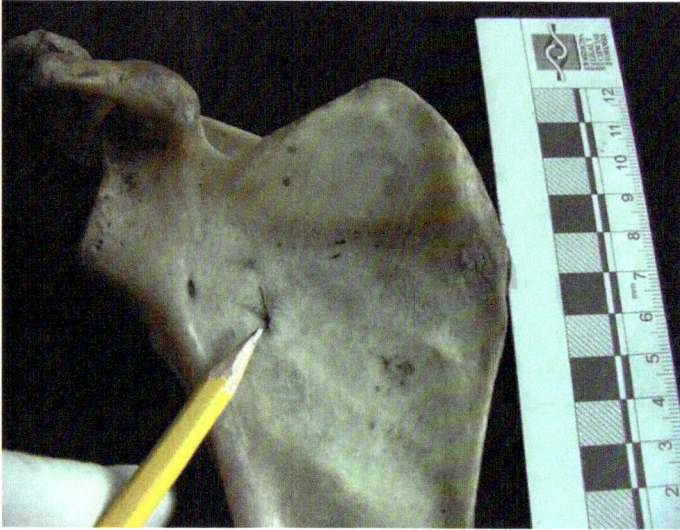

FIGURE 2.6 Anterior view of scapula with bone defect generated by sharp force (piercing) mechanism. Source: *César Sanabria-Medina, National Group of Forensic Pathology, INMLCF, Bogotá D.C., Colombia.*

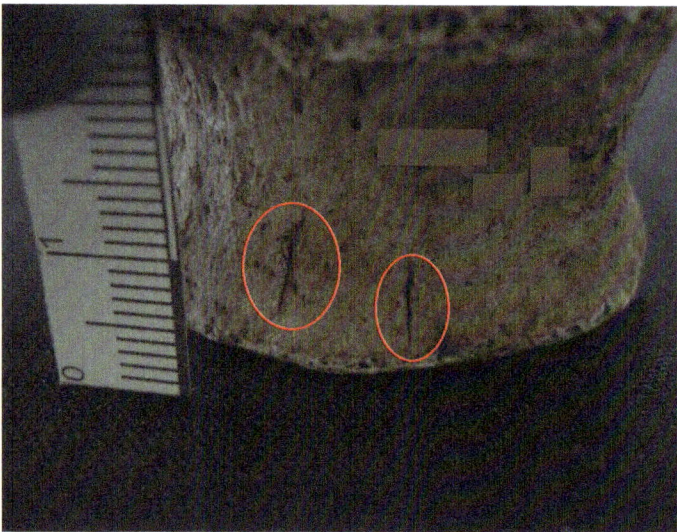

FIGURE 2.7 Anterior view of the body of lumbar vertebra. Note two defects generated by sharp force (piercing) mechanism. Source: *Mónica Chapetón, Forensic Anthropology Group, Regional Bogotá, INMLCF, Bogotá D.C., Colombia.*

and depending on the force used to injure, fractures or breaks may radiate away from the edges of the defect. Peripheral bone losses are not characteristic of this type of injury.

Incised Wounds

Their appearance has the form of linear striations that create discontinuity on the surface of the bone tissue, as a result of the transversal movement of a sharp-edged element (sharp or serrated). Generally, these wounds tend to be of greater length than width. It is common to find these kinds of superficial and shallow marks (false starts) in joints and adjacent areas. In cases of gutting and decapitation these are often found in the cervical spine. When incised alterations are generated by the use of a sharp-edged tool, the aspect on its transverse view will resemble a "V" (Fig. 2.8), whereas in the case of a serrated edge tool it will be "U" shaped (Fig. 2.9). The relative orientation of these defects will depend on the angle and direction of impact on the bone (Kimmerle and Baraybar, 2008).

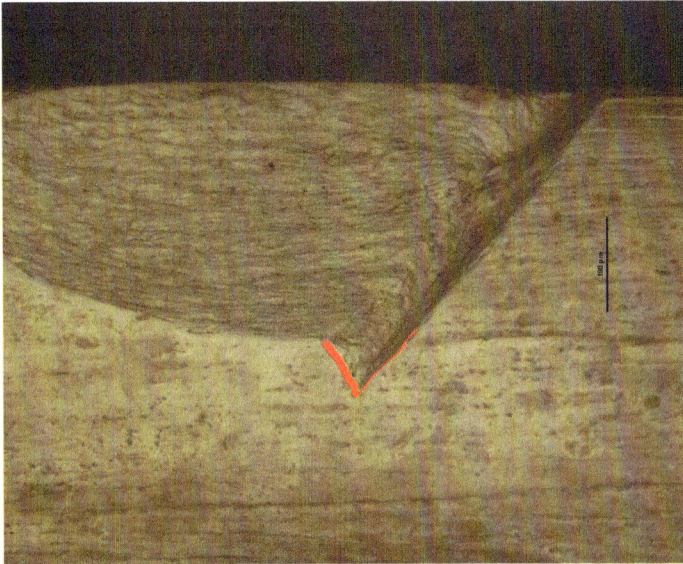

FIGURE 2.8 Detail of the anterior aspect of the left femur. Note the injury associated to blunt force mechanism with a sharp-edged tool. Notice the "V" shape of the defect and the associated bone loss. Source: *Juan Manuel Guerrero R., National Group of Forensic Pathology, INMLCF, Bogotá D.C., Colombia.*

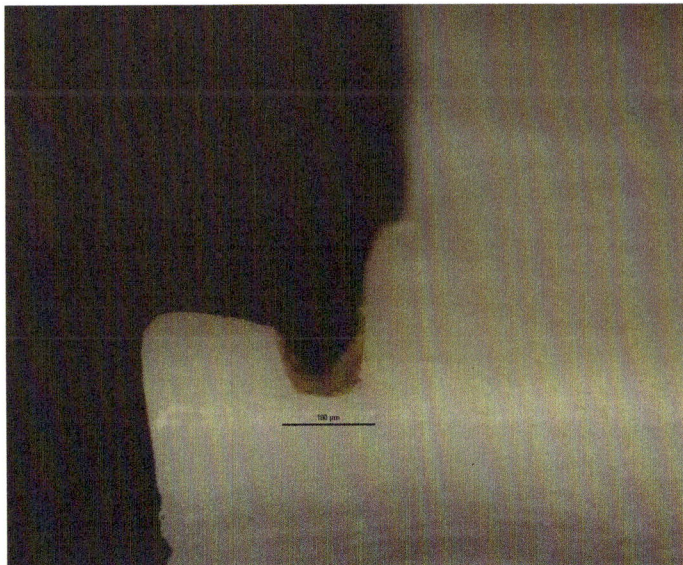

FIGURE 2.9 Detail of the anterior aspect of a left rib. Notice the kerf floor generated with a serrated blade. Notice the "U" shape of the defect. Source: *Juan Manuel Guerrero R., National Group of Forensic Pathology, INMLCF, Bogotá D.C., Colombia.*

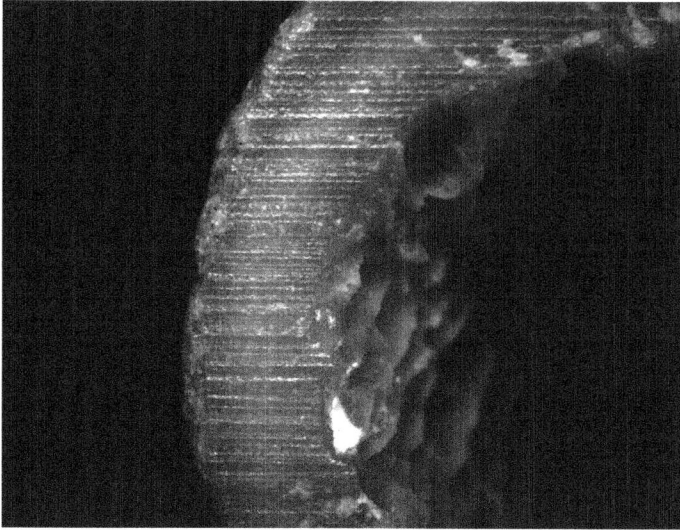

FIGURE 2.10 Detail of diaphyseal cut of a pig femur with endless saw (seen in Fig. 2.3). The photograph was taken with a stereomicroscope 20×, which displays the striations and allows the researcher to measure the spaces between them. Source: Taken from Arias-Quintero, J.D., Yury Viviana López, T.Y.V.Y., Pérez, T.P.D., 2011. Estudio experimental de marcas de corte en hueso producidas por dos agentes mecánicos: motosierra y sierra sinfín. Monografía de grado para optar al título de Antropólogo. Universidad de Antioquia, Facultad de Ciencias Sociales y Humanas, Departamento de Antropología, Medellín, Colombia, with permission of the authors.

An important aspect in the examination and interpretation of sharp injuries is the use of adequate equipment to magnify the image of a bone structure. For example, a stereomicroscope allows to observe in great detail the morphology of the floors and walls of the defect, besides other signs that might help establish the type of tool used (Figs. 2.10 and 2.11).

Slicing Wounds

These injuries result from the mechanical action generated by long or heavy tools with sharp edges, and/or a thick blade (blunt force mechanism with a sharp-edged tool), such as machetes, axes, and swords, among others. Its main function is to slice hard material, such as bone, through the efficient use of released energy during the momentum. Generally, this force exceeds the resistance capacity of bone, thus continuous or comminuted fractures may be produced.

According to Kimmerle and Baraybar (2008) and Symes et al. (2012), when the force generated by a heavy sharp tool is excessive, bone responds in a similar manner to that of a blunt force mechanism; this results in an injury that starts as an incised defect, and ends in a typical fracture associated to compression/tension mechanism. These types of defects are denominated in some Spanish-speaking countries as corto-contundente (sharp-blunt injuries). Depending on the type of tool used, the force generated, and the anatomical location of the trauma, these injuries may be accompanied by comminuted fractures and/or loss of bone tissue (Figs. 2.12—2.15).

INTERPRETATION AND DOCUMENTATION OF BONE INJURIES

During the medicolegal necropsy, part of the protocol requires an extensive documentation of trauma signs present in the body, in both soft and bone tissues, which includes

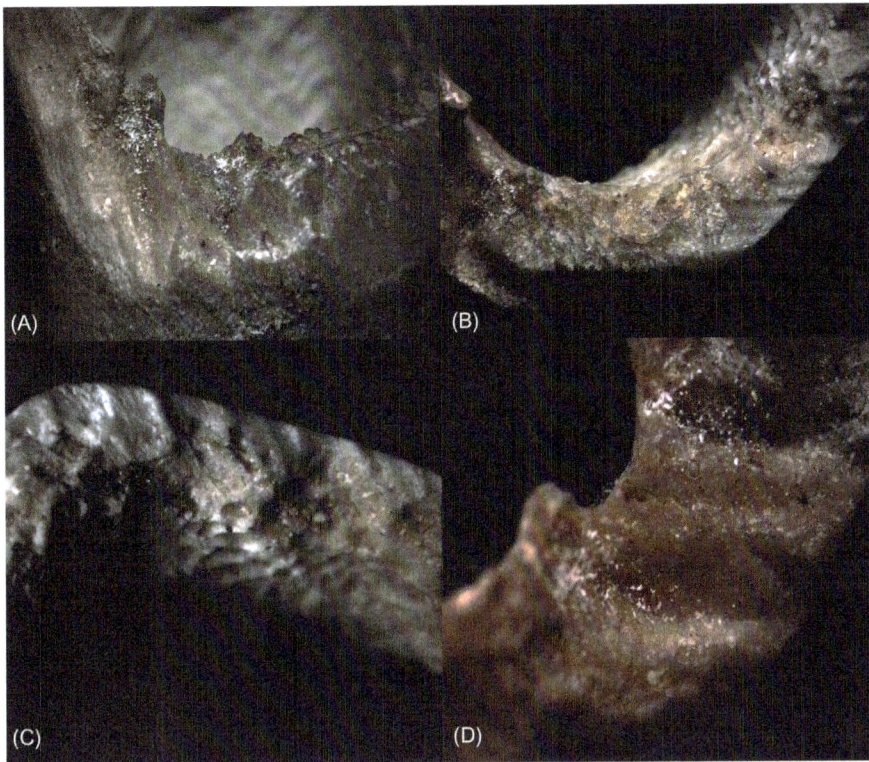

FIGURE 2.11 Details of walls of cuts on pig femurs with Stihl M250 chainsaw. The photographs were taken with stereomicroscope 20×. Microscopic surface level MS1-C2-S2. (A) Irregular edge; steep, with presence of notches. (B) Striated walls with wrinkled appearance. (C) Wall with striations. (D) Striations with remarkable distances between each other. Source: *Taken from Arias-Quintero, J.D., Yury Viviana López, T.Y.V.Y., Pérez, T.P.D., 2011. Estudio experimental de marcas de corte en hueso producidas por dos agentes mecánicos: motosierra y sierra sinfín. Monografía de grado para optar al título de Antropólogo. Universidad de Antioquia, Facultad de Ciencias Sociales y Humanas, Departamento de Antropología, Medellín, Colombia, with permission of the authors.*

multiple photographic and radiographic records, as well as the production of bone casts that display the analyzed injuries (Sanabria-Medina et al., 2016). These documentation procedures are of great importance in the context of death investigations, as they are part of the judicial investigation, and can be used as evidence to support or discard a criminal conduct.

In addition to the previous technical/scientific procedures that could be considered part of "routine," there is an additional one, not less important, which in addition to being useful to the judicial investigation; is also part of the prevention policies of this type of crime. It consists on the *systematized*, rigorous, and interdisciplinary *analysis* of some variables related to dismemberment, such as (1) the geographical location of the body or its parts, (2) the sex of the victim, (3) the biological age of the victim, (4) the ancestry of the victim, (5) the social and/or economic position of the victim and the occupation of the victim(in identified bodies), (6) the anatomical distribution and types of cuts, (7) the

FIGURE 2.12   Overview of proximal epiphysis of femur with trauma caused by blunt force mechanism with sharp-edged tool (machete). Source: *Juan Manuel Guerrero R., National Group of Forensic Pathology, INMLCF, Bogotá D.C., Colombia.*

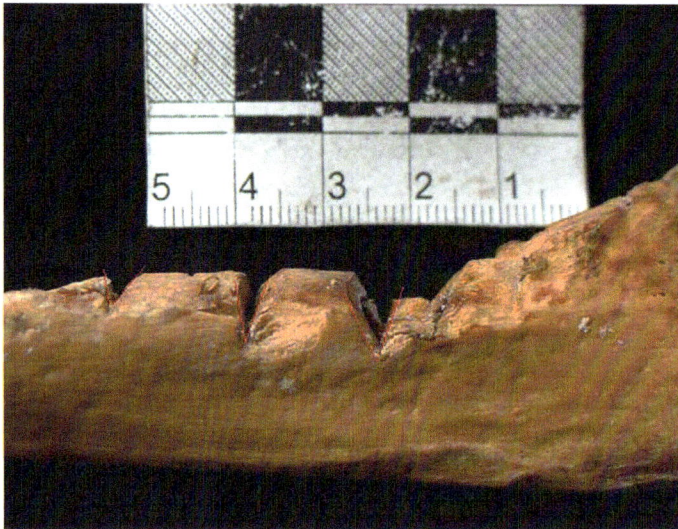

FIGURE 2.13   Panoramic of traumas by blunt force mechanism with sharp-edged tool in a distal portion of the humeral diaphysis (machete). Note the "V" shaped defects. Source: *César Sanabria-Medina, National Group of Forensic Pathology, INMLCF, Bogotá D.C., Colombia.*

mechanism used (sharp force or blunt force mechanism with a sharp-edged tool or the combination of both), and (8) the particular or individualizing characteristics (class characteristics) of the used tool, which usually leaves marks on the bone. Such variables are useful, for instance, to establish the modus operandi of the perpetrator(s), and may help to confirm or discard the uniprocedence of serial killings as well as to make comparisons with weapons or tools confiscated from suspects.

The interpretation of tool marks in bone tissue is of great value when it fulfills two requirements that are considered essential in the examination of bone trauma: (1) the actor

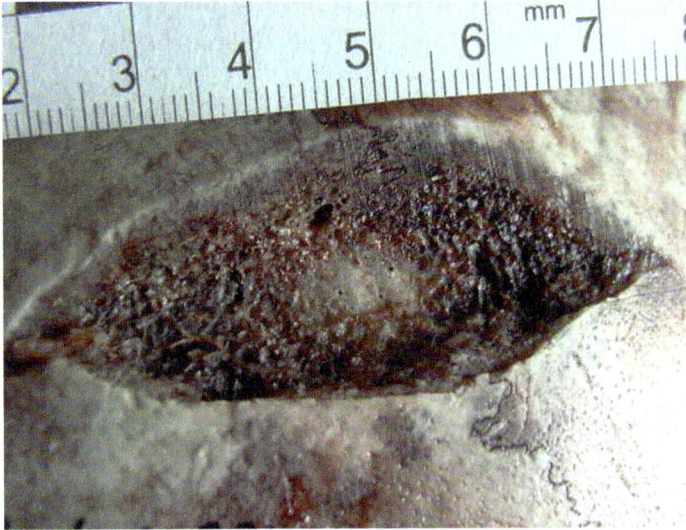

FIGURE 2.14 Slicing wound by blunt force mechanism with sharp-edged tool on the external surface of the skull with cortical exposure. The tool utilized was machete. Note the vertically oriented striations on the superior portion of the cut. Source: *César Sanabria-Medina, National Group of Forensic Pathology, INMLCF, Bogotá D.C., Colombia.*

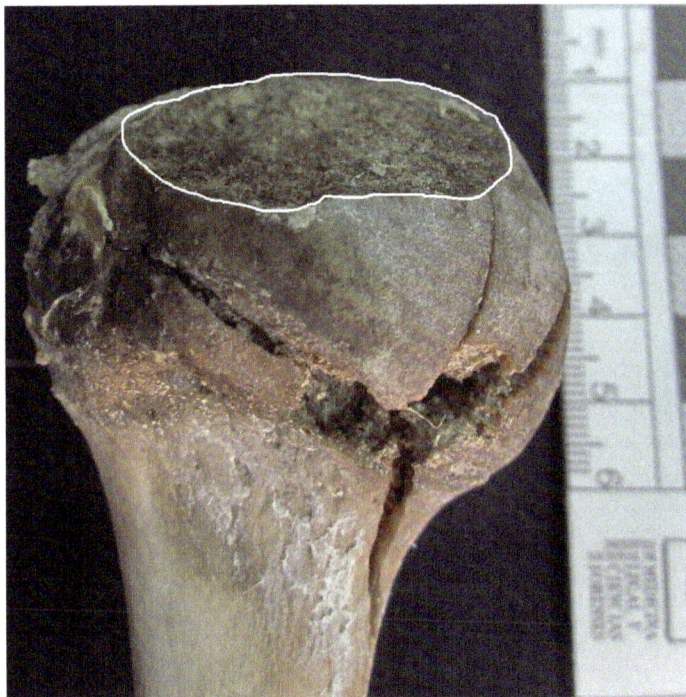

FIGURE 2.15 Slicing wound by blunt force mechanism with sharp-edged tool to the head of the humerus. Fractures radiate away from the wound in inferior and superior directions. Source: *César Sanabria-Medina, National Group of Forensic Pathology, INMLCF, Bogotá D.C., Colombia.*

must be identified accurately (if the bone marks are the product of human action versus animal bites and scratches) as well as the agent (knife, saw, etc.); (2) the interpretation contemplates a differential diagnosis (intentionally generated cut marks versus those produced by taphonomic agents either biological, physical, or chemical) and the distribution and recurrence of tool marks can be analyzed with high resolution equipment, for example, by using experimental models designed for these purposes (Blumenschine et al., 1996).

ON THE TEMPORALITY OF BONE TRAUMA ASSOCIATED WITH DISMEMBERMENT AND DECAPITATION

Due to the legal implications that these traumas may entail, for example, establishing torture signs or other cruel and inhumane treatment, a classic question from the authority is whether the injuries produced during decapitation, dismemberment, or quartering occurred while the victim was still alive or if he/she had already died. It is also of their interest that the chronological sequence of each cut can be established.

Forensic interpretation of trauma that affects bone tissues is a complex task in which the ideal analysis is performed from a hierarchical or multilevel perspective involving macroscopic and microscopic analysis. Microscopic analysis in particular, including histological, molecular, and atomic studies, not only reinforces and complements the information obtained from macroscopic findings, but also can provide data to the investigation that cannot be obtained through other methods (Crowder and Stout, 2012).

There seems to be a consensus on the fact that contemporary practices of dismemberment in criminal contexts occur in a postmortem period (Di Nunno et al., 2006; Cangrejo and Tejada, 2014; Konopka et al., 2007; Porta et al., 2016). Even in some pre-Columbian historical contexts, such as central California (3000−500 BC), it has been reported that this practice was performed after the victim had died in a war context (Andrushko et al., 2010).

Establishing with certain reliability the moment of occurrence or the temporality of bone trauma during dismemberment is perhaps one of the most complex demands in the medicolegal investigation of deaths, particularly because injuries occur systematically, one after the other, in intervals of time that generally do not exceed minutes or perhaps hours. This means that the changes that will occur in soft tissues and underlying bones are usually similar (hemorrhages, blood infiltrations in the bone, morphology of the cuts, fractures and fissures, among others). Thus, it is unlikely to find significant differences between one and the other, or to determine the sequence in which they occurred.

In cases of cut throat, decapitation or beheading, dismemberment, and quartering it is unusual and practically impossible to find typical vital reactions or signs (swelling, infection, reparation/remodeling, among others) different from hemorrhage. These vital reactions are more likely to be encountered in a victim who survives at least a few days to these types of trauma.

The diagnosis of the temporality of bone trauma is a scientific exercise whose assessment depends on several factors that require an interdisciplinary analysis that contemplates the joint evaluation of the available information, and the macro- and microscopic findings; more so when forensic practitioners are faced with skeletonized cases that show signs of dismemberment. According to Cattaneo et al. (2010), it is important that the study of the vitality of fractures in dry bone can be explored and performed from histopathological perspective.

At present, the macroscopic studies that forensic anthropologists conduct to determine the temporality of bone traumatisms have notable limitations, particularly in those cases in which the authority requires to establish if the trauma occurred while the individual was alive.

The diagnosis of the temporality or moment of occurrence of bone trauma may fall in the ground of uncertainty, even when microscopic studies are applied. For such reasons, from the forensic anthropology perspective it is possible to argue that trauma is clearly antemortem when signs of remodeling/repair/healing can be observed or postmortem, when there is evidence to establish that the organic content and humidity/moisture of bone have completely disappeared (Guerrero, 2016).

As different authors suggest, the term *perimortem* must be used by forensic anthropologists when referring to the taphonomic analysis—presence/absence of viscoelastic properties—of bone trauma and not to establish its temporality or moment of occurrence. This can be considered ambitious and certainly compromising, unless the case presents enough evidence to support temporality. An inaccurate diagnosis on the temporality of bone trauma can lead to insurmountable errors on the part of the authority when legal decisions are made, for example, to typify a trauma as torture when this was not the case, or worse, to emit a misdiagnosis that would lead to a mistaken legal decision when torture was in fact part of a case (Guerrero, 2016).

When the diagnosis is conclusively perimortem—in taphonomic terms—this implies that it must be based on the presumption that the trauma occurred when the bone still retained an organic matrix, totally or partially intact, and still had viscoelastic properties, but not because it occurred around the time of death. Conducting the analysis in terms of temporality of the injury may lead to biases that could be objected, particularly by peer counterparts in the context of trials or public hearings (Guerrero, 2016).

RECOMMENDATIONS FOR THE ANALYSIS, INTERPRETATION, AND DOCUMENTATION OF BONE TRAUMA BY SHARP FORCE OR BLUNT FORCE MECHANISM WITH A SHARP-EDGED TOOL IN CASES OF DISMEMBERMENT

Bone injuries by sharp force or blunt force mechanism with a sharp-edged tool are typical in cases of cut throat, decapitation or beheading, dismemberment, and quartering. Their correct analysis, interpretation, and documentation will be a key to establish the cause, manner, and mechanism of death, as well as the identification of the tool used and how it was manipulated, in addition to the number of events. Proper analysis, interpretation, and documentation of trauma will determine the success of the medicolegal necropsy in the judicial process.

For the abovementioned, the documentation and analysis of bone trauma associated to cases of dismemberment must be a process that provides clues to the death investigation. Additionally, it must be very rigid in the sense of following the protocols framed in existing manuals of best practices. As indicated by these manuals, statements that cannot be supported with physical evidence should be avoided (SWGANTH, 2011).

A CASE STUDY

This is the case of a 34-year-old peasant who left his farm to go to the village to buy some groceries. Since he did not return home, the next day, his relatives began the search and finally found his body lying next to a road. The corpse had the hands and feet tied, and presented macroscopic signs of cut throat, dismemberment, and quartering. After finding him, his relatives proceeded to bury his body in the courtyard of the house where they lived, without reporting what happened to the authorities. That is, without a medico-legal necropsy that could establish his identity, and the cause and manner of death.

By the time of the events (2001), the region had a strong influence of paramilitary groups, and the majority of forced disappearances perpetrated by these illegal groups were not reported to the authorities. As mentioned in the beginning of the chapter, once the paramilitary groups signed the peace treaty with the Colombian State (Law 975 of 2005), the process of searching for disappeared victims began. The present case corresponds to one of the almost 7000 bodies recovered between 2005 and 2017. Its location and subsequent necropsy occurred in 2012, 11 years after the peasant went missing.

Body Identification

The forensic identification process was achieved via genetic analysis by matching the victim's genetic profile with the biological samples of the presumed relatives.

Trauma Analysis

The analysis of the body established the presence of bone trauma compatible with *cut throat*, *dismemberment*, and *quartering* perpetrated with sharp force and blunt force mechanism with a heavy sharp-edged tool (Fig. 2.16), possibly machete. No additional injuries that could have suggested the use of other tools were found.

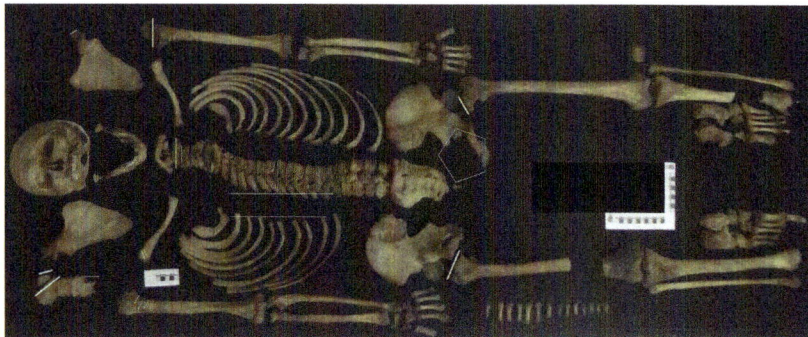

FIGURE 2.16   Skeleton examined during necropsy. Lines indicate areas with traumas.

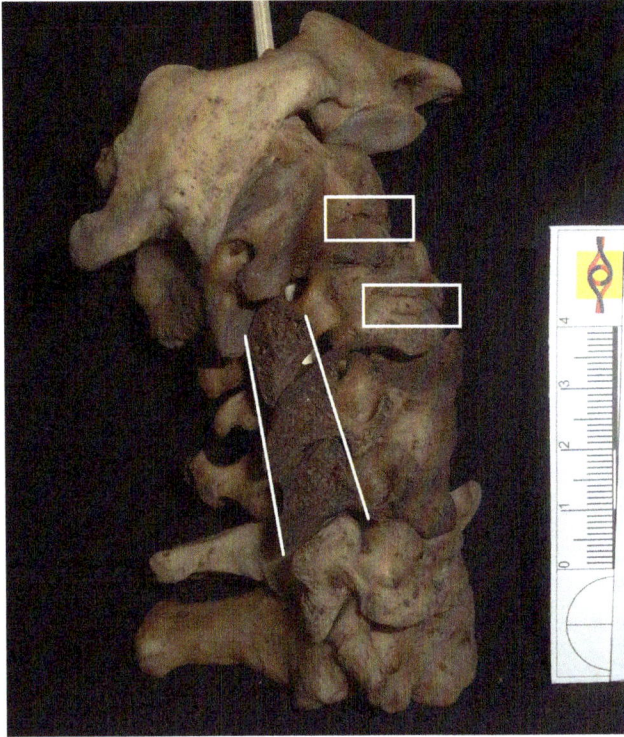

FIGURE 2.17 Rectangles enclose three deep horizontal cuts on the anterior surfaces of C2 and C3 related to the cut throat. Lines enclose bone losses by complete cuts in right transverse processes of C3, C4, and C5, not directly related to the cut throat.

Cut Throat

The presence of three deep horizontal cuts on the anterior surfaces of C2 and C3, (Fig. 2.17, rectangles) confirmed that the victim was cut throat; decapitation was dismissed because the cervical spine was articulated at the time of the analysis. Additional bone losses and cuts located on the cervical spine were found to be associated with other events unrelated to the cut throat, all of which will be presented later.

Dismemberment

The upper and lower limbs were separated from the body by the application of sharp force and blunt force mechanism with a heavy sharp-edged tool, possibly a machete.

Upper limbs: The upper left limb was separated at the level of proximal third of humerus in at least three events using blunt force mechanism with a heavy sharp-edged tool: the first cut sectioned the upper third of the acromion (Fig. 2.18) with a medial–lateral trajectory and a posterior–anterior direction; the other two are complete cuts corresponding to slicings that produced avulsion of the upper and midsection of the humeral head (Fig. 2.19). Probably, the upper third of the humeral head remained attached to the glenoid cavity of the scapula and separated during the process of decomposition of the body. Unlike the dismemberment observed in the upper left limb, the right was separated by

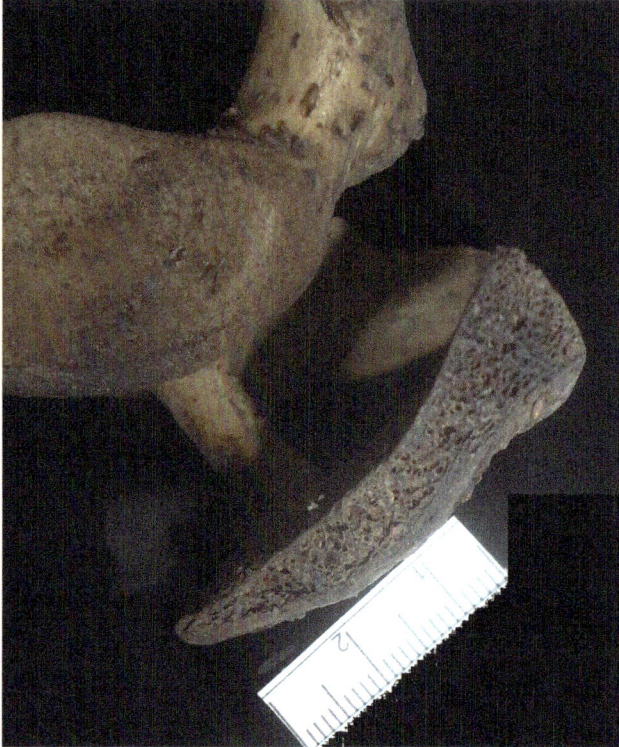

FIGURE 2.18   The upper left limb was separated at the level of proximal third of humerus in at least three events using blunt force mechanism with a heavy sharp-edged tool. First cut sectioned upper third of acromion.

FIGURE 2.19   Two complete transverse cuts produced avulsion of the upper and midsection of humeral head left.

sharp force mechanism only at the joint and surrounding areas at the proximal end of the humerus (Figs. 2.20 and 2.21) and the acromial portion of the right clavicle (Fig. 2.22). Several false starts observed are the result of some of the multiple cuts performed by the perpetrator to achieve the separation of the arm, which only sectioned soft tissues (skin, muscle, and tendons). The reason as to why the victimizer opted to use this mechanism to separate the arm is unknown, since it is clear that blunt force mechanism with a heavy sharp-edged tool demands less time investment. It was also impossible to establish with certainty which of the two arms was separated first. However, within the hypotheses

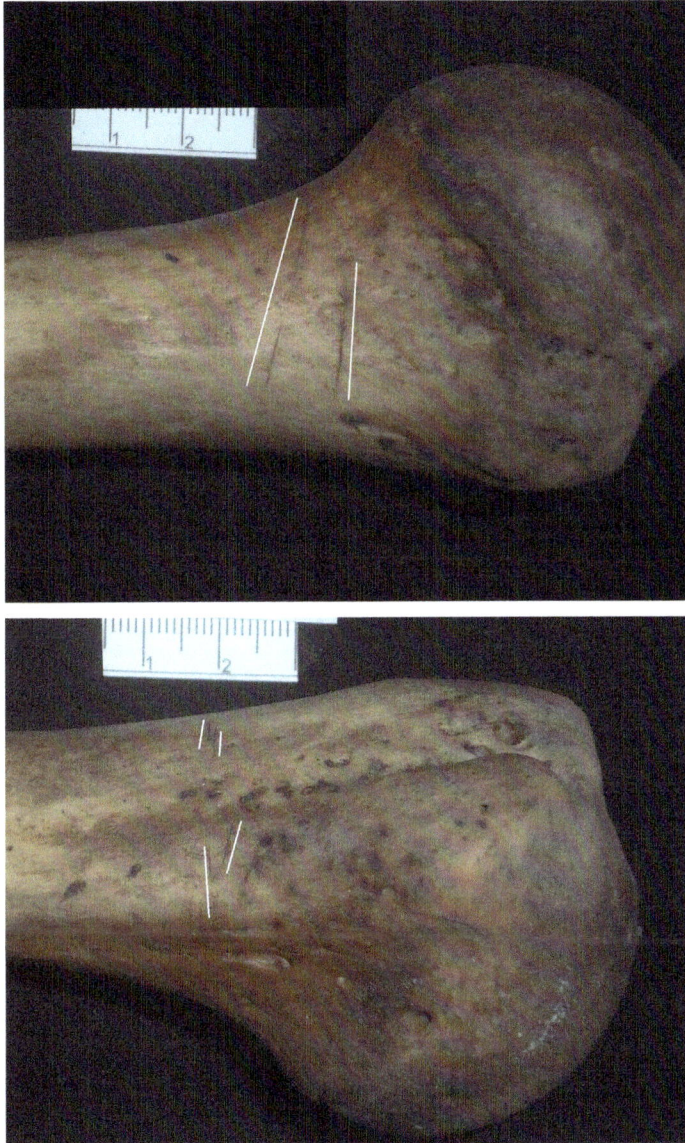

FIGURES 2.20, 2.21, AND 2.22 The upper right limb was separated by sharp force mechanism only at the joint and surrounding areas at the proximal end of the humerus.

discussed, it could be inferred that the first arm separated was the right because there, the perpetrator could have realized that the application of sharp force mechanism involves more effort and time, as opposed to the blunt force mechanism with a heavy sharp-edged tool, which is much more effective in terms of time and energy investment.

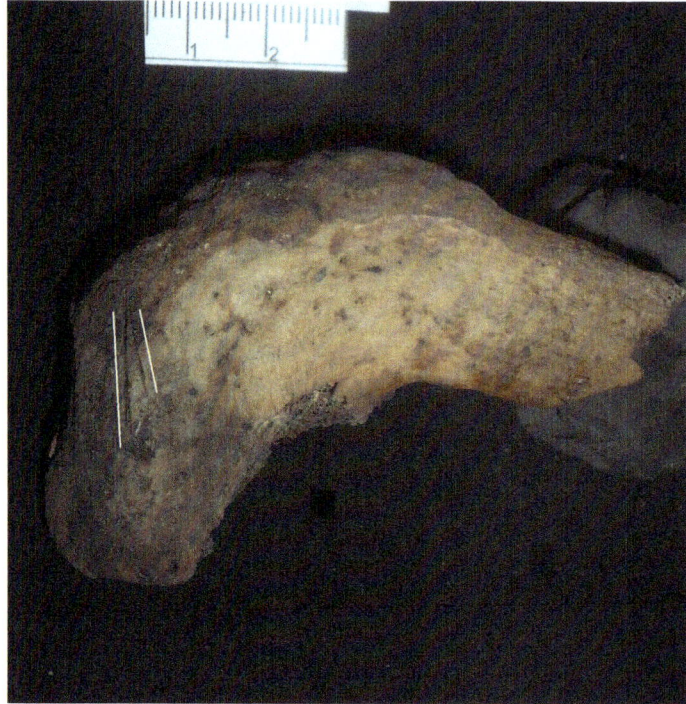

FIGURES 2.20, 2.21, AND 2.22   Continued

Lower limbs: Injuries were produced with blunt force mechanism with a heavy sharp-edged tool in femoral heads. However, to achieve the final objective, there was a slight variation between the procedures. The left lower limb displays a complete cut resulting from a single vertical movement, with superior−inferior trajectory, that sectioned the posterior portion of the femoral head and the upper portion of the greater trochanter (Fig. 2.23) This implies that the anterior portion of the femoral head kept articulated in its original location, that is to say, inside the acetabulum. Thus, judging by the fractures present and by the bone losses that compromise the lower portion of the femoral head, and partially the ischium (Fig. 2.24), the perpetrator proceeded to apply torsion forces to achieve the total separation of the limb, since the cut was not enough to achieve it. The right lower limb was separated by applying a blunt force mechanism with a heavy sharp-edged tool through a single complete cut that sectioned the superior, posterior, and inferior edges of the acetabulum as well as the femoral head (Fig. 2.25, line).

Quartering

The case presents signs of dismemberment manifested by complete cuts made by blunt force mechanism with a sharp-edged tool in different areas of the thorax and surrounded by false starts. As a result of these cuts the right dorsal column was separated from the coastal grid by at least 11 events (Figs. 2.26 and 2.27). Transverse processes of T10, T11,

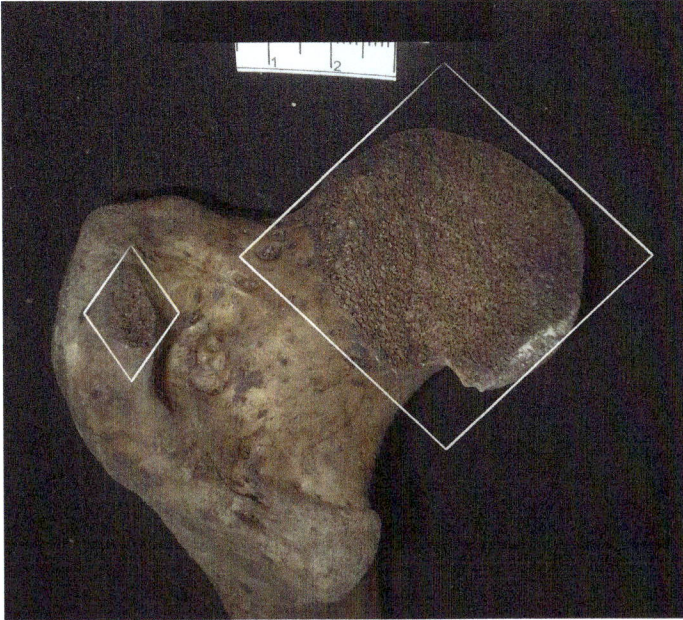

FIGURE 2.23 The left lower limb displays a complete cut resulting from a single vertical movement, with superior–inferior trajectory that sectioned the posterior portion of the femoral head and the upper portion of the greater trochanter.

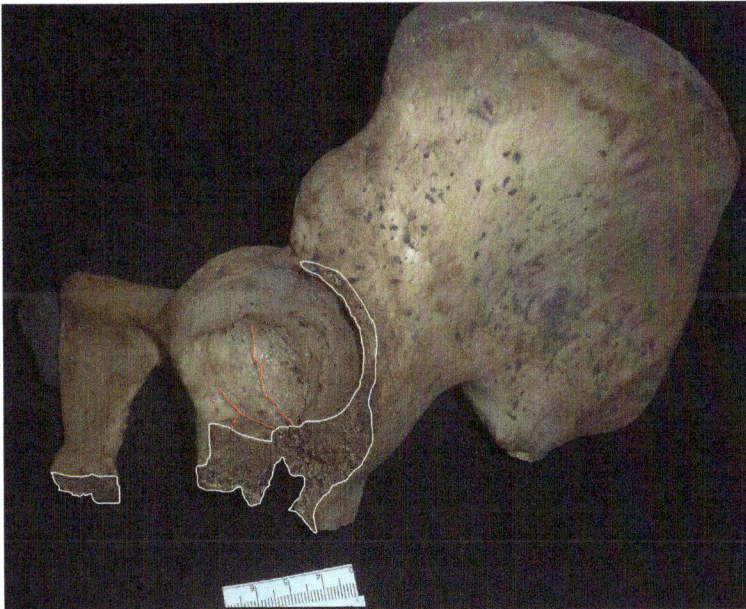

FIGURE 2.24 Fractures present and the bone losses that compromise the lower portion of the femoral head and partially the ischium, suggested the perpetrator applied torsion forces to achieve the total separation of the limb, since the cut was not enough to achieve it.

and T12 were separated by tearing or pulling off. The rib heads were not recovered, but it was clear that they were sectioned from their original locations by the complete cuts present in the dorsal column as well as in the posterior region of right ribs no. 2 to no. 10. In the anterior region of the thorax, two injures were found to be associated to blunt force mechanism with a sharp-edged tool that sectioned the sternum. One was a slicing cut that

FIGURE 2.25 The right lower limb was separated by applying a blunt force mechanism with a heavy sharp-edged tool through a single complete cut that sectioned the superior, posterior, and inferior edges of the acetabulum as well as the femoral head.

separated the uppermost left portion of the manubrium (Fig. 2.28A and B); the second was a complete diagonal cut that separated the remaining left portion of the manubrium (Fig. 2.28A and B).

In addition to the aforementioned injuries, superficial cuts were found on the left zygomatic bone as well as on the zygomatic process of the same side (Figs. 2.29 and 2.30, lines). Because these injuries are not necessarily lethal and taking into account the defenselessness of the victim, it is possible to infer that they are more compatible with torture practices than with the intention of separating or detaching specific areas of the face.

DISCUSSION

In the case presented, it was possible to determine that the bone injuries corresponding to criminal activities of cut throat, dismemberment, and quartering occurred during perimortem events (the use of the term *perimortem* for the different trauma of the present case is raised from the taphonomic context and not from the temporality or time of occurrence of each trauma, that is, it indicates that these occurred when the bone still had soft tissues around it or presence of marrow in its inside, variables that confer viscoelastic properties to the bone tissue, and make the difference with the alterations that occur during events postmortem when the bone is dry and/or dehydrated.) It was not possible to establish chronological sequence of the different traumas, or if the individual was still alive when the perpetrator initiated such procedures. The context in which the body was found, the versions of the circumstances surrounding the death and the different findings by the necropsy allowed to conclude that the manner of death was homicide and that the cause of death was associated to "... injuries by blunt force mechanism with a sharp-edged tool

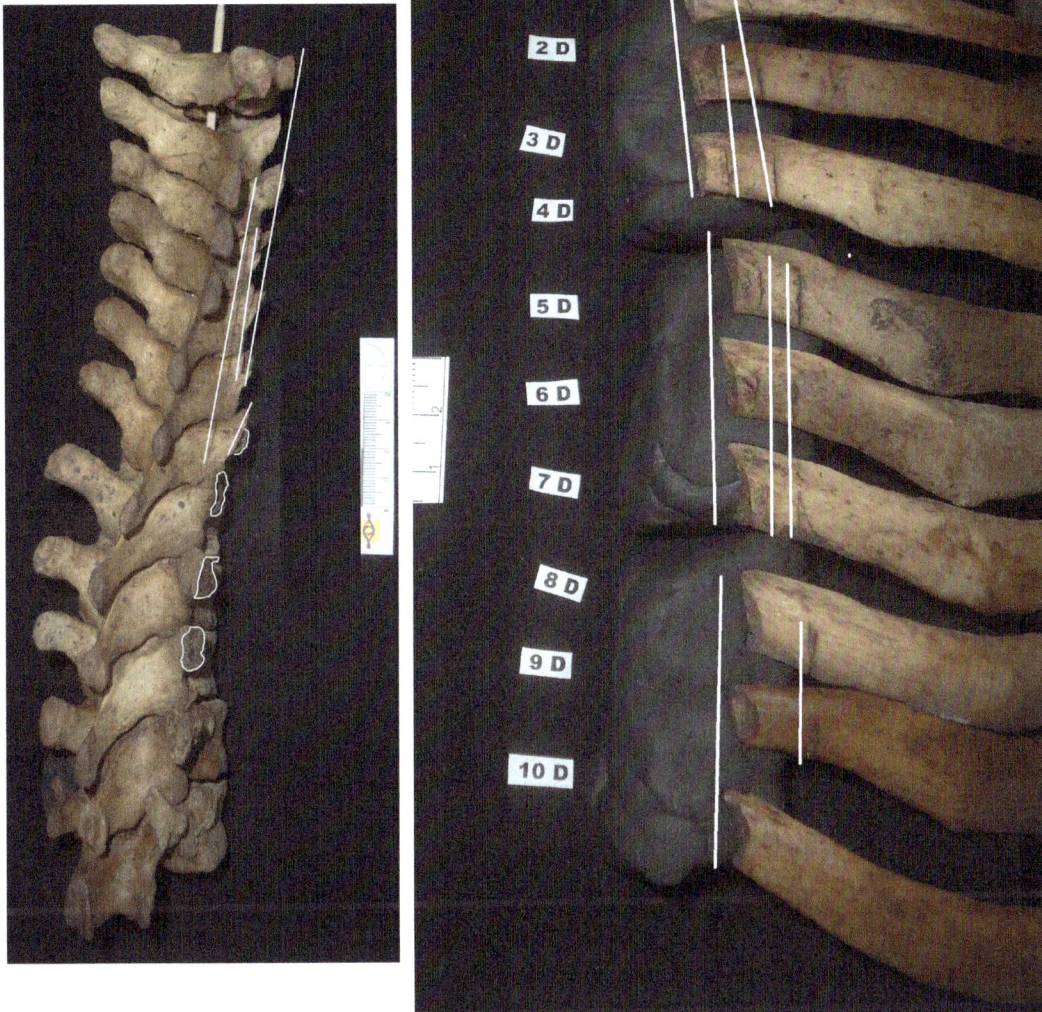

FIGURES 2.26 AND 2.27   The right dorsal column was separated from the costal grid by at least 11 events.,

with pattern of cut throat, dismemberment and quartering pattern." This cause of death is in accordance with recommendations by Morcillo-Méndez and Campos (2012). However, and in the absence of conclusive evidence, it was not possible to determine what trauma caused the death, as it could have happened during the cut throat or the dismemberment of one of the arms or the legs, since there are important veins and arteries that if seriously injured would have inexorably generated a hypovolemic shock. Likewise, the possibility that previous to the occurrence of the cut throat, dismemberment, and quartering, the victim received a lethal injury either sharping, piercing, or stabbing to a vital organ

FIGURE 2.28   (A and B) First cut separated the uppermost left portion of the manubrium; the second was a complete diagonal cut that separated the remaining left portion of the manubrium.

(compromising only soft tissues) remains open. Given the state of skeletonization of the body this hypothesis cannot be confirmed or dismissed.

Regarding the trauma to the malar bone and the zygomatic process, these are injuries that are not necessarily fatal, which together with the defenselessness of the victim—established by the ropes on the hands and feet—the contextual information, and the antecedents of the paramilitaries' modus operandi, allowed us to infer that they are more compatible with torture practices than with the intentionality of separating some segment from the affected areas.

On the other hand, the topographical location of the injuries in posterior and anterior thoracic regions allowed forensic practitioners to establish that the murderer had to perform maneuvers to place the body in different anatomical positions (supine and prone). However, it was not possible to determine the chronological order of the wounds.

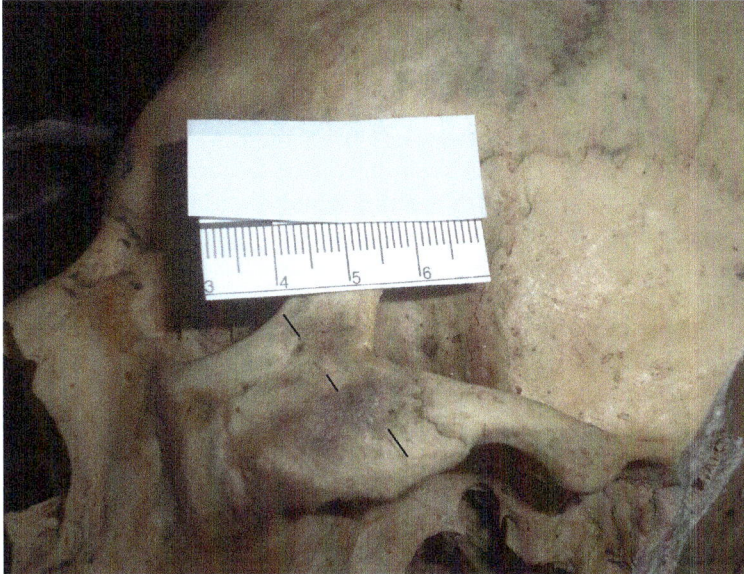

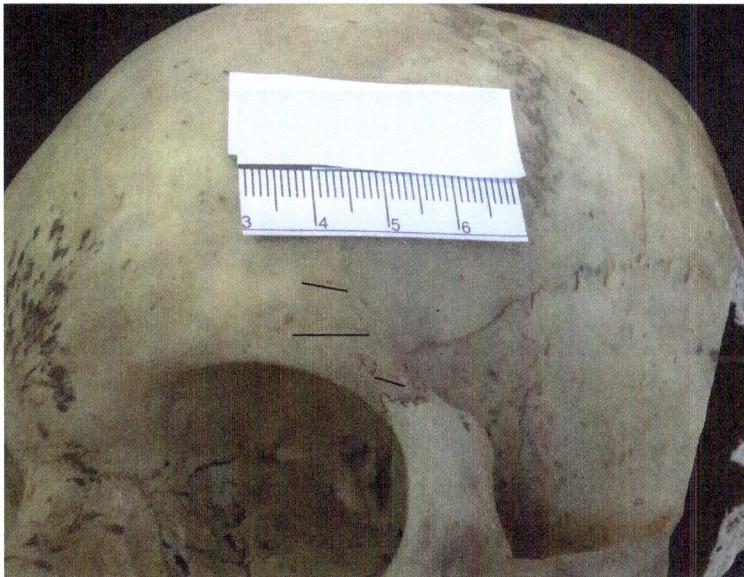

FIGURES 2.29 AND 2.30 Superficial cuts were found on the left zygomatic bone, as well as on the zygomatic process of the same side.

FINAL CONSIDERATIONS

The analysis, interpretation, and documentation of bone injuries by cut throat, decapitation, dismemberment, and quartering in skeletonized bodies requires experience, skill, and insight by forensic experts, but also demands from them to be aware of the legal norms that typify and sanction these criminal conducts. Not less important is the interpretation of the entire case, which is the result of a serious analysis of various variables, such as the existing testimonies about the case, the context of the findings and the injuries found in the body. If the study is not carried out in this manner, there will be situations that will prevent the expert from interpreting some findings as possible evidence of crimes other than homicide. For example, as observed in the case discussed, the victim's helplessness and the presence of nonfatal injuries to the face, examined in the context of the case, are already suggesting a type of possible torture, or other cruel, inhumane, or degrading treatment outlined in the four Geneva Conventions of International Humanitarian Law.

For the aforementioned, the study carried out from a forensic anthropology perspective in support of the medicolegal necropsy cannot be limited to describe a biological profile and simply document trauma. This will result in an incomplete and undoubtedly inefficient expert report that will be incapable of using the findings as evidence to support the perpetration of one or more crimes, and will ultimately be detrimental to the surviving victims. Morales (2011:24) describes this situation in a very comprehensive manner: *"An expert opinion of this type, which is inadequate, insufficient and out of context, will not be read as an expression of conceptual poverty, but as scientifically supported truth, backed by the signature of an expert and may well contribute to the filing of a case due to the lack of evidence."*

Acknowledgments

Special thanks to colleague María Isabel Cardona, a forensic anthropologist of the Institute of Legal Medicine of the city of Barranquilla, Colombia, who facilitated the case presented in this chapter and made important comments on our analysis and interpretation of it.

Many thanks to colleague Alexandra López Cerquera, doctoral candidate in the Department of Anthropology of the University of Tennessee, for her support in the translation and her important comments on the text.

References

Acevedo, T., 2011. Las extremidades de Galán. <http://www.elespectador.com/noticias/cultura/extremidades-de-galan-articulo-244107>.

Andrushko, V.A., Schwitalla, A.W., Walker, P.L., 2010. Trophy-taking and dismemberment as warfare strategies in prehistoric central California. Am. J. Phys. Anthropol. 141, 83–96.

Arias-Quintero, J. D., López-Tobón. Y. V. and Pérez-Torres, P. D. 2011. Estudio experimental de marcas de corte en hueso producidas por dos agentes mecánicos: motosierra y sierra sinfín. Monografía de grado para optar al título de Antropólogo. Universidad de Antioquia, Facultad de Ciencias Sociales y Humanas, Departamento de Antropología, Medellín, Colombia.

Blumenschine, R.J., Marean, C.W., Capaldo, S.D., 1996. Blind tests of inter-analyst correspondence and accuracy in the identification of cut marks, percussion marks, and carnivore tooth marks on bone surfaces. J. Archaeol. Sci. 23 (4), 493–507. Available from: https://doi.org/10.1006/jasc.1996.0047.

Cangrejo, J.Y., Tejada, A., 2014. Abordaje de la necropsia médico legal en cuerpos desmembrados. In: Téllez, N. (Ed.), Patología Forense un enfoque centrado en derechos humanos. Universidad Nacional de Colombia, Instituto Nacional de Medicina Legal y Ciencias Forenses, Bogotá D.C., pp. 703–717.

Caracol Radio, 2012. Fiscalía desconoce número de víctimas de paramilitares: Corporación Nuevo Arco Iris. Disponible en <http://www.caracol.com.co/noticias/judiciales/fiscalia-desconoce-numero-devictimas-de-paramilitares-corporacion-nuevo-arco-iris/20120514/nota/1687599.aspx>.

Cattaneo, C., Andreola, S., Marinelli, E., Poppa, P., Porta, D., Grandi, M., 2010. The detection of microscopic markers of hemorrhaging and wound age on dry bone: a pilot study. Am. J. Forensic Med. Pathol. 31 (1), 22–26.

Centro Nacional de Memoria Histórica, 2014. Textos corporales de la crueldad. Memoria histórica y antropología forense. Bogotá, D.C., Colombia.

Centro Nacional de Memoria Histórica, 2016. Hasta encontrarlos. El drama de la desaparición forzada en Colombia. Bogotá, D.C., Colombia.

Christensen, A., Passalacqua, N.Y., Bartelink, E., 2014. Forensic anthropology. Current Methods and Practice. Academic Press, Oxford.

Crowder, C.Y., Stout, S., 2012. Bone remodeling, histomorphology and histomorphometry. In: Crowder, C., Stout, S.B. (Eds.), Bone Histology: An Anthropological Perspective. CRC Press, Raton.

Delabarde, T., Ludes, B., 2010. Missing in Amazonian jungle: a case report of skeletal evidence for dismemberment. J. Forensic Sci. 55 (4), July 2010.

Di Nunno, N., Costantinides, F., Vacca, M., Di Nunno, C., 2006. Dismemberment: a review of the literature and description of 3 cases. Am. J. Forensic Med. Pathol. 27, 307–312. Más allá de adentrarse en las motivaciones psicológicas, psiquiátricas o conductuales del victimario responsable de un desmembramiento, esta breve definición resume genéricamente los aspectos procedimentales de este tipo de maniobra.

Dirkmaat, D.C., Cabo, L.L., Ousley, S.D., Symes, S.A., 2008. New perspectives in forensic anthropology. Am. J. Phys. Anthropol. 2008 (Suppl. 47), 33–52.

Ehrlich, E., Rothschild, M.A., Pluisch, F., Schneider, V., 2000. An extreme case of necrophilia. Leg. Med. 2, 224–226.

El Espectador, 2009. Los hornos del terror en el Catatumbo. Disponible en <http://www.elespectador.com/impreso/salvatore-mancuso/articuloimpreso140079-los-hornos-del-horror-el-catatumbo>.

El mundo. es Internacional, 2011. Columna internacional. Colombia busca a 10.000 víctimas de los paramilitares en ríos y fosas comunes. Disponible en <http://www.elmundo.es/elmundo/2008/11/28/internacional/1227860352.html>.

Gibelli, D., Mazzarelli, D., Porta, D., Rizzi, A.Y., Cattaneo, C., 2012. Detection of metal residues on bone using SEM-EDS—Part II: Sharp force injury. Forensic Sci. Int. 223, 91–96.

González, T.Y., 1985. El sacrificio humano entre los mexicas. Instituto Nacional de Antropología e Historia – Fondo de Cultura Económica, México, p. 257.

Guerrero, R.J.M., 2016. Análisis de traumatismos óseos por mecanismos de fuerza cortante. In: Sanabria-Medina, C. (Ed.), Patología y antropología forense de la muerte: la investigación científico-judicial de la muerte y la tortura, desde las fosas clandestinas, hasta la audiencia pública. Forensic Publisher, Bogotá D.C., pp. 711–718.

Human Rights Watch, 2014. La crisis en Buenaventura – Desapariciones, desmembramientos y desplazamiento en el principal puerto de Colombia en el Pacífico. Impreso en Estados Unidos de América, https://www.hrw.org/es/report/2014/03/20/la-crisis-en-buenaventura/desapariciones-desmembramientos-y-desplazamiento-en-el.

Humprey, J.Y., Hutchinson, D., 2001. Macroscopic characteristics of hacking trauma. J. Forensic Sci 46 (2), 228–233.

Işcan, M., Steyn, M., 2013. The Human Skeleton in Forensic Medicine, third ed. Charles C. Thomas, Springfield.

Kimmerle, E., Baraybar, J., 2008. Skeletal Trauma: Identification of injuries resulting from human rights abuse and armed conflict. CRC Press, Boca Ratón, FL.

Konopka, T., Bolechała, F., Strona, M., 1991. An unusual case of corpse dismemberment. Am. J. Forensic Med. Pathol. 12, 291–299.

Konopka, T., Strona, M., Bolechała, F., Kunz, J., 2007. Corpse dismemberment in the material collected by the Department of Forensic Medicine, Cracow, Poland. Leg. Med. 9, 1–13.

Lewis, J.E., 2008. Identifying sword marks on bone: criterial for distinguishing between cut marks made by different classes of bladed weapons. J. Archaeol. Sci. 35, 2001–2008. Available from: https://doi.org/10.1016/j.jas.2008.01.016.

Marciniak, S.M., 2009. A preliminary assessment of the identification of saw marks on burned bone. J. Forensic Sci. 54 (4), 779–785. Available from: https://doi.org/10.1111/j.1556-4029.2009.01044.x.

Memoria Histórica de la Comisión Nacional de Reparación y Reconciliación - Primer Informe, 2008. Trujillo Una Tragedia que no cesa. Editorial Planeta Colombia S.A, Bogota, D.C., Disponible en: <www.cnrr.org.co/new/newnoticias/08/-septiembre/memoria/Resumen ejecutivo.pdf>.

Morales, R.M., 2011. La necropsia medicolegal en víctimas de desaparición forzada: documentación de la tortura y la violencia sexual. Editado por Instituto Nacional de Medicina Legal y Ciencias Forenses y Programa de las Naciones Unidas para el Desarrollo (PNUD) / Programa Fortalecimiento a la Justicia en Colombia. In: Sanabria-Medina, C. (Ed.), Patología y antropología forense de la muerte: la investigación científico-judicial de la muerte y la tortura, desde las fosas clandestinas, hasta la audiencia pública. Forensic Publisher, Bogotá D.C., pp. 711–718. , 2016.

Morcillo-Méndez, M.D.Y., Campos, I.Y., 2012. Dismemberment: cause of death in the Colombian armed conflict. Torture 2 (1), 5–13.

Pijoan, C., Pastrana, A., 1987. Método para el registro de marcas de corte en huesos humanos. In: El caso de Tlatelcomila, Tetelpan, D.F. (Eds.), Estudios de antropología biológica: III Coloquio de antropología física, Juan Comas 1984. Instituto de investigaciones antropológicas, Universidad Nacional Autónoma de México, México, pp. 419–432. , Disponible en: <http://books.google.com.co/books?id = CUsuEn4n1cQC&lpg = PA419&ots = Onj1-VAvmX&dq = carmen%20pijoan%20metodologia%20para%20el%20analisis%20de%20marcas%20de%20corte&pg = PA432#v = onepage&q&f = false>.

Porta, D., Amadasi, A., Cappella, A., Mazzarelli, D., Magli, F., Gibelli, D., 2016. Dismemberment and disarticulation: A forensic anthropological approach. J. Forensic and Legal Med 38, 50–57.

Quatrehomme, G.A., 2007. A strange case of dismemberment. In: Brikley, M.B., Ferlini, R. (Eds.), Forensic Anthropology: Case Studies in Europe, 2007. Humana Press, Totowa, NJ, pp. 99–119.

Rajs, J., Lundstrom, M., Broberg, M., Lidberg, L., Lindquist, O., 1998. Criminal mutilation of the human body in Sweden—a thirty-year medico-legal and forensic psychiatric study. J. Forensic Sci. 43, 563–580.

Quevedo-Hidalgo, H.A., 2008. Escuela de la muerte: una mirada desde la antropología forense. Universitas Humanística No.66: 139–153 Bogotá, D.C., Colombia.

Reichs, K., 1998. Postmortem dismemberment: recovery, analysis and interpretation. In: Reichs, K. (Ed.), Forensic Osteology: Advances in the Identification of Human Remains, second ed. Charles C Thomas, Springfield, pp. 353–388.

Sanabria-Medina, C., Osorio, H., 2015. Ciencias forenses y antropología forense en el posconflicto colombiano. Revista Criminalidad 57 (3), 119–134. Available from: http://www.scielo.org.co/pdf/crim/v57n3/v57n3a09.pdf.

Sanabria-Medina, C., Coello, H.J.E., Osorio, R.H., 2016. Traumatismos óseos por impacto de proyectil de arma de fuego. In: Sanabria-Medina, C. (Ed.), Patología y antropología forense de la muerte: la investigación científico-judicial de la muerte y la tortura, desde las fosas clandestinas, hasta la audiencia pública. Forensic Publisher, Bogotá D.C., pp. 569–636.

Sierra, L.M., 2007. *Colombia busca a 10.000 muertos.* En: El Tiempo, abril 24 de 2007, Santafé de Bogotá. Available from: <http://www.eltiempo.com/archivo/documento/CMS-3525023>.

Symes, S.A., 1992. Morphology of Saw Marks in Human Bone: Identification of Class Characteristics. Dissertation, University of Tennessee, Knoxville, TN.

Symes, S.A., Smith, O.C., Gardner, C.D., Francisco, J.T., Horton, G.A., 1995. Anthropological and pathological analysis of sharp trauma in autopsy [Abstract]. Proc. Am. Acad. Forensic Sci. 177–178. 1995.

Symes, S., Berryman, H., Smith, O.C., 1998. Saw marks in bone: introduction and examination of residual kerf contour. In: Reichs, K.J. (Ed.), Forensic Osteology II. C.C. Thomas, Springfield, IL.

Symes, S., Williams, J., Murray, E., Hoffman, J., Holland, T., Saul, J., et al., 2002. Taphonomic context of sharp-force trauma in suspected cases of human mutilation and dismemberment. In: Haglund, W.Y., Sorg, M. (Eds.), Advances in Forensic Taphonomy: Method, Theory, and Archaeological Perspectives. CRC Press, Boca Raton, FL, pp. 403–434.

Symes, S., Rainwater, C.W., Cabo, L.L., Chapman, E.N., Wolff, I., 2005. Knife and Saw Toolmark Analysis in Bone: A Manual Designed for the Examination of Criminal Mutilation and Dismemberment. National Institute of Justice Grant. Available from: <www.ncjrs.gov/pdffiles1/nij/grants/232864.pdf>.

Symes, S., L'Abbé, E., Chapman, E., Wolff, I.Y., Dirkmaat, D., 2012. Interpreting traumatic Injury to bone in medi-colegal investigations. In: Dirkmaat, D. (Ed.), A Companion to Forensic Anthropology. Wiley-Blackwell, Chichester, pp. 340–389.

Scientific Working Group for Forensic Anthropology (SWGANTH), 2011. Trauma analysis. recuperado de. Available from: <http://swganth.startlogic.com/Trauma%20Rev0.pdf>.

Verdad Abierta.com, 2009. In forme especial: *Los cuatro días que estremecieron al Naya*. Disponible en: <http://www.verdadabierta.com/nunca-mas/40-masacres/1135-tres-dias-que-sacudieron-el-naya>.

Verdad Abierta.com, 2011. Columna, A su hermano lo lanzaron vivo a los cocodrilos: desmovilizados. Disponible en <http://www.verdadabierta.com/component/content/article/3686-a-su-hermano-lo-lanzaronvivo-a-los-cocodrilos-desmovilizados>.

Walker, P.L., Long, J.C., 1977. An experimental study of the morphological characteristics of tool marks. Am. Antiquity 42 (4), 605–616. Disponible en: <www.anth.ucsb.edu/.../PLW%201977%20Tool%20Mark%20Morphology.pdf>.

Dismemberment in Brazil: From Early Colonization to Present Days

Aluisio Trindade Filho[1,2] *and Marcos Paulo Salles Machado*[2,3]

[1]Civil Police Department of the Federal District, Brasilia, Brazil [2]Brazilian Association of Forensic Anthropology (ABRAF), Brasilia, Brazil [3]Civil Police Department of Rio de Janeiro, Rio de Janeiro, Brazil

INTRODUCTION

In the context of a violent death, the occurrence of mutilation of the body has the power to cause deep repulsion in people, often times more than the death itself. Dismemberment is a type of mutilation consisting in the removal, in life or after death, of parts of the body, normally the head or limbs, or cutting the body in half. Dismemberment may result from an accident, suicide, or homicide. Accidental dismemberments often involve means of transport, especially airplane crashes. In countries with an extensive railway network, there is occasional decapitation by the wheels of the compositions, due to suicidal acts (Zoja et al., 2009). Decapitation has also been reported during the suicidal act by hanging when the body is heavy enough and the rope is thin, resistant, and inflexible (usually nylon) or when the act involves a jump from a great height (Rothschild and Schneider, 1999). When dismemberment follows a homicide, the former is often seen by society as a more hideous crime than the homicide itself (Dogan et al., 2010).

Dismemberment can be classified as (1) defensive, when the reason is to facilitate the disposal and concealment of the corpse, to get rid of evidence, or to make it difficult to identify the victim; (2) aggressive, when the impulse to dismember arises from fury, indignation, or emotional unrest of the aggressor; (3) offensive, when dismemberment is part of the motivation for homicide, with extreme disdain for the dead; (4) necromaniac, whose purpose is to use some part of the body as a trophy, symbol or fetish, and death may not necessarily result from homicide (Häkkänen-Nyholm et al., 2009; Gupta and Arora, 2013;

Rajs et al., 1998). A very sharp cutting weapon (razors, knives) and other cutting tools like machete, axe, or saw are the most used instruments for dismemberment. If the body parts are found in one place, they are almost certainly parts of the same body. The issue is more complex when segments are found distant from each other, especially when the time lag between locating all of them is large. In either scenario, efforts should be made to correlate body segments by juxtaposition of section surfaces.

Soft tissue may eventually help if the victim had a tattoo or scar that is still preserved in the section line. More reliable is the juxtaposition of the sectioned bone surfaces. If the discovery of human remains occurs when the skeletonization process is already ongoing, the use of anthropological methods with complete maceration of the human remains is encouraged. This eases the task of juxtaposing the bone surfaces and allows for better photographic documentation. Maceration also provides important clues to clarifying the cause of death. If still unclear, the alternative is to collect samples of biological material from each body segment to perform genetic analyses, looking for an allelic profile that is identical for all analyzed segments.

Bone lesions produced by actions other than those that caused the dismemberment are very likely to be related to the mechanism or even the cause of death. As the dismemberments are almost always performed with the use of cutting instruments, the detection of traumas caused by blunt forces or firearms in the skeleton and in body sections located far from the bone edges are likely related to the cause of death. Radiological study is always performed in these cases, especially when firearm projectile or metallic fragments are found amongst the human remains.

In Brazil, from its discovery by the Portuguesein the year 1500 to the present day, cases of dismemberment have been reported. The purpose of this text is to shed light on the postmortem dismemberment in the country.

FRAMEWORK OF VIOLENCE IN PRESENT-DAY BRAZIL

Brazil is a country endowed with enormous natural wealth. At the same time, it also presents severe educational and economic discrepancies between the upper class and the poor, who normally reside in the outskirts of the bigger cities. Furthermore, Brazil has extensive and poorly protected territorial boundaries with nations that are major drug producers, which facilitates drug and arms trafficking to Brazil's large consumer population, and further makes the country a route for international trafficking.

According to demographic data gathered by IBGE (Brazilian Institute of Geography and Statistics), in 2014 Brazil reached 202 million inhabitants (ftp://ftp.ibge.gov.br/ Estimativas_de_Populacao/Estimativas_2014/estimativa_dou_2014.pdf). The Mortality Information System (SIM) of the Ministry of Health shows that, in the same year, there were approximately 59,600 homicides in Brazil—equivalent to a rate of 29 homicides per 100,000 inhabitants, slightly more than 10% of the total of homicides registered in the world (http://infogbucket.s3.amazonaws.com/arquivos/2016/03/22/atlas_da_violencia_2016.pdf).

The country is a federation made up of 26 states plus the Federal District. Possession of arms is prohibited to citizens (except in very specific cases) as is the trade and use of drugs. Each state has very particular cultural, social, and economic characteristics, especially in terms of violence and of the *modus operandi* of criminals. One of the most important states in the country is the state of Rio de Janeiro, whose capital, also called Rio de Janeiro, presents characteristics that reveal the widespread disparity of the country. While it has sophisticated districts, pockets of poverty and misery are spread over large areas, mainly in the north zone and in the suburb called Baixada Fluminense. This is one of the most violent suburbs of the city of Rio de Janeiro, with 48 homicides per year for every 100,000 inhabitants, most of them related to drug trafficking.

The Federal District, home of the capital of the country since 1960, is the smallest unit of the federation in terms of territorial extension. Although Brasília is its only municipality, there are 30 localities (similar to suburbs) within it called administrative regions. Conceived to be an administrative city with slow population growth, Brasília has been experiencing one of the country's highest demographic increases since its founding due to the intense migration from other states, mostly of unskilled workers belonging to the lower social classes. Together with other reasons, this reproduced in the Federal District the pattern of the great Brazilian urban agglomerations, with the creation of areas of poverty that have, as a corollary, an explosion of crime. Data from 2014 depict a homicide rate of 33.1 per 100,000 inhabitants, with drug trafficking playing a relevant role in the genesis of this violence (http://infogbucket.s3.amazonaws.com/arquivos/2016/03/22/atlas_da_violencia_2016.pdf).

DISMEMBERMENT IN BRAZIL

Historical Perspective

The reasons for dismemberment in Brazil are very diverse and vary over time: religious and cultural motivations, punishment and intimidation of the population by the State, and demonstration of power by criminals. Dismemberment can also be done as a way of facilitating the transport and concealment of the cadaver or of hindering the victim's identification.

Upon landing from a transatlantic journey on the east coast of a land later to be called Brazil, the Portuguese settlers encountered a native human population that they subsequentlynamed *indigenous*, a term already attributed to the inhabitants of the "New World" since the arrival of Christopher Columbus in the Caribbean Islands almost a decade earlier. The time was the beginning of the 16th century and after a few years, most of the coast of this new land would have been visited. The recently arrived people were quick to realize that this population was made up of people with homogenous physical characteristics, formed by diverse ethnic groups and numerous tribes with cultural features extremely different from European standards.

One of the behaviors that caused most repulsion and fear among the Portuguese was the praxis of executing the captured enemies and subsequently producing their dismemberment, to feed themselves on their flesh as part of an elaborate and complex ritual witnessed through the contact with the Tupinambás, Caetés, Potiguares, and Tamoios tribes.

In the accounts of Hans Staden, a German mercenary who sailed to Brazil with the Portuguese, after killing the hostage with a blow to the nape of the neck, "they cut the legs of the deceased above the knees and the arms close to the trunk" (http://www.historia-net.com.br/conteudo/default.aspx?codigo = 612).

Execution and subsequent dismemberment were attributed to the Indians believing that, by eating the flesh of an enemy warrior, they would thus acquire their power, knowledge, and qualities. But the reason for such a practice could be explained by hatred and contempt for the enemy and to avenge the death of their friends killed in a war. Archeological studies proved this to be a very old practice among part of the Amerindian tribes that inhabited all the American territory (Andrushko et al., 2010; Allen and Jones, 2014). It is not known, however, exactly how many indigenous groups practiced anthropophagy. To the best of current knowledge, the habit was extinguished in the 17th century, when catechization and imposition by force ended with this repulsive law in the territories controlled by the Europeans.

The history of Brazil registers two famous cases of sentencing to death for the crime of sedition in which after execution by hanging, the dismemberment was executed as part of the conviction. This was the case of Joaquim José da Silva Xavier, nicknamed Tiradentes, involved in a separatist movement. Tiradentes was hanged in 1792 and then dismembered, so that the parts of his body were scattered at strategic points, his head being reserved for public exposure in the main square of the capital of the state of Minas Gerais (Fig. 3.1). A similar fate befell the five leaders of the state of Paraiba in the Revolution of 1817. Condemned after being defeated in a separatist revolt that aimed to implant a republic in the northeast of the country along the lines of that adopted by the United States, after execution by hanging all five had their heads and hands cut off and exposed in public places

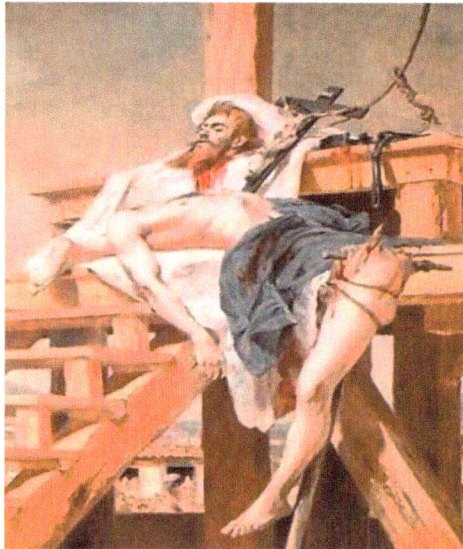

FIGURE 3.1　The dismemberment of Tiradentes. Oil on canvas, Pedro Américo, 1893. http://www.ensinarhistoriajoelza.com.br/tiradentes-esquartejado-uma-leitura-critica/.

FIGURE 3.2 Heads of Lampião and some members of his group. http://www.fotografiaecultura.com/2012/08/ 27/decapitacao-de-lampiao/ Source: *By Lauro Cabral de Oliveira, 1938.*

of the state capital. In both episodes, the section of the bodies and exposure of the parts in public places aimed to intimidate the population and curb other insurgencies.

In the 1920s and 1930s the gang of Lampião (Lampion)—as Virgulino Ferreira da Silva, the most famous Robin Hood—like-bandit of Brazil became known—spread terror and looting through the cities of the northeast countryside. When he was surprised by police forces in the countryside in 1938, Lampião, his wife Maria Bonita, and nine other members of the group were shot dead. The police, in a rather inhuman way to current standards, but following the custom of the time, cut off the heads of the 11 corpses and exposed them in an uninterrupted way through several cities of the northeast and even of the south of the country, as a way of rejoicing in the feat achieved (Fig. 3.2).

Current Situation

In a small but significant number of homicides committed in Brazil, the crime has been followed by the dismemberment of the corpse, usually soon after death, although in some cases longer time spans may separate both events. Little statistical data on dismemberment rates for Brazil can be found. In the Federal District, a survey coordinated by one of the authors found that approximately 4350 cadavers whose death was related to a homicide were necropsied in the Institute of Forensic Medicine between 2012 and 2016 (unpublished data). Seventeen such homicides, (0.4% of the cases) involved severe mutilations on the face and other parts of the body produced by sharp and blunt forces (the cases of corpse incineration after a homicide are not considered here). Among them, nine were dismembered, a rate of 1 in every 480 autopsies, a number close to the 1 in every 500 cases described in German statistics, quoted by Konopka (Konopka et al., 2006). Three of the nine corpses showed vital signs on the section edges (one of them beheaded at the victim's request during a psychotic outbreak). In the other six cases, the dismemberment occurred after death. A study carried out between 2000 and 2003 in some of the main Brazilian capitals indicated mutilations in 7.8% of the 42,433 corpses examined in the city of Rio de Janeiro,3% of the 48,405 corpses examined in the city of São Paulo,1.6% of the 7378 corpses examined in the city of Goiânia, 0.9% of the cadavers examined in the city of Belém, and 0.3% of the 13,677 corpses examined in the city of Porto Alegre (Lessa, 2010).

In Brazil, the motivations for dismemberment following a homicide are various. In the so-called Yoki case, in 2012, a high-ranking businessman was shot dead by his wife in their apartment and dismembered in seven parts after around 10 hours following the murder (head, abdomen, upper, and lower limbs). The motivation for the dismemberment was to facilitate the transport of the body into two large suitcases, and its subsequent disposal in an empty piece of land roughly 30 km away from their apartment so to conceal the murder—a typical case of defensive dismemberment. In other cases, dismemberment is performed due to outrage, as in cases in which it is performed after the lynching by members of the community of someone believed to have committed a serious crime (aggressive), such as rape; or by hatred of the victim, as after a murder due to the victim's sexual orientation (offensive). However, most dismemberments following homicides are associated with criminal organizations. In organized crime, relationships are dictated by the "rule by the strongest," which encourages the practice of barbaric acts against disaffected persons. One of the ways of displaying power in such an environment is to dismember the corpses of individuals from rival groups, members of the same group who fall into shame, or members of the public safety forces. Such demonstration of power is a common motivation for dismemberments carried out by gangs of drug dealers, who often post pictures of the dismembered corpse on social networks. This also seems to be the motivation for the dismemberments in the successive rebellions in Brazilian prisons of the north and northeast regions of the country in early 2017. In these rebellions, members of two of the largest criminal organizations, called the First Command of the Capital (PCC) and Red Command (CV), the latter allied with a minor faction, engaged inside the prisons for the control of the regional drug and arms trafficking. As a result, approximately 130 prisoners lost their lives. In the observed scenes of barbarism, several victims were tortured, shot, or stabbed, and later subjected to decapitations and deprivation of other parts of their bodies. Overall, these episodes in the prisons fall into the offensive type, with public demonstration of immense contempt for the body of the deceased victim. It is possible to draw a parallel between these episodes in Brazilian prisons and the practices of extremists groups, such as the Islamic State and Mexican drug cartels. By their magnitude, these events even seem to aim to terrorize society, already numbed to such horrors by the grim routine of daily displays of news of homicides in Brazilian media. A mutilation would show the horror, the revolt, and the fear that a "simple murder" can no longer evoke (http://sylviacolombo.blogfolha.uol.com.br/2017/01/08/por-que-decapitar/).

As often mentioned in publications on the subject, the corpse is generally sectioned in preferred areas, which differs from accidental mutilation. Routine segments of choice are the neck, the three large joints of the upper limbs (shoulder, elbow, and wrist), the abdomen, and the three large joints of the lower limbs (hip, knee, and ankle), although other areas may be chosen, especially if the author has no knowledge of human anatomy or dissection skills. In this way, the body can be split between two or up to

15 parts. Two when just one division occurs, in general in the neck or abdomen, and 15 if the three joints of the upper and lower limbs are sectioned bilaterally in addition to the neck and abdomen.

For the complete clarification of the facts, the forensic pathologist and the forensic anthropologist usually work together, with the participation of the necropapiloscopist and the forensic geneticist, contingent on the case characteristics. The information from the forensics expert who attended to the crime scene adds elements for the distinction between homicide, accident, and suicide.

Under Brazilian law, the legal framing of those who dismember a corpse may derive from the application of two articles of the Penal Code:Article. 211.—Destroy, subtract or hide corpse or part of it: Penalty—imprisonment, from 1 (one) to 3 (three) years, and fine; Art. 212.—Vilipend corpse or its ashes: Penalty—detention, from 1 (one) to 3 (three) years, and fine (http://www.planalto.gov.br/ccivil_03/decreto-lei/Del2848compilado.htm).

CASE EXAMPLES

Case 1

In February 2004, in Brasília, Distrito Federal (DF), human remains of a dismembered female dead body, found in an open area covered by grass in Taguatinga, DF, were referred for examination (Fig. 3.3). They arrived already identified by the police as a 27-year-old woman and at that time it was not part of the routine in the morgue to technically confirm identification. Multiple skull fractures and subgaleal ecchymosis clarified the cause of death. The dismemberment occurred in the neck, at the C3 and C4 levels, in the abdomen involving the L3 and L4, and in the distal thirds of the thighs, just above the distal epiphysis of the femurs. The vertebral lesions showed cutting marks, with some irregularity at the edges (Fig. 3.4). The section in the humeri and femurs showed linear superficial marks and irregular fractures with a butterfly-shaped fracture in the left femur, suggesting that these bones were divided by sharp and blunt forces produced by a heavy-edged instrument (Fig. 3.5).

Later on, a rusty machete probably used to cut the dead body into pieces was found close to the place where the human remains were discovered (Fig. 3.6). Additionally, there was an incomplete fracture in the distal part of the diaphysis of the right humerus with a fragment pulled out, interpreted as an unsuccessful attempt of dismemberment. The investigation showed that the victim was part of a gang of users and drug dealers and was killed by members of the group itself. Although the perpetrators have never confessed to the crime, the motivation for the homicide appears to have been internal struggles. The fact that the corpse was found on easy-to-reach land in an urban area suggests that the dismemberment was carried out by the criminals with the purpose to demonstrate power to the rival gangs. The perpetrators were eventually indicted only for the murder.

Case 2

A partly skeletonized human body was found in an open area in Brasília on March 4, 2012, severed into four parts (Fig. 3.7), each of them inside a plastic bag. The biological

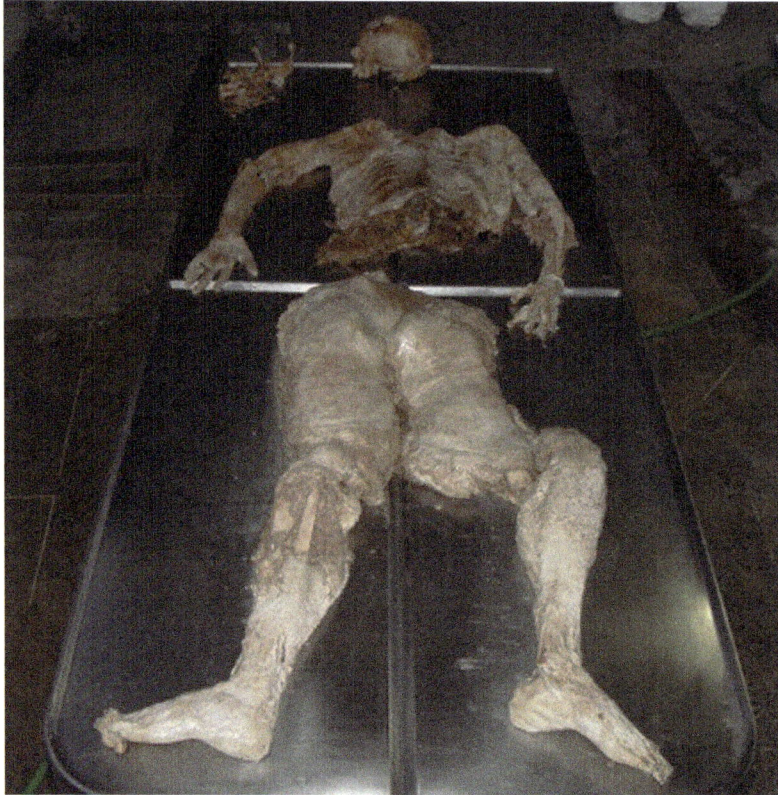

FIGURE 3.3   Segmented human remains as they arrived to the autopsy.

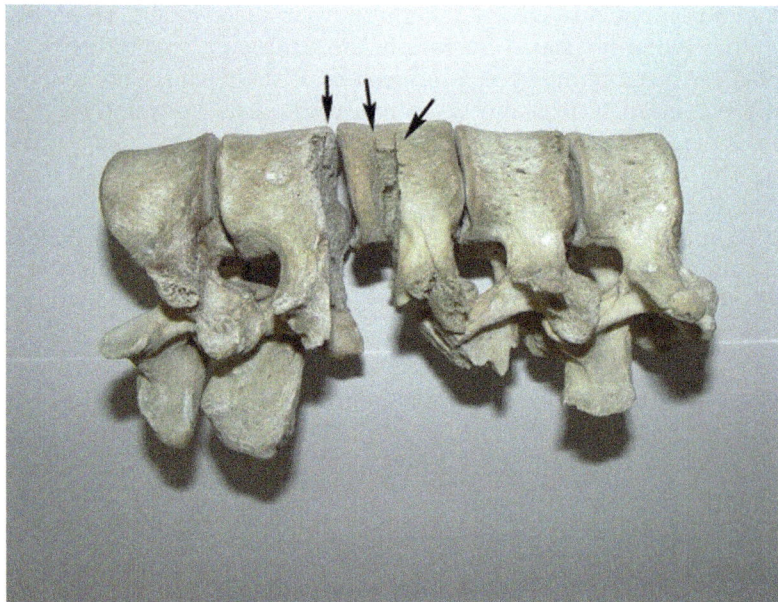

FIGURE 3.4   L3 and L4 cutting marks (*arrows*).

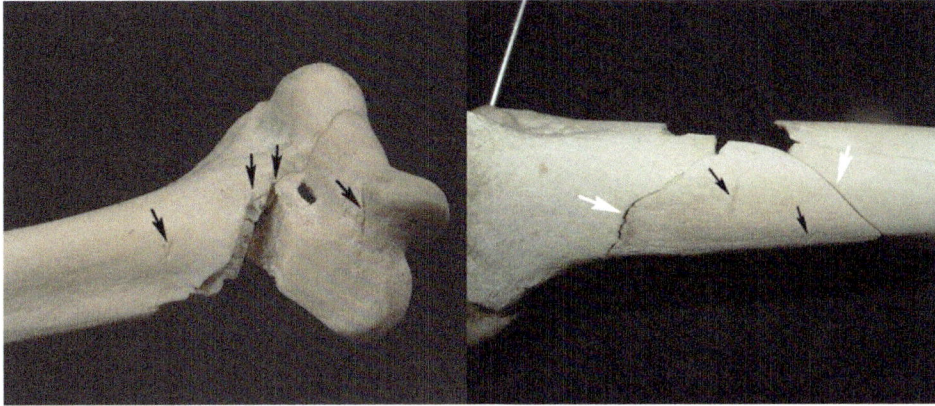

FIGURE 3.5   Fractures due to sharp forces (*black arrow*) in the distal segment of right humerus and left femoral shaft, the latter depicting a butterfly fracture due to blunt forces (*white arrows*).

FIGURE 3.6   Machete probably used to cut the dead body.

FIGURE 3.7   Dismembered human remains as they arrived to the morgue.

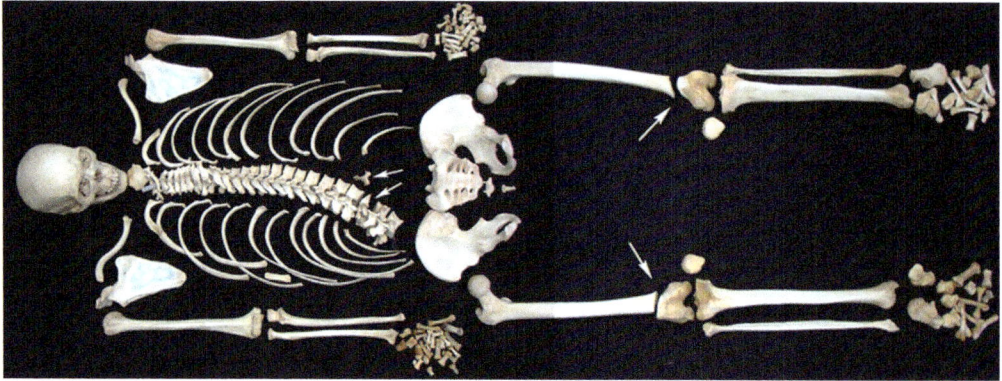

FIGURE 3.8   Sections at the level of the third lumbar vertebra and above the femoral condyles (*arrows*).

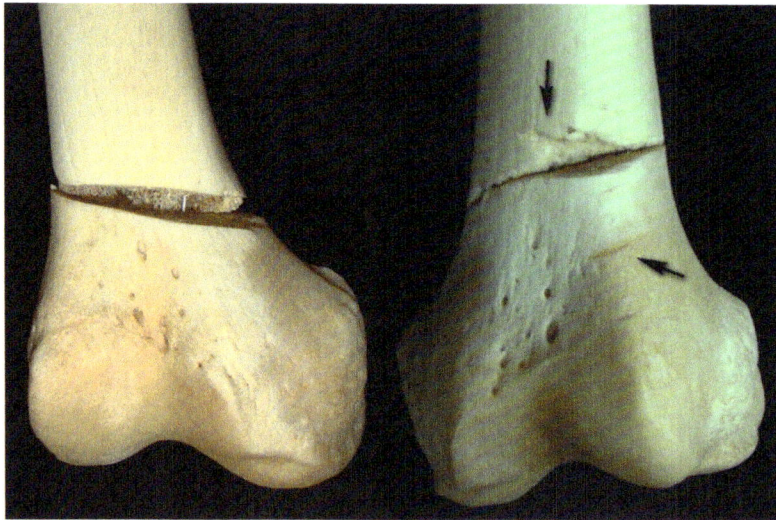

FIGURE 3.9   Right and left femur divided by sharp forces; false start marks (*arrows*).

profile pointed to a young male. Segmentations were performed in the lower abdomen, in the third lumbar vertebra, and in the thighs, just above the distal femoral epiphyseal line (Fig. 3.8).

Cut marks on the three bones were clear, with no evidence of hematological deposition. There were four typical superficial false start cuts in the anterior surface of the left femur, in the vicinity of the section line, not found in the right femur, suggesting that dismemberment was performed first on the right thigh (Fig. 3.9).

The perfect juxtaposition of the two segments of the third lumbar vertebra and of the femurs proved they were parts of the same individual.

The lesions described for the three bones are compatible with fractures produced by sharp instruments and blunt objects. The cause of the death remained unknown. The identification was established by necropapiloscopy as being a 25-year-old male. The inquiry did not reveal the motivation of the murder. The authorship of dismemberment could not be established.

Case 3

In May 2012, in a vacant lot in Brasília, DF, close to the South Lake, a cephalic pole, trunk, and proximal part of the upper limbs of a human individual were found in a plastic bag (Fig. 3.10). Data from the biological profile was compatible with a subadult male. The inventory showed that the distal portions of the humeri were sectioned transversally at the level of the epiphyses, with the distal segments corresponding to the trochlea, capitula, and lateral epicondyles missing (Fig. 3.11).

In the trunk, the third lumbar vertebra presented a transverse section with identical characteristics to the humeri, resulting in the loss of the lower half of the vertebra. On the anterior face of the distal part of the right-sided humerus, there were four linear and superficial transversal lesions interpreted as false starts (Fig. 3.11). These marks may mean that the author of the dismemberment had no knowledge of human anatomy, dissection skills, or common abilities in certain professions, such as physicians, veterinarians, butchers, or hunters. It also suggests that the section was firstly performed on the right humerus so that when practicing the cut on the left side the perpetrator already had in mind where to work with the harmful instrument. The distal body segments did not come for examination.

In September 2013, in an empty area covered by grass about 8 km away from the previous one, the distal part of a partially charred human skeleton was found by members of

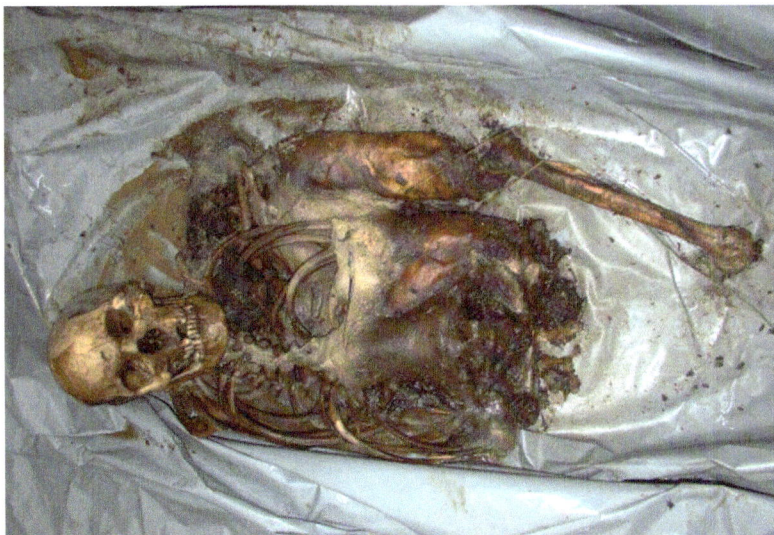

FIGURE 3.10 Upper half of the human dead body.

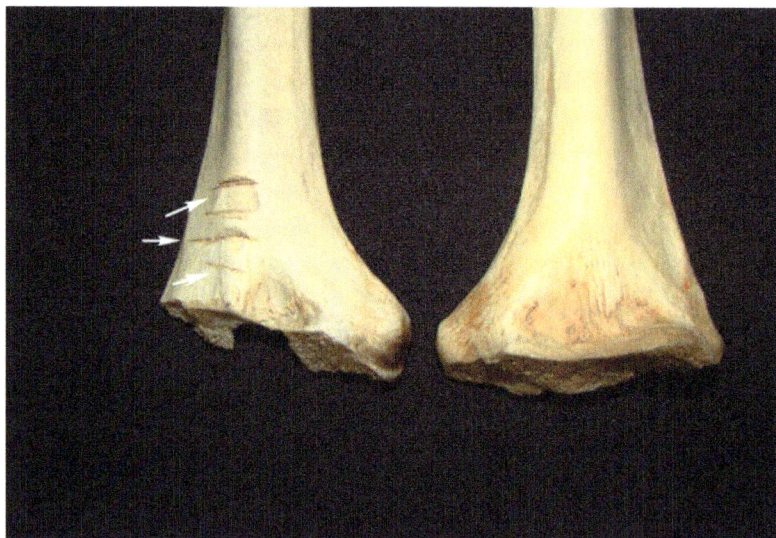

FIGURE 3.11   Humeri section lines; false starts (*arrows*).

the fire department on duty to fight a wildfire. Examination of this skeleton showed that it was composed of forearms, hand bones, distal segment of the lumbar spine, pelvis, and bones of the lower limbs. These were exactly the bony elements missing in the case above (Fig. 3.12). Also found was part of the lower half of a lumbar vertebra and part of the distal epiphysis of a right humerus.

The juxtaposition of the lumbar vertebra fragment to the proximal half of the third lumbar vertebra of the preceding case indicated a perfect fit (Fig. 3.13). The same occurred with the distal epiphysis of the right humerus, the fit of a notch near the lateral edge of the bone being noteworthy. The two halves of the skeletons were judged to be parts of the same individual. The characteristics of the bone lesions suggest the use of a heavy sharp instrument, maybe of the machete type, used with great energy not with a sliding movement, but with the application of pressure. The cause of death was not evident. However, the motivation for dismemberment must have been defensive as the body parts were disposed far apart from one another. The identification of the deceased, a 19-year-old male, was established by the fitting of a removable dental prosthesis brought by family members, as well as by medical history reporting an old facial trauma. The cause of the death could not be clarified. So far no one has been charged with the crime.

In these three caseworks described, evidence of the use of blunt and sharp forces at sites outside the joints suggests a specific lack of skill on the part of the aggressors.

Case 4

A fragmented skull and the first three cervical vertebrae in an advanced state of decomposition were found in the city of Rio de Janeiro and sent to the Forensic Anthropology

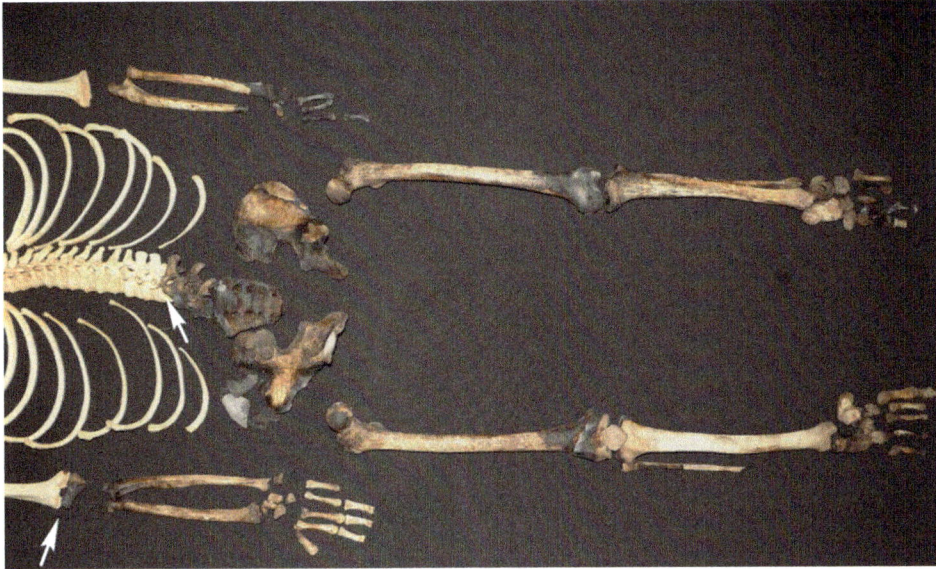

FIGURE 3.12   Distal half of the skeleton already juxtaposed to the proximal one (*arrows*).

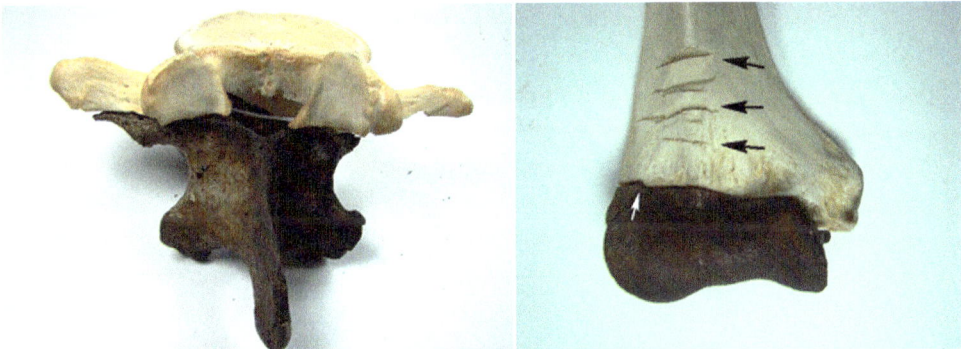

FIGURE 3.13   Juxtaposition of the fragments of the third lumbar vertebra and the distal epiphysis of the right humerus. *Black arrows* point to false starts. *White arrow* depicts a perfect indentation matching.

Service of the Afrânio Peixoto Medical-Legal Institute. The biological profile evaluation indicated a 35- to45-year-old male. The lower edge of the C3 displayed a lesion with a regular surface cut with loss of part of the blades, spinal apophysis, and lower articular surfaces. The upper edge of the spinal process of C2 was also sectioned with similar characteristics. The analysis was exclusively macroscopic. A heavy cutting instrument caused the fractures in both vertebrae. The impact in the C3 was interpreted as strong enough to cause decapitation. The damage in C2 suggested an attempt of beheading,

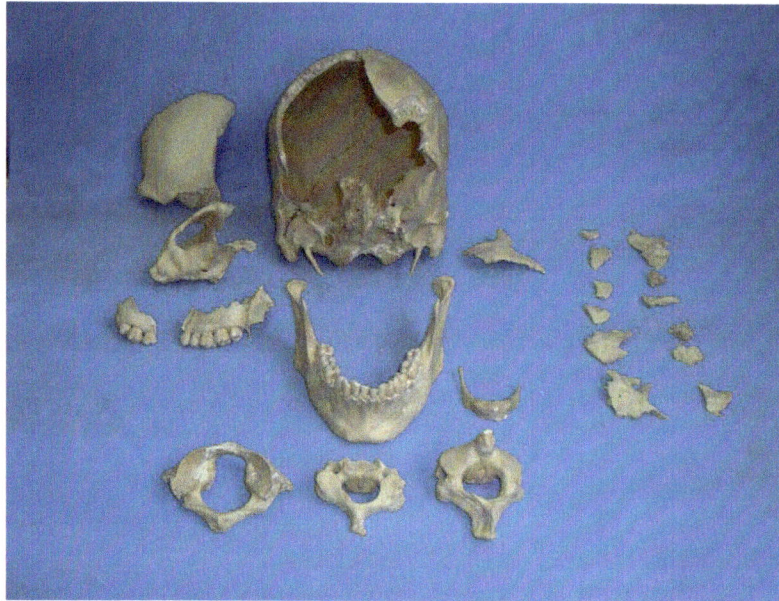

FIGURE 3.14 Fragmented skull, after maceration. The comminuted fracture is in relation with the referred GSW.

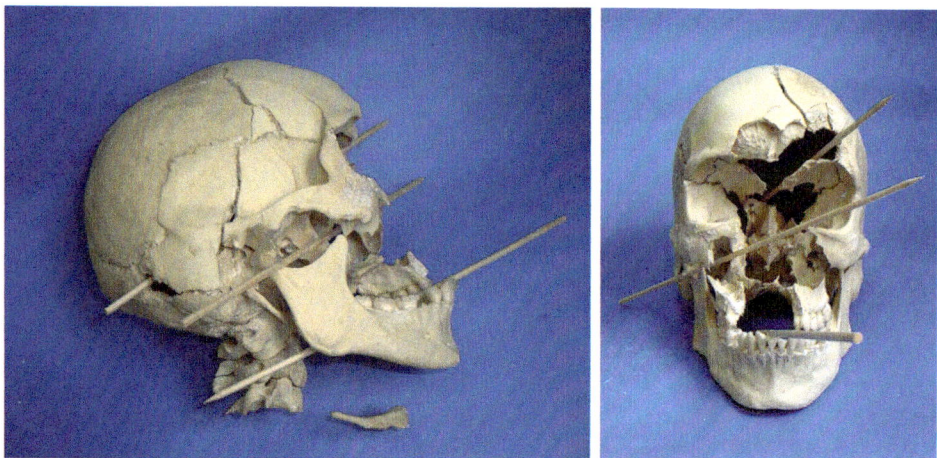

FIGURE 3.15 Reconstructed skull with the indication of the pathway of the projectile [bullet holes (rods)]. Decapitation occurred at the level of C3.

frustrated by the resistance provided by the odontoid apophysis. The hyoid was fractured, and part of the left upper corner was missing (Figs. 3.14–3.17). We were able to detect at least three gunshot wounds to the head (Fig. 3.15), which were related to the cause of death. The individual remained unidentified.

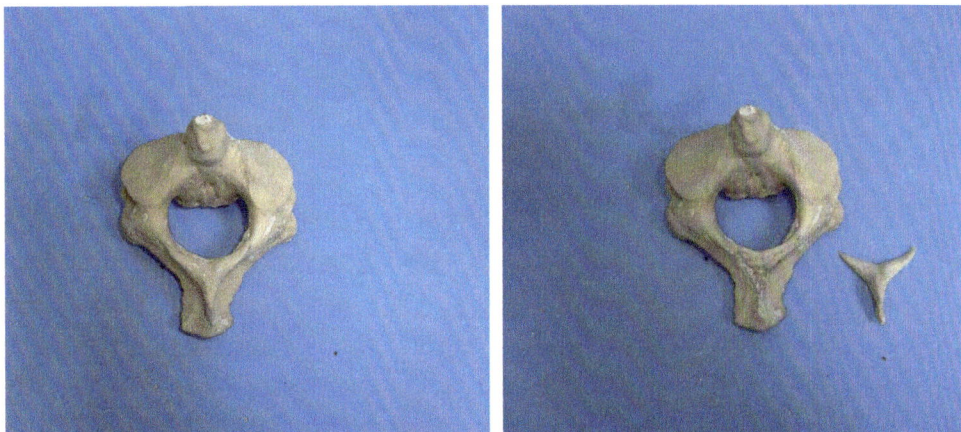

FIGURE 3.16   Pullout of the upper edge of the spinous process of C2.

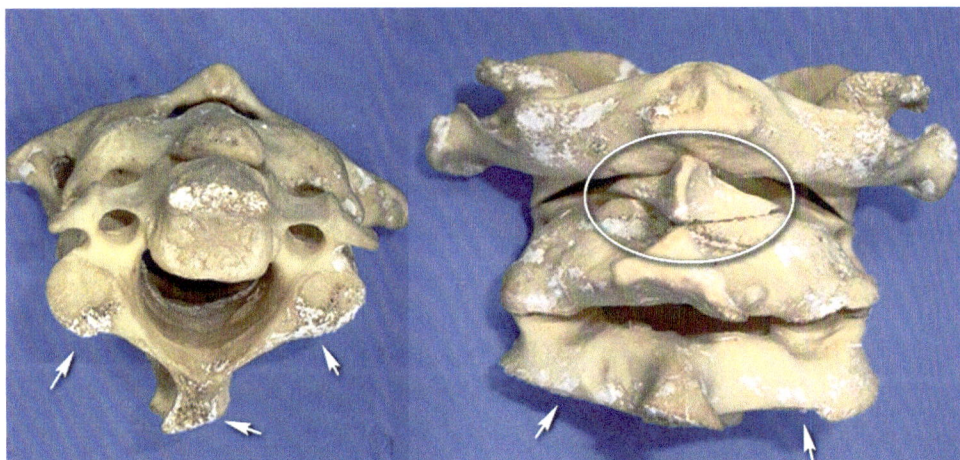

FIGURE 3.17   C1 to C3. Inferior border of C3 missing segments (*arrows*); clear cut edge fractures in superior aspect of C2 spinous process (*circle*).

Case 5

Two partially skeletonized and incomplete corpses (named A and B) composed of the lumbar vertebrae, the pelvic region, and the femurs were found (Figs. 3.18–3.20) at the same site. The remains belonged to two adult male individuals. Both showed signs of traumatic action at the level of their lumbar vertebrae, lower abdomen, and above the knee region (individual A) and at the proximal ends of the tibias (individual B) suggesting that they were dismembered in about the same way. The femurs of individual A were

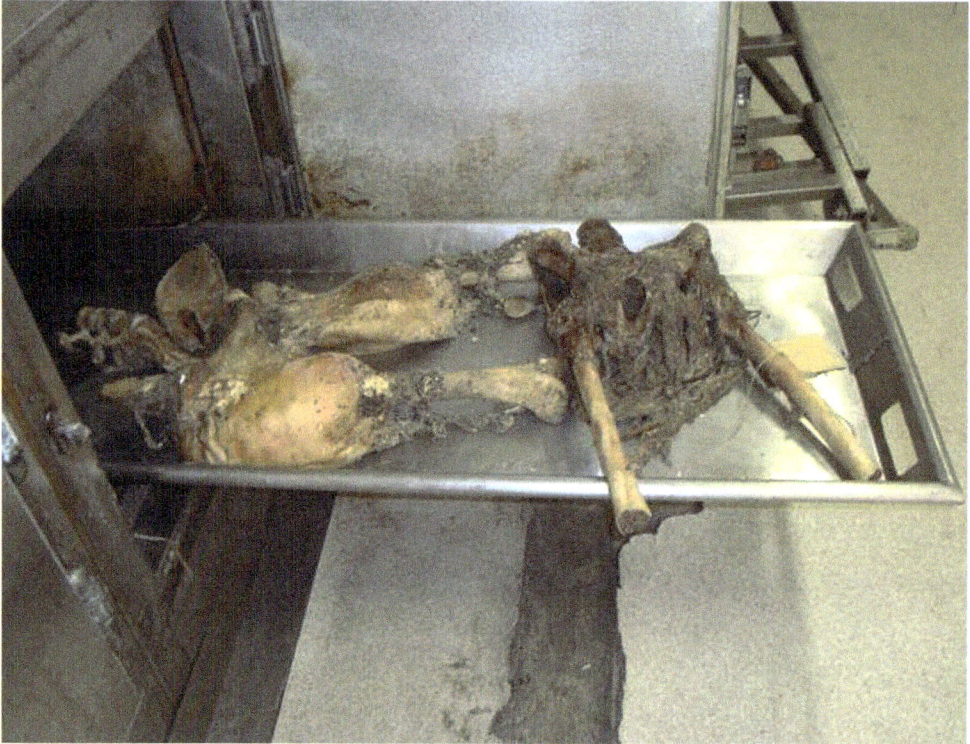

FIGURE 3.18   Human remains of the two corpses as they were found.

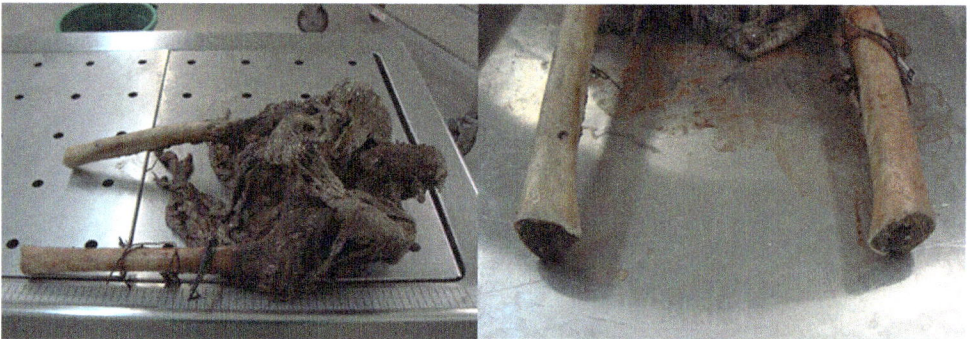

FIGURE 3.19   Individual A, adult male, was represented by lumbar vertebrae, pelvic bones, and both femurs, still in articulation. He was severed at lumbar level and in a symmetric way in the distal ends of the femurs.

symmetrically severed above their distal ends whereas the tibial plates of individual B were completely separated due to the cuts. The analysis was only macroscopic. The cuts were consistent with a heavy tool such a machete, which caused mixed lesions designated in Portuguese as *corto-contundente*. Besides, individual B displayed perforating injuries in

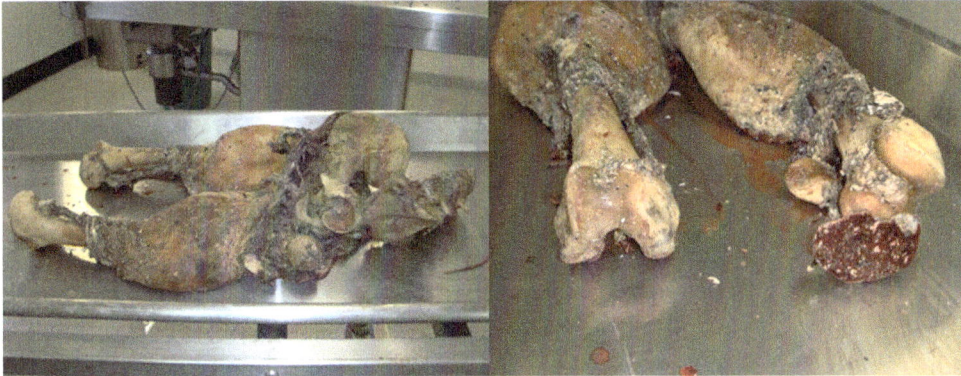

FIGURE 3.20   Individual B was also in an advanced state of preservation. The body of this adult male was also severed at lumbar level, that is, lower abdomen. Besides, he was shot in the pelvis.

FIGURE 3.21   Skeleton A after maceration: L3 and distal epiphysis of the femurs exhibit clear cut sections.

the sacrum and left iliac consistent to a (using again Portuguese terminology) *perfuro-contundente* action, that is, a gunshot wound (GSW). We interpreted that a GSW killed at least one of the victims and that both were dismembered after death (Figs. 3.21 and 3.22). Identification was not attained.

FIGURE 3.22   Skeleton B after maceration: L3 and proximal epiphysis of the right tibia clear cut sections; gunshot wounds seen in right side of sacrum.

CONCLUSION

The globalized and computerized world allows the exchange of information in volume and time never experienced before. Understanding the type of violence, its causes, and modus operandi plays an important role in the search for solutions. The dismemberment of bodies soon after death in a context of violence in Brazil can be due to multiple motivations and has changed over time. From the sociocultural practices of pre-Columbian cultures through the episodes of conviction through the legal process, it has reached a point in the present day where cases of occasional dismemberment by a casual crime merge with overwhelming crimes perpetrated by drug cartels. This problem has reached a magnitude that justifies preemptive State actions. Uniting the various body segments, identifying the victim, and elucidating the cause of death are the major challenges for experts who deal with these cases.

Acknowledgments

The authors would like to thank Dr. Malthus Fonseca Galvão for Figures 3.3 to 3.6 and Dr. Elvis Adriano da Silva Oliveira for Figures 3.7 to 3.10 and Figure 3.12.

References

Allen, M.W., Jones, T.L., 2014. Violence and Warfare Among Hunter-Gatherers, first ed. Left Coast Press, Inc, Walnut Creek, California, USA.

Andrushko, V.A., Schwitalla, A.W., Walker, P.L., 2010. Trophy-taking and dismemberment as warfare strategies in prehistoric central California. Am. J. Phys. Anthropol. 141, 83—96.

Dogan, K.H., Demirci, S., Deniz, I., Erkol, Z., 2010. Decapitation and dismemberment of the corpse: a matricide case. J. Forensic Sci. 55, 542–545.

Gupta, R., Arora, V., 2013. Profile of mutilation-murder in northern medico-legal jurisdiction of Himachal Pradesh, India. J. Indian Acad. Forensic Med. 35, 151–155.

Häkkänen-Nyholm, H., Weizmann-Henelius, G., Salenius, S., Lindberg, N., Repo-Tiihonen, E., 2009. Homicides with mutilation of the victim's body. J. Forensic Sci. 54, 933–937.

Konopka, T., Bolechała, F., Strona, M., 2006. An unusual case of corpse dismemberment. Am. J. Forensic Med. Pathol. 27, 163–165.

Lessa, A., 2010. Períciasforenses e justiça criminal sob a ótica da antropologiaforense no Brasil. [Forensic investigation and criminal justice from the perspective of forensic anthropology in Brazil]. Segurança, Justiça e Cidadania 44, 153–172.

Rajs, J., Broberg, M., Lidberg, L., Lindquist, O., 1998. Criminal multilation of the human body in Sweden—a thirty-year medico-legal and forensic psychiatric study. J. Forensic Sci. 43, 563–580.

Rothschild, M.A., Schneider, V., 1999. Decapitation as a result of suicidal hanging. Forensic Sci. Int. 106, 55–62.

Zoja, R., Battistini, A., Gentile, G., 2009. Death with complete decapitation: report of four suicides by train. Am. J. Forensic Med. Pathol. 30, 303–306.

Further Reading

ftp://ftp.ibge.gov.br/Estimativasde_Populacao/Estimativas_2014/estimativa_dou_2014.pdf (accessed 29.03.17.).

http://infogbucket.s3.amazonaws.com/arquivos/2016/03/22/atlas_da_violencia_2016.pdf (accessed 30.03.17.).

http://www.historianet.com.br/conteudo/default.aspx?codigo = 612 (accessed 29.03.17.).

http://sylviacolombo.blogfolha.uol.com.br/2017/01/08/por-que-decapitar/ (accessed 30.03.17.).

BRASIL. DECRETO-LEI No 2.848, DE 7 DE DEZEMBRO DE 1940. Código Penal. <http://www.planalto.gov.br/ccivil_03/decreto-lei/Del2848compilado.htm> (accessed 14.05.17.).

Postmortem Criminal Mutilation in Panama

José Vicente Pachar Lucio

Forensic Pathology, Medico Legal Institute of Panama, Republic of Panama

The Central American region of Costa Rica, Nicaragua, Honduras, and El Salvador along with Mexico has one of highest crime levels in the world. In recent decades, three of these countries (Guatemala, El Salvador, and Nicaragua) have experienced internal conflicts along with major human rights violations resulting in thousands of human and material losses. Although to a lesser degree, Honduras also experienced armed conflict, while Costa Rica had minor violent outbreaks within regions. Panama faced a difficult internal political conflict that culminated in the US invasion in 1989. Toward the end of the last decade, democratization of the region, specifically Nicaragua, Costa Rica, and Panama, resulted in positive outcomes with a notable decrease in violence. However, in the remaining countries, including Mexico, there has been an increase in criminality with extreme forms of cruelty such as dismemberment. To date, because there is an absence of academic training and scientific research in forensic pathology and anthropology, the study of postmortem dismemberment is limited and is primarily realized through the examination of published information within the region that reflects the technical, operative, and financial limitations of this expertise. Another major limitation is the lack of standardized reporting for these types of cases among government agencies.

Because of an increase in criminal activity from narcotraffickers, paramilitary groups, gangs, and *maras* or transnational associated gang organizations, a high incidence of homicides, femicides, and dismemberments have been reported in Mexico, Guatemala, Honduras, and El Salvador (Rosales Huerta, 2013; Fragoso, 1998; Alerta por descuartizados El Salvador; A los "Chirizos" atribuyen crímenes de desmembrados Honduras, 2013). For example, on May 13, 2012, 49 dismembered bodies were found in one day in Nuevo Leon in Mexico (Suman, 2013). In Guatemala, 188 cases of mutilation (decapitation and dismemberments) were reported for 2012 by the National Institute of Forensic Sciences (INACIF; INACIF, 2013). Conversely, a total of 19 of these types of cases were registered for 2008−16 by the Department of Forensic Pathology in Panama City, Panama.

63

When examining on a case-by-case basis the distinctive characteristics of dismemberments in the region, their distinction doesn't allow them to be easily classified into known published categories (Encuentran, 2013; Cuatro descuartizados frente a secundaria en Chilpancingo México, 2013; Hallan, 2013; Cadáver fue desmembrado con motosierra El Salvador, 2013; Hallan cuerpos desmembrados dentro de sacos Honduras, 2013; Byard et al., 2002). This new scenario has forced medicolegal practitioners in the region with a deficiency in forensic pathology and anthropology, to update their knowledge and work these cases in an individual and empirical manner. In this chapter, the most common types of criminal dismemberment observed in the region are presented and regional protocols are proposed for the approach and study of these cases.

CRIMINAL DISMEMBERMENT IN PANAMA

In a retrospective examination of the 2008–13 archives of the judicial morgue from the Department of Forensic Pathology, Institute of Legal Medicine and Forensic Sciences, in Panama City, nine cases of criminal mutilation were found (seven fragmented bodies and two body parts). Of these nine cases, seven were found in high crime urban sectors and two in rural areas. Seven bodies were complete, naked, or seminaked. Of these, five were wrapped in plastic bags or synthetic material; one body was decapitated, quartered, naked, and left aboveground; and another was buried fully clothed. The other two recorded cases corresponded to one male torso wrapped in synthetic material and right foot both found at different times on a Panama City beach.

The profiles of the complete bodies were young males with a mean age of 20 years with known police records and gang membership. Five were identified via fingerprints or secondary methods such as tattoos and two via DNA. According to DNA, the body parts did not correspond to any of the individuals nor were any additional parts recovered. In six of the cases, cause of death was established with three from sharp force trauma, two from gunshot wounds to the head, and one by mechanical asphyxia. Proof of postmortem dismemberment was evidenced by the absence of any signs of vital reaction to the sectioned borders of the neck and extremities. Five of the cases had similar modes of fragmentation and in every case the genital area was intact. In six of the cases, transection through bone was conducted with a blunt-sharp implement (e.g., machete), in one case a hammer, in one case a manual saw, in one case a large nonserrated knife; for the foot the instrument used was indeterminate. In the following years, from 2013 to 2016, 10 cases with similar characteristics were recorded.

CASE REPORT

A decapitated, dismembered female without hands was recovered from a river near a highway close to Panama City on September 17, 2017 (Fig. 4.1). The body was recovered by civil protection officers. The analysis was performed at the mortuary of the Forensic Sciences and Medicolegal Institute of Panama, in the city of La Chorrera, by the author.

FIGURE 4.1   Nude and dismembered body immersed in water.

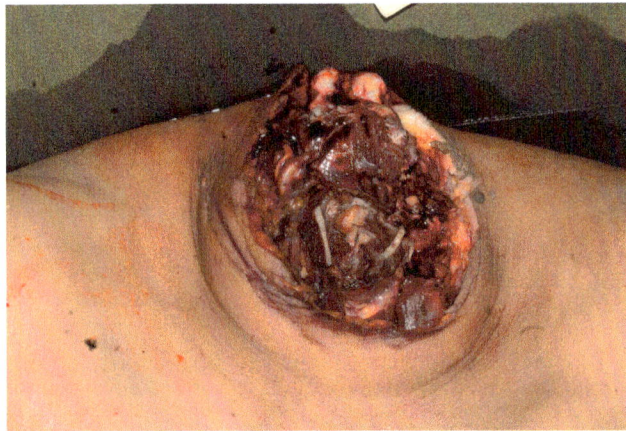

FIGURE 4.2   Decapitation by full neck section.

Missing persons data and postmortem data were obtained using Interpol Disaster Victim identification forms. Although general identification was possible using matching data (anthropological characterization of ancestry, sex, age, scars, recognition of scars, etc., by next-of-kin), positive identification was impossible using conventional methods such as fingerprints or odontology due to absence of those parts. There were no identifiable peri-mortem injuries on the remains available for autopsy and thus, cause of death was not determined. However, the dismembered sections showed evidence of sharp force on the neck and wrists (Figs. 4.2–4.3). Further investigations of the missing person's last movements led to the original crime scene to an urban transport bus. Although the primary crime scene had been washed away, remnants of blood stains were enough to recon-struct the events. Bloodstain pattern analysis revealed evidence of significant bloodshed

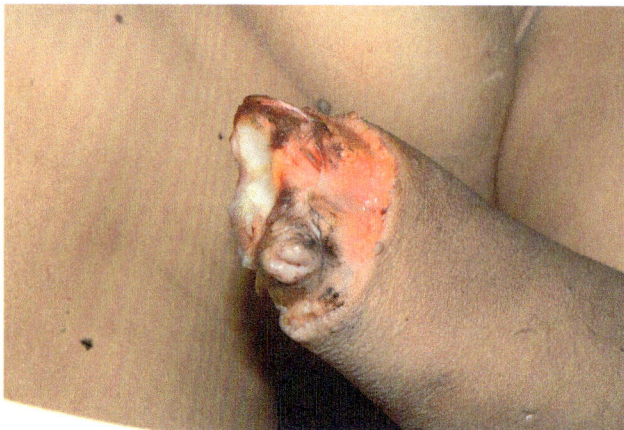

FIGURE 4.3   Section and disarticulation of the left hand.

either before or after death. The victim was sexually assaulted and died of suffocation based on the police investigation. Decapitation and dismemberment were done postmortem with a serrated knife based on the pattern observed on the edges of the skin and were consistent with the account of a hunter's knife described by a witness to the judicial authorities.

Soft tissue from the sectioned planes was sampled for histological analysis and no signs of vital reaction were observed. Positive identification was done via DNA, which confirmed the identification of the missing person.

PROPOSED ADDITIONAL CLASSIFICATION OF DISMEMBERMENT

Classification of dismemberment according to Saville et al. (2007) is based on the extension of amputations and includes localized, generalized, defensive, aggressive, offensive, and necromanic (see Chapter 12 this volume for detailed description). In addition, another form, communication, has also been described generally associated with criminal groups such as narcotraffickers and *maras* as a means of settling old scores and to scare and intimidate rivals (Pavón Cuellar and Albarrán Díaz, 2012). After examining the available cases of dismemberment from Mexico and Central America, some of these can be classified into the defensive type but many include additional elements of intent such as written notes, labeled body parts, pictorial or signs of violence of a psychological, psychiatric or symbolic etiology such as mutilation of the tongue, genitals, removal of the face and scalp, signs of torture, placing anatomical parts in public places or using them as trophies, fetishes, and photographic and video dissemination (Fragoso, 1998; Alerta por descuartizados El Salvador; A los "Chirizos" atribuyen crímenes de desmembrados Honduras, 2013; INACIF, 2013; Encuentran, 2013; Cuatro descuartizados frente a secundaria en Chilpancingo México, 2013; Hallan, 2013; Cadáver fue desmembrado con motosierra El Salvador, 2013; Hallan cuerpos desmembrados dentro de sacos Honduras, 2013). This information regarding motives specific to the region suggests that a *mixed* and *indeterminate* type should be added to the classification. A mixed type would include when two or more types of the original classification are encountered. For example, an offensive (genital) and/or aggressive type associated with the transmission of message by sending photographs by cell phone to family members. An indeterminate type would include cases in which the state of fragmentation does not allow for classification into an existing type.

DISCUSSION

In some of the countries of the region, extreme forms of violence such as dismemberments are clear manifestations of symbolic criminal activities along with mass disappearances and the discovery of clandestine burials are contextually tied to the increase and consolidation of narcotraffickers and other criminals. For example, in the recorded cases of mutilation in Mexico, is not only an elaborate exercise in violence resulting in death but also includes the dramatization of said mutilation. In other words, the intent is to cast a terrorizing death scene that shows the level of violence and cruelty that they are capable of. In addition, these mutilations are almost always accompanied by an elaborate declaration that allows the perpetrators to express their justification for their actions through written notes, as if violence exercised on the body need be accompanied by an explanation. Thus, this is the reason that Pavón Cuellar and Albarrán Díaz (2012) assert that in the interpretation of this type of mutilation the cadaver must be considered as the instrument of discursive action and that the body itself is solely the literal means of a bloody declaration (narcotrafficker discourse).

In El Salvador, Honduras, and Guatemala, the high crime index is longstanding and is part of a trail of violence including stoning, burning, and torture. It stands out that many cases of dismemberment and mutilation have taken place in penitentiaries overrun by gangs in constant turf wars inside and outside the jails. In addition, the proliferation of interment and concealment of bodies documented by the increase number of burial pits and clandestine cemeteries impedes the discovery and identification of the victims, which masks the reality of these cases. Another area worthy of mention is the sheer number of dismembered female bodies, reflecting the gravity and cruelty of femicides in the region (Instituto Interamericano de Derechos Humanos, 2006).

As previously mentioned, one of the many difficulties found in the record and analysis of these cases is a set of forensic protocols specific to these types of cases even though the constitutional configuration of the regional judiciary institutions envisions a coordinated and permanent interagency design, in practice, however, the actions of these medicolegal institutions continue to be fragmented and dysfunctional, with competing practices that impede an integrated function (Instituto Universitario de Opinión Pública Iudop, 2014). For this reason, investigations of criminal dismemberment must be consistent with an interinstitutional protocol (Pachar, 2015) that begins at the crime scene and the circumstances surrounding the scene, through the autopsy and determination of the type of dismemberment. The use of said protocol would facilitate medicolegal practice and scientifically ground police and judicial investigations, which will be conducive to the study and analysis on a national and regional level.

References

A los "Chirizos" atribuyen crímenes de desmembrados (Honduras). Disponible en <http://www.laprensa.hn/Secciones-Principales/Sucesos/A-Los-Chirizos-atribuyen-crimenes-de-desmembrados#.UWQV8JNO5hA>. Consultado el 10 de abril de 2013.

Alerta por descuartizados (El Salvador). Disponible en <http://www.elsalvador.com/noticias/2006/06/19/nacional/nac9.asp>.

Byard, R.W., James, R.A., Gilbert, J.D., 2002. Diagnostic problems associated with cadaveric trauma from animal activity. Am. J. Forensic Med. Pathol. 23 (3), 238–244.

Cadáver fue desmembrado con motosierra (El Salvador). Disponible en: <http://elmundo.com.sv/cadaver-fue-desmembrado-con-motosierra>. Consultado el 16 feb, 2013.

Cuatro descuartizados frente a secundaria en Chilpancingo (México). Disponible en <http://guerreronoticias.com/2009/12/cuatro-descuartizados-frente-a-secundaria-en-chilpancingo>. Consultado el 16 feb. 2013.

Encuentran 14 cadáveres descuartizados en México. Disponible en <http://www.lavoz.com.ar/noticias/mundo/encuentran-14-cadaveres-descuartizados-mexico>. Consultado el 10 de abril de 2013.

Fragoso, J.M., 1998. Feminicidio sexual serial en Ciudad Juárez: 1993–2001. Fuentes 18, 18.

Hallan 27 cuerpos descuartizados en Guatemala. Disponible en <http://spanish.peopledaily.com.cn/31614/7380874.html>. Consultado el 10 de abril de 2013.

Hallan cuerpos desmembrados dentro de sacos (Honduras). Disponible en: <http://laprensa.hn/Secciones-Principales/Sucesos/Hallan-cuerpos-desmembrados-dentro-de-sacos#.UR_toh03Z60>. Consultado el 16 feb. 2013.

INACIF – Guatemala. Datos Numéricos. Disponible en <www.inacif.gob.gt/estadisticas/anual/AnualM2012>. Consultado el 13 feb. 2013.

Instituto Interamericano de Derechos Humanos, 2006. I Informe regional: situación y análisis del femicidio en la región Centroamericana / Instituto Interamericano de Derechos. Humanos. IIDH, San José, Costa Rica.

Instituto Universitario de Opinión Pública (Iudop). La situación de la seguridad y la justicia 2009–2014: entre expectativas de cambio, mano dura militar y treguas pandilleras / Aguilar, Jeannette (Coord.). [et al.]. 1a ed. San Salvador, El Salv.: Instituto Universitario de Opinión Pública (Iudop), 2014.

Pachar, J.V., 2015. La investigación pericial forense de los cuerpos mutilados. Rev. Cienc. Forenses Honduras 1 (2), Año.

Pavón Cuellar, D., Albarrán Díaz, L., 2012. "Narco mensajes y cadáveres: el discurso del narcotráfico y su violenta literalidad corporal". En: Garate Martínez, I., Marinas Herreras, J.M., y Orozco Guzmán M. (coord.). Estremecimiento de lo real: ensayos psicoanalíticos sobre cuerpo y violencia (pp. 191–204).

Rosales Huerta G. Hallazgos necrópticos observados en piel y hueso que dejan los instrumentos utilizados en el desmembramiento criminal en cadáveres ingresados al servicio médico forense del distrito federal en el periodo de enero de 2008 a enero de 2010. Disponible en <http://www.repositoriodigital.ipn.mx/handle/123456789/12229>. Consultado el Feb 15, 2013.

Saville, P.A., Hainsworth, S.V., Rutty, G.N., 2007. Cutting crime: the analysis of the "uniqueness" of saw marks on bone. Int. J. Legal Med. 121, 347–357.

Suman 49 los cuerpos descuartizados, encontrados en una carretera de Nuevo León. Disponible en: <http://www.excelsior.com.mx/2012/05/13/nacional/833706>. Consultado el 10 de abril de 2013.

Dismemberment in South Africa: Case Studies

Maryna Steyn and Desiré Brits

Human Variation and Identification Research Unit (HVIRU), School of Anatomical Sciences, University of the Witwatersrand, Johannesburg, South Africa

INTRODUCTION

South Africa is unfortunately a country plagued by violence and crime and its murder rates are amongst the highest in the world (Vincent, 2008). Also known as the "Rainbow Nation," the country has a large variety of peoples with various different belief systems. While some areas are highly developed, other regions and pockets of the community have retained more traditional belief systems. South Africa has become a haven for refugees and migrants from all over Africa, adding to the problems with personal identification of victims and lack of reporting of missing individuals. The combination of the high levels of crime and the difficulties experienced with personal identification results in the fact that a large number of bodies are buried annually as unidentified paupers, and the associated crimes never solved (L'Abbé and Steyn, 2012; Bernitz et al., 2015; Steyn et al., 2016).

Worldwide bodies are most often dismembered in an attempt to hide/dispose of the body or make it unidentifiable (Symes et al., 2002; Christensen et al., 2014). While these are also motivations for dismemberment in South Africa, we have an additional different cause for dismemberment, namely muti/medicine murders (Scholtz et al., 1997; Steyn, 2005). *Muti* or *muthi* indicates a strong medicine, and in traditional belief systems human body parts are believed to be particularly strong medicine with various parts used for specific purposes (Ngubane, 1986; Scholtz et al., 1997; Labuschagne, 2004; Ashforth, 2005; Bishop, 2012). Human remains are particularly sought after as they are believed to contain the essence of the life of the individual/victim (Labuschagne, 2004; Vincent, 2008) and as such are very powerful. Body parts are usually harvested from live victims to ensure that this essence of life is retained within the remains to make powerful muti (Labuschagne, 2004). Fig. 5.1 shows two muti/medicine shops from the Limpopo Province of South Africa. These are common around the country, although the majority would only sell

FIGURE 5.1   (A and B) Muti shops in the Limpopo Province, South Africa.

traditional herbal and other medicines. The selling of human body parts is of course illegal and condemned by the vast majority of southern Africans and traditional healers. Body parts may be obtained by actually killing an individual, or by sourcing remains from deceased individuals, although removing body parts from the living makes for even stronger muti (Labuschagne, 2004; Vincent, 2008).

Ngubane (1986) mentioned that ritual killings for medicinal purposes in traditional societies are sometimes the work of a group of people. These people would typically be a group with some common interests, for example, the advancement of a business. The victim may have personal or physical qualities that are needed for a specific purpose, and therefore may sometimes be someone close to the members of the group or the person harvesting the remains. Vincent (2008), for example, describes in some detail the murder of 21-month-old Theophilus Mabuda by his father, a traditional healer. Minnaar et al. (1991) mentioned that these ritual murders may in some cases be seen to be for the common good of the group, and are therefore not necessarily seen as murder. Nowadays muti killings are however more frequently sought by individuals for *personal gain* (Vincent, 2008).

Steyn (2005) reported on a muti-related case where the remains of at least two individuals were used to construct a series of medicine pots (two of these were made from human skulls). These pots were filled with human body parts, herbs, and other items. Other cases described in the literature include a small series of decapitations reported on in İşcan and Steyn (2013), which may have been muti-related, as well as cases described in a paper by Scholtz et al. (1997). As can be expected, many of the murders occur in more remote areas, such as Limpopo Province, Northern Zululand, Swaziland, Mpumalanga, and Venda but it is not uncommon in the cities (Labuschagne, 2004; Vincent, 2008). Cases are reported from time to time in the general media. For example, on August 26, 2016 News24 (a South African news website) reported that the body of a 3-year-old toddler was found in the Eastern Cape with its arms and legs removed. On August 10, 2016, News24 reported that two individuals were arrested for trying to sell a human head in Durban, KwaZulu-Natal. According to a police spokesperson the head had been burned beyond recognition. The two men (aged 20 and 24, respectively) apparently wanted to sell the head to informal traders. According to News24 this particular area is a popular place for sangomas (traditional doctors) to sell traditional medicine. Another, suspected muti reported by News24 (January 12, 2017) describes the theft of skeletal remains from a cemetery in Nelspruit, Mpumalanga, where the graves of an individual buried in 1968 and another from 2013 were robbed and emptied.

Unfortunately no statistics are available in South Africa regarding body dismemberments or muti-related killings as the manner of death in death registers are mainly recorded as either homicide (murder) or unknown. It has, however, been estimated that there are anything between 15 and 300 muti-related killings per year (Labuschagne, 2004) while others estimate this figure to be as high as 250 per year in the Limpopo Province alone (Vincent, 2008). Although this source is somewhat dated, Vincent (2008) mentioned that some people suggested that "South Africa is currently witnessing what is described as an 'epidemic' of occult-related violent crime" (p. 43). She described in some detail the possible reasons for this "epidemic."

In this chapter we will discuss four recent cases of dismemberment. Case 1 is a muti-related case, whereas for Case 2 very little information is available. Case 3 demonstrates some cut/chop marks of the vertebrae commonly associated with dismemberment. Case 4 is an example of presumable dismemberment in combination with postmortem damage most likely associated with skeletal processing. It should be kept in mind that these four cases reflect the experience of the authors, and may not necessarily be representative of all cases in the country. Also, it only reflects what is seen on skeletal tissue and does not include signs of dismemberment on soft tissues.

CASE STUDY 1

In 2014, police apprehended a man in the Gauteng province of South Africa carrying a suspicious-looking bucket with a lid. Upon opening the bucket, a human head was found inside. According to information received, the remains were destined to be used for muti. The remains were defleshed/cleaned and were found to comprise of a human cranium and mandible (Figs. 5.2 and 5.3) and first cervical vertebra (atlas). Also included were five vertebrae of a young animal. The right ramus of the mandible was missing.

Age estimation of the victim was difficult as no postcranial remains were available. The third molars of this individual had erupted and were worn and there were also several antemortem tooth losses. The synchondrosis sphenooccipitalis was obliterated and several

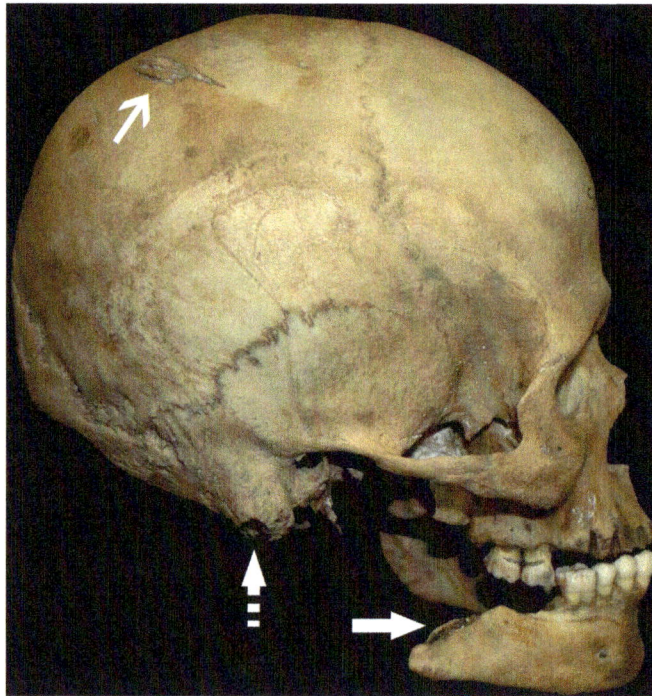

FIGURE 5.2   Case 1: skull in right view. Note the fractured mandible (*solid arrow*), missing tip of the mastoid process (*dashed arrow*), and lesion on the cranium (*line arrow*).

FIGURE 5.3   Close-up view of the injury on the skull.

cranial sutures were closed. A lower canine was present and was used to calculate the age using the Lamendin method adapted for South Africans (Ackermann and Steyn, 2014). The formula for "South African blacks, both sexes, lower canine" was used, and an estimate of 37.314 ± 12.85 years was obtained. This individual was most probably a middle-aged adult, most likely in his/her 30s or 40s.

Sex was similarly difficult to estimate from the skull only and the cranial features were very ambiguous with a medium-sized nuchal crest, small mastoid processes, sharp-ish supraorbital margins, medium-sized supraorbital ridges, and roundish chin. A FORDISC3.1 (FD3) analysis (not shown here) indicated a male individual (with posterior probabilities of 70% when run for sex and ancestry and 93% when run for sex only) (Jantz and Ousley, 2005). This individual was thus assessed to have been male. The morphological features and FD3 analysis, using a custom South African database, suggested an individual of African descent, but the possibility of other genetic influences cannot be excluded as the posterior probabilities were low.

Evidence of blunt force trauma with a sharp object (chop wound) was visible on the right parietal area (Figs. 5.2 and 5.3). This lesion was ± 32 mm to the right of the sagittal suture, and ± 50 mm behind the right coronal suture. It was about 35 mm in length, and showed a linear defect with parallel hinge fractures driven inwards (Kimmerle and Baraybar, 2008; İşcan and Steyn, 2013). Small areas of bone loss (bone wastage) were evident. This lesion did not penetrate into the skull. The left zygomatic bone was fractured with bone loss, but it could not be ascertained when this injury occurred.

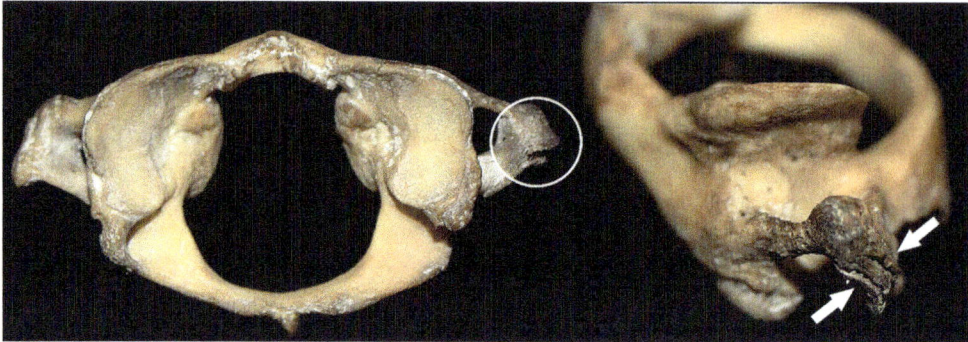

FIGURE 5.4   Traumatic changes to the first vertebra. Note the two cut/chop marks on the transverse process (*solid arrows*).

The right side of the mandible showed evidence of blunt force trauma (possibly with a sharp object), with a fracture through the gonial area (Fig. 5.2). The ramus was not present. A small area of bone loss could also be seen on the tip of the right mastoid process (Fig. 5.2). In addition to the evidence of blunt force trauma to the skull, two cut/slice/chop marks could be observed on the right transverse process of the atlas (Fig. 5.4), with a slight area of bone loss. Some bone loss could also be observed on this vertebra on the inferior aspect of the right superior articular process. These three lesions (on the mandible, mastoid, and inferior part of the atlas) may be part of the same incident of trauma, with a chop wound type of injury sustained from the right side.

No other cut marks could be observed on the remains available.

It seems plausible that the individual received at least two blows with an object, such as a machete, spade, axe, or panga. One of these blows left the injury on the right parietal bone, while another, much more violent blow fractured the mandible, chopped off a bit of the right mastoid, and left a small indentation on the atlas. A different, smaller instrument was then probably used to dismember the individual, leaving the two marks observed on the right transverse process of the atlas. While the evidence for dismemberment was unequivocal, it was interesting to note how little evidence of this was preserved in the skeleton, in particular the vertebrae themselves.

CASE STUDY 2

In 2004, a fully fleshed human skull with hair and soft tissue was found floating in a dam in the greater Ekurhuleni municipal area (Gauteng Province). The remains comprised of a human cranium, mandible, and five cervical vertebrae. Although still a subadult, the characteristics of the skull (e.g., vertical forehead, small mastoids, sharp orbital margins, no supraorbital ridges) and mandible (e.g., pointed chin) tentatively suggested a female individual. The remains were generally delicate in appearance. All present teeth were permanent but the third molars were only in the early phases of eruption. The synchondrosis sphenooccipitalis and all the other cranial sutures were still open. The cranial and dental characteristics indicated a young individual who had probably been about 17 ± 2 years old.

The characteristics of the face and skull indicated an individual of black African origin. The skull appeared long and low, although mesocephalic. In 2004 FORDISC did not contain a custom South African database, and therefore discriminant function analysis (İşcan and Steyn, 1999) was conducted. These provided mixed results; function 1 (cranial dimensions) indicated an individual of African affinity, while functions 2 (vault) and 3 (face) indicated European affinity. This individual was thus most likely of mixed descent.

Both zygomatic arches and both mandibular condyles were broken (or eroded). It was difficult to determine whether this happened perimortem or postmortem. Cut marks were visible on the anterior surfaces of the bodies of vertebrae C4 and C5 (Fig. 5.5). Cut marks on C4 extended to the transverse processes. Some loss of bone on the vertebral body was evident. The cut mark on C5 ran obliquely on the body of the vertebra and small marks were also visible on the right transverse process.

The observed cut marks were most probably made by a sharp object used during the process of decapitation of the individual. It is also not unusual to have cut marks on the anterior surfaces of cervical vertebrae when an individual's throat is sliced, but the facts that there were more than one mark and that only the head was found suggest that this is a case of dismemberment. The motive for the decapitation was not clear and the victim was, to our knowledge, not identified.

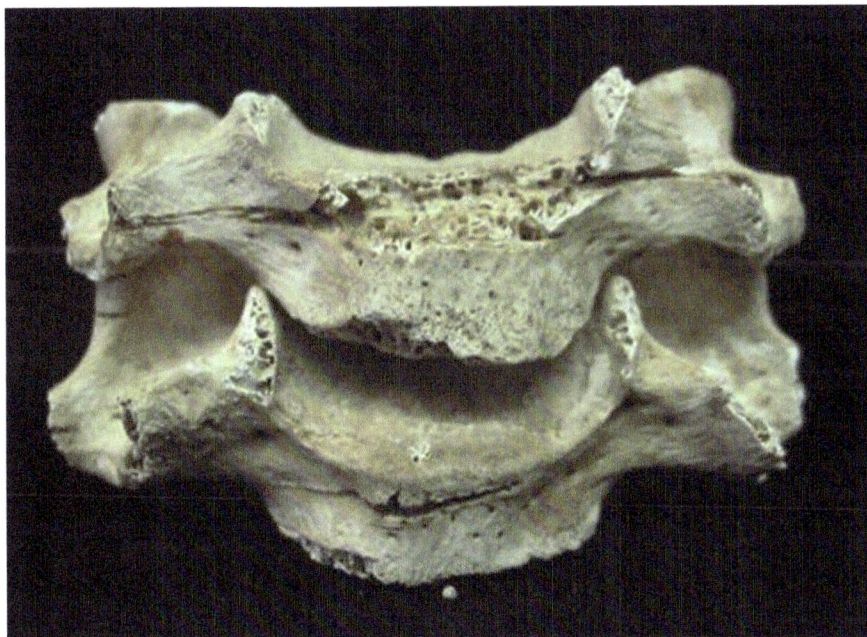

FIGURE 5.5   Case 2: cut marks on the bodies and transverse processes of C4 and C5. Source: *From İşcan, M.Y., Steyn, M., 2013. The Human Skeleton in Forensic Medicine. Charles C. Thomas, Springfield. Fig. 9.16; published with permission of Charles C. Thomas.*

CASE STUDY 3

In 2016, a forensic medical practitioner from the Forensic Pathology Services (FPS) requested forensic anthropological analysis of a decapitation injury with transection of the cervical spine. The fresh transected vertebrae were macerated by the FPS and the skeletonized remains, which comprised of three cervical vertebrae (two complete and one fragmentary), presumably C2—C4, along with a number of vertebral fragments were submitted for forensic anthropological analysis.

All three cervical vertebrae along with a number of the vertebral fragments showed evidence of sharp force trauma. These bone severing incisions were presumed to be cut/slice/chop marks (Symes et al., 2012; Berryman et al., 2013; İşcan and Steyn, 2013; Christensen et al., 2014) and were not consistent with saw marks. Multiple straight-line bone severing cut/chop marks orientated in various directions were observed.

The body of the axis had been completely transected from the vertebral arch in the posterior aspect of the superior articular facets (Figs. 5.6 and 5.7). The cut/slice/chop mark had a smooth appearance inferiorly but appeared more jagged superiorly. The rugged appearance of the superior aspect of the cut/slice/chop mark might have been produced when the weapon was removed from the bone causing the weakened bone to fail and break (sharp-blunt trauma) (Fig. 5.7).

A bone severing cut/slice/chop mark was also visible on the anterior surface of the body of the third cervical vertebra, which severed the anterosuperior aspect of the body as well as the superior tip of the left anterior tubercle of the transverse process and the left uncinate process (Fig. 5.6). Peeling or shaving defects were noted on the anterosuperior

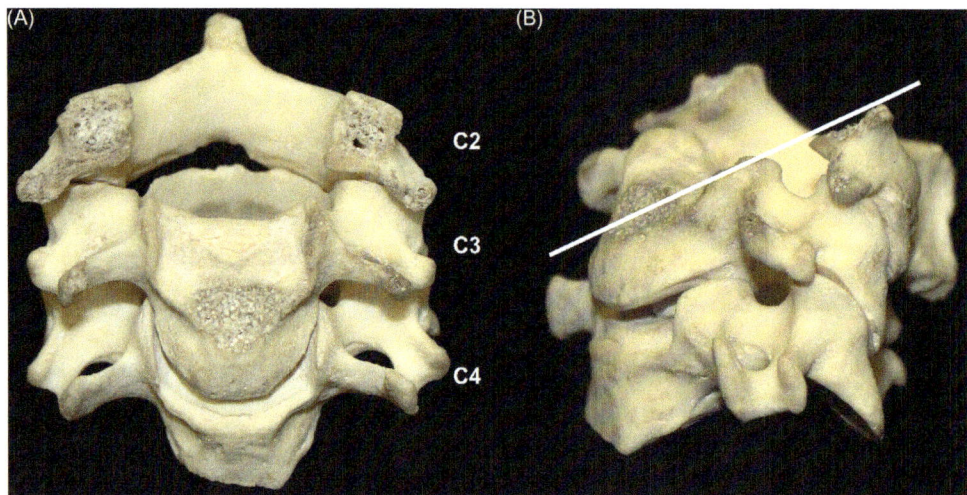

FIGURE 5.6   Case 3: cervical vertebrae (C2—C4). (A) Note the transected body of the axis, as well as the cut/chop marks on the superior aspect of the body of the 3rd and the inferolateral aspect of the body of the 4th cervical vertebrae. (B) The trauma observed on the second and third vertebrae is likely due to a single anterior cut/slice/chop from an inferior to superior direction.

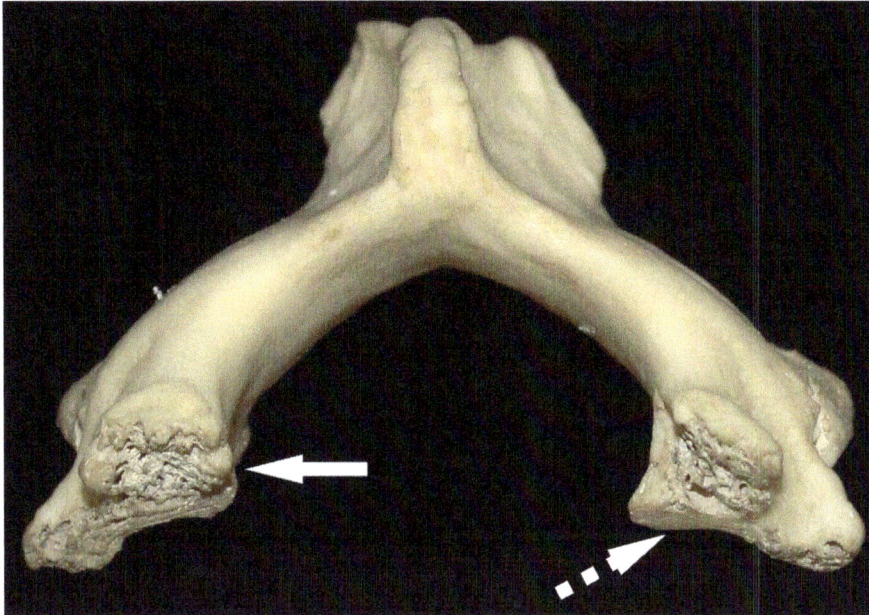

FIGURE 5.7   The anterosuperior view of the axis demonstrating the smooth incisions inferiorly (*dashed arrow*) and jagged area (*solid arrow*) superiorly.

aspect of the left transverse process and the anterior aspect of the anterior tubercle of the right transverse process (Fig. 5.6). It is likely that the sharp force trauma observed on the second and third cervical vertebrae was due to a single anterior cut/slice/chop from an inferior to superior direction.

An oblique cut/slice/chop mark was also present on the inferior surface of the body of the fourth cervical vertebrae, which severed the anterior margin of the right inferolateral aspect of the body (Fig. 5.6). This cut/slice/chop mark extended toward the inferior aspect of the anterior tubercle of the right transverse process. The cut/slice/chop mark severed the anterior tubercle of the right transverse process and may have caused the weakened posterior tubercle of the right transverse process to break off (Fig. 5.6). It is possible that this anterior cut/slice/chop was directed from left to right.

From the forensic anthropological analysis, it seems that there were at least two separate cuts/slices/chops executed with a long and heavy weapon (Kimmerle and Baraybar, 2008), such as machete or panga. Unfortunately no other skeletal elements were sent for forensic anthropological analysis and as such it is unknown if any other part of the body showed signs of dismemberment or attempted dismemberment.

CASE STUDY 4

Advanced decomposed and partially skeletonized remains were recovered from a river in Gauteng in August 2012. The adhering desiccated tissue and mud were cleaned and macerated by the FPS in 2014 and only a selected number of skeletal elements were submitted in 2016 for forensic anthropological analysis. This included the cranium, mandible, five vertebrae (four cervical and one lumbar), sacrum, three coccygeal vertebrae, left and right os coxae, the broken right femur, and the proximal part of the left femur.

The age of the victim was assessed from both cranial and postcranial elements. All permanent teeth, including the maxillary third molars, were erupted although the right third maxillary molar was not in full occlusion. Overall the dentition showed little to no dental wear. All available epiphyses as well as the sphenooccipital synchondrosis were fused, which is indicative of an adult individual (Scheuer and Black, 2004). No osteoarthritic growth was noted around the available joint surfaces nor were any osteophytes associated with the available vertebrae. Age was also estimated with transition analysis (Boldsen et al., 2002, 2011) based on the effects of aging as assessed from the cranial sutures, the pelvic symphyses, and auricular surfaces of the pelvis. Based on this analysis the individual was most probably a young to middle-aged adult, most likely between 26 and 40 years.

Morphological features of the pelvis such as the presence of a ventral arc, subpubic concavity, and a narrow ischiopubic ramus were indicative of a female individual (Phenice, 1969; Klales et al., 2012). Likewise, morphological features of the skull including sharp supraorbital margins as well as the limited projection of the glabellar area and the mental eminence were also indicative of a female individual (Walker, 2008; Krüger et al., 2015).

Ancestry was assessed based on morphological (Hefner, 2009) and metric analyses of the skull. FD3 in combination with a custom South African database comprised of black, colored, and white South Africans was used for metric analysis (Jantz and Ousley, 2005). Results suggested an individual of African descent.

Some postmortem damage was noted on the skull just superior to the right mastoid process. Signs of presumable postmortem thermal damage were also visible on the right femur. The thermal damage was localized. An area of charring was present on the posteriorlateral surface of the proximal shaft along with a heat border suggesting that some tissue still adhered to the bone when burned (Christensen et al., 2014). The irregular burning pattern is however indicative of a body that might not have been fully fleshed when burnt. A transverse postmortem fracture was also associated with the area of thermal damage. The shaft of the left femur was transected proximally, presumably postmortem. Saw marks were visible on the compact bone and ran perpendicular to the shaft of the bone. A breakaway spur, commonly associated with saw marks (Christensen et al., 2014), could be seen on the posterolateral aspect of the shaft (Fig. 5.8).

The atlas, axis, and two additional cervical vertebrae along with a lumbar vertebra were included in the skeletal remains received for forensic anthropological analysis. Presumable perimortem sharp force trauma was observed on the two lower cervical vertebrae, which did not appear to follow in sequence. Sharp trauma was noted on the lateral margin of the right inferior articular facet of what was believed to be the 3rd cervical vertebra (Fig. 5.9). A peeling/shaving defect was also noted on the inferior aspect of the right transverse process (Fig. 5.9). The superior aspect of the right anterior tubercle of the transverse process was damaged and broken off. Likewise, the superior aspect of the right anterior tubercle of the transverse process of the lower cervical vertebra (presumably C5) was also broken off. A cut mark was also present on this vertebra on the lateral aspect of the right superior articular facet and process along with presumable scrape marks just superior to the cut mark on the posterior aspect of the superior articular process (Fig. 5.10).

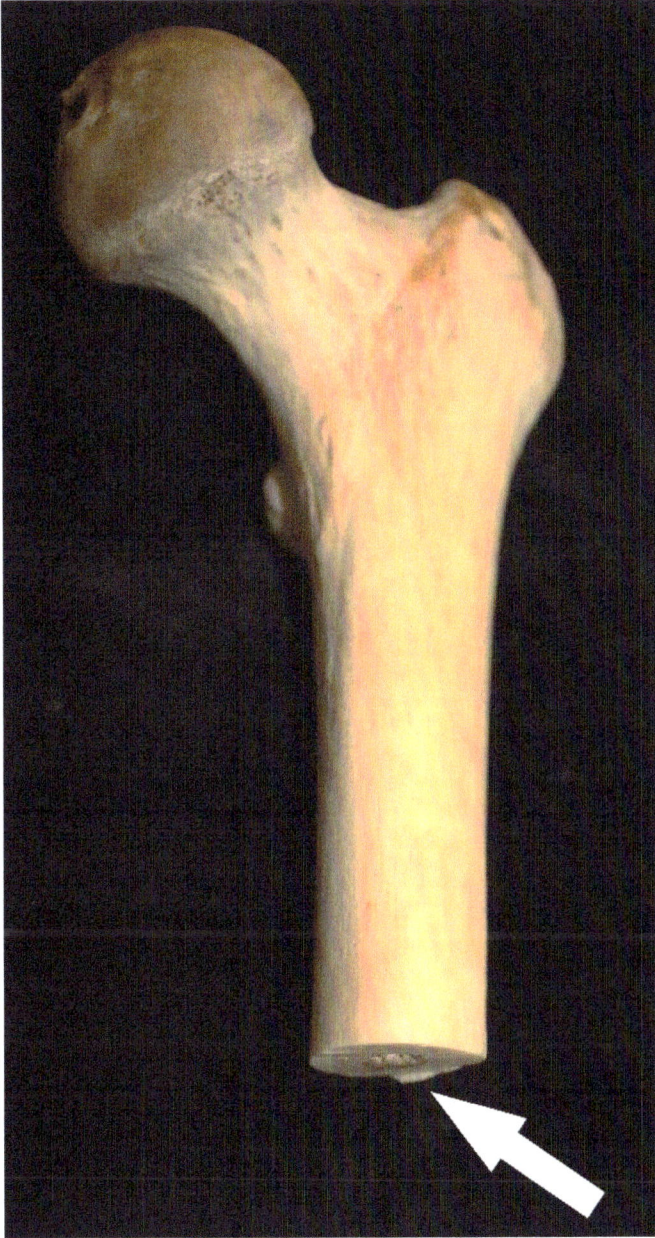

FIGURE 5.8 Case 4: left proximal femur with saw marks that run perpendicular to the long axis of the bone with a breakaway spur (*solid arrow*) on the posterolateral aspect of the shaft.

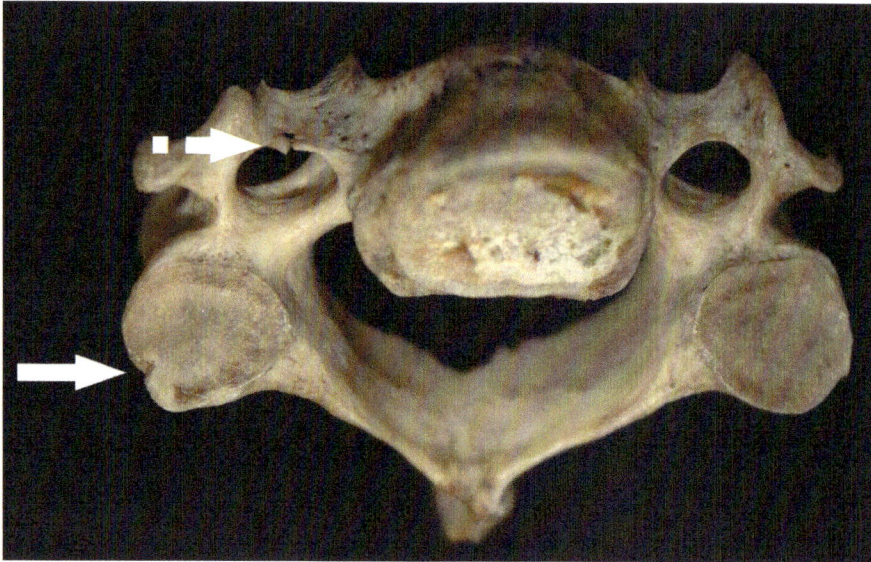

FIGURE 5.9   Sharp trauma to the lateral margin of the right inferior articular facet (*solid arrow*) with a peeling/shaving defect on the inferior aspect of the right transverse process (*dashed arrow*).

FIGURE 5.10   Cut mark on the lateral aspect of the right superior articular facet and process (*solid arrow*) with presumable scrape marks (*dashed arrow*).

It seems plausible that the left femur was transected postmortem in an attempt to dismember the individual. Damage to the two cervical vertebrae are, however, thought to be associated with processing/maceration damage as the spinal column was intact according to the forensic pathologist's report, indicating that the damage had to have been sustained after the initial autopsy/examination.

DISCUSSION

In this chapter we reported on three or possibly four cases of dismemberment, of which at least one is associated with muti/medicine murders. It is interesting to note that all of the confirmed muti-related cases involved the head and neck, and that in our context and experience dismemberment of peripheral body parts as far as the skeleton is concerned is rare. When dealing with harvesting body parts for muti, many other parts of the body are used but these mainly involve soft tissues such as the genitals, breasts, tongues, hands, etc. and may not leave signs on the skeleton. Literature on muti and muti-related killings is relatively scarce and further complicating the understanding thereof is the often contradicting literature available (Labuschagne, 2004; Vincent, 2008). It should however be kept in mind that these traditional practices are mainly carried forward from one generation to the next based on word of mouth and as such practices often differ (Labuschagne, 2004).

Unfortunately dismemberment and/or muti-related killings happen with relatively high frequency in South Africa, but there are very limited statistics available (Labuschagne, 2004; Vincent, 2008). Adults and children, friends, and/or family members can be potential victims. Interestingly, the elderly are not usually used for muti as it is believed that their muti will be less powerful (Labuschagne, 2004). An important requirement when harvesting organs for muti is that the victim possesses the necessary qualities sought by the client.

Victims of muti-related killings are rarely buried (Labuschagne, 2004) and when the remains of these individuals are recovered there is also often a long delay in submission of these cases to forensic anthropologists. There is also often a lack of will from officers to try and solve these cases. This can be related to the more traditional beliefs of some investigators or the rumors surrounding the involvement of politicians and/or esteemed businessmen that cause the investigators to fear the consequences of their involvement in such investigations (Labuschagne, 2004). Likewise, community members are often also reluctant to testify in these cases for fear of being targeted (Vincent, 2008), which results in the fact that conviction rates are low, and it is hard to get good feedback on motivations and outcomes.

It is interesting to note that more than one weapon may be used in cases of dismemberment, as illustrated in Case 1. In this case, it seems that a larger weapon (axe, machete, or panga) was used to kill the individual, whereas another instrument was used for the dismemberment. This clearly shows some preplanning of the event.

It may be assumed that operators who source material for the muti trade may have some experience with dismemberment thus leaving limited evidence of cut marks. Even so, cut marks should always be visible as it is nearly impossible to dismember a fresh body without leaving any traces. One of us (MS) was involved in an alleged case of dismemberment where the body of a hefty female was stuffed in the trunk of a car. According to witnesses, the body had then gone into rigor and could not be taken out to be buried. The body was then allegedly dismembered to some extent and eventually stuffed into an animal burrow. The remains were submitted for analysis, but no signs of cut marks could be found on any part of the skeleton, and the conclusion was made that dismemberment in this case was highly unlikely (much to the dismay of the prosecutors). To our knowledge, no cases of dismemberment have been reported in the literature without any cut or chop marks on the skeleton.

In South Africa, forensic anthropologists do not attend crime scenes and rarely receive background information pertaining to cases. As such trauma analyses and the interpretation thereof are limited to skeletal analysis. Often some relevant information is provided by the forensic pathologist that can be of vital importance as is illustrated in Case 4. Without the pathologists' notes on the vertebral column the associated vertebral damage could have been interpreted as an attempt at decapitation. The analyst should therefore be very careful not to overinterpret the evidence, and make sure that there is sufficient evidence to suggest dismemberment. Nevertheless, in this case, some uncertainty remains as to what happened to the femur.

In conclusion, here we reported on three, possibly four cases of dismemberment. In a country plagued by crime and violence the problems with large numbers of unidentified bodies are exacerbated by many factors, amongst them the muti trade, which is possibly the most likely cause for dismemberment in the region.

Acknowledgments

The authors would like to acknowledge the National Research Foundation for funding of research. We are also grateful to our colleagues in the South African Police Services and Forensic Pathology Services for referring cases to us, as well as to Mr. N. Bacci, Mr. T. Meadows, Dr. J. Myburgh, and Dr. T. Houlton for their assistance with the cases and photographs.

References

Ackermann, A., Steyn, M., 2014. A test of the Lamendin method of age estimation in South African canines. Forensic Sci. Int. 236, 192.e1–192.e6.

Ashforth, A., 2005. Muthi, medicine and witchcraft: regulating 'African science' in post-apartheid South Africa? Soc. Dyn. 31, 211–242.

Bernitz, H., Kenyhercz, M., Kloppers, B., L'Abbé, E.N., Labuschagne, G.N., Olckers, A., et al., 2015. The history and current status of forensic science in South Africa. In: Ubelaker, D.H. (Ed.), The Global Practice of Forensic Science. Wiley-Blackwell, pp. 241–250.

Berryman, H.E., Shirley, N.R., Lanfear, A.K., 2013. Low velocity trauma. In: Tersigni-Terrant, M.A., Shirley, N.R. (Eds.), Forensic Anthropology: An introduction. CRC Press, Boca Raton, pp. 271–290.

Bishop, K.M., 2012. Anglo American media representations, traditional medicine, and HIV/AIDS in South Africa: from muti killings to garlic cures. GeoJournal 77, 571–581.

Boldsen, J.L., Milner, G.R., Konigsberg, L.W., Wood, J.W., 2002. Transition analysis: a new method for estimating age from skeletons. In: Hoppa, R.D., Vaupel, J.W. (Eds.), Paleodemography: Age Distributions From Skeletal Samples. Cambridge University Press, Cambridge, pp. 73–106.

Boldsen, J.L., Milner, G.R., Hylleberg, R., 2011. ADBOU Age estimation software. Version 2.0.

Christensen, A.M., Passalacqua, N.V., Bartelink, E.J., 2014. Forensic Anthropology: Current Methods and Practice. Academic Press, San Diego.

Hefner, J.T., 2009. Cranial nonmetric variation and estimating ancestry. J. Forensic Sci. 54, 985–995.

İşcan, M.Y., Steyn, M., 1999. Craniometric assessment of population affinity in South Africans. Int. J. Legal Med. 112 (2), 91–97.

İşcan, M.Y., Steyn, M., 2013. The Human Skeleton in Forensic Medicine. Charles C. Thomas, Springfield.

Jantz, R., Ousley, S.D., 2005. FORDISC 3.1. Computerized Forensic Discriminant Functions. Version 3.1. The University of Tennessee, Knoxville, TN.

Kimmerle, E.H., Baraybar, J.P., 2008. Skeletal Trauma. CRC Press, Boca Raton.

Klales, A.R., Ousley, S.D., Vollner, J.M., 2012. A revised method of sexing the human innominate using Phenice's nonmetric traits and statistical methods. Am. J. Phys. Anthropol. 149, 104–114.

Krüger, G.C., L'Abbé, E.N., Stull, K.E., Kenyhercz, M.W., 2015. Sexual dimorphism in cranial morphology among modern South Africans. Int. J. Legal Med. 129, 869–875.

L'Abbé, E.N., Steyn, M., 2012. The establishment and advancement of forensic anthropology in South Africa. In: Dirkmaat, D.C. (Ed.), A Companion to Forensic Anthropology. Wiley-Blackwell, pp. 626–638.

Labuschagne, G., 2004. Features and investigative implications of muti murder in South Africa. J. Invest. Psychol. Off. Profil. 1, 191–206.

Minnaar, A.V., Offringa, D., Payze, C., 1991. To live in fear: witch burning and medicine murder in Venda. Report to the Human Sciences Research Council, Pretoria, South Africa.

Ngubane, H., 1986. The predicament of the sinister healer: some observations on 'ritual murder' and the professional role of the inyanga. In: Last, M., Chavunduka, G.L. (Eds.), The Professionalisation of African Medicine. Manchester University Press, Manchester, pp. 189–204.

Phenice, T.W., 1969. A newly developed visual method of sexing the os pubis. Am. J. Phys. Anthropol. 30, 297–302.

Scheuer, L., Black, S., 2004. The Juvenile Skeleton. Academic Press, London.

Scholtz, H.J., Phillips, V.M., Knobel, G.J., 1997. Muti or ritual murder. Forensic Sci. Int. 87, 117–123.

Steyn, M., 2005. Muti murders from South Africa: a case report. Forensic Sci. Int. 151 (2/3), 279–287.

Steyn, M., L'Abbé, E.N., Myburgh, J., 2016. Forensic anthropology as practiced in South Africa. In: Ubelaker, D., Blau, S. (Eds.), Handbook of Forensic Anthropology and Archaeology, second ed. Left Coast Press, Walnut Creek, CA.

Symes, S.A., Williams, J.A., Murray, E.A., Hoffman, J.M., Holland, T.D., Saul, J.M., et al., 2002. Taphonomic context of sharp-force trauma in suspect cases of human mutilation and dismemberment. In: Haglund, W., Sorg, M. (Eds.), Advances in Forensic Taphonomy. CRC Press, Boca Raton, pp. 403–434.

Symes, S.A., L'Abbé, E.N., Chapman, E.N., Wolff, I., Dirkmaat, D.C., 2012. Interpreting traumatic injury to bone in medicolegal investigations. In: Dirkmaat, D.C. (Ed.), A Companion to Forensic Anthropology. Wiley-Blackwell, Chichester, pp. 340–389.

Vincent, L., 2008. New magic for new times: muti murder in democratic South Africa. Tribes Tribals 2, 43–53.

Walker, P.L., 2008. Sexing skulls using discriminant function analysis of visually assessed traits. Am. J. Phys. Anthropol. 136, 39–50.

A Dismemberment Case From Portugal: How a Dozen Bones Can Tell the Story

Eugénia Cunha[1,2]

[1]National Institute of Legal Medicine and Forensic Sciences, Lisbon, Portugal [2]Centre for Functional Ecology, Department of Life Sciences, University of Coimbra, Coimbra, Portugal

INTRODUCTION

Although criminal behavior related to human dismemberment and mutilation has been recognized and investigated in Portugal, we here present a case of dismemberment that is quite uncommon in the country. The case calls attention to the importance of a good recovery, to the need for good complicity between several experts intervening in this type of case, and, above all, to the major contribution forensic anthropology can give. The goal is therefore to highlight the importance of interdisciplinary work and the role forensic anthropology can play in dismemberment cases.

THE CASE

During the follow up of a light fire in the woods in an outdoor site, the police found some dry bones nearby in ripped plastic bags between the burned vegetation (Fig. 6.1). All the recovery was performed by law enforcement officials. The first set of bones was delivered to the National Institute of Legal Medicine and Forensic Sciences (NILMFS), south delegation, in Lisbon where they were analyzed by the author. The good state of preservation of the bones, which were not affected by the fire, immediately made her think that the recovery was incomplete. Therefore, she insisted that the police should return to the recovery site to enlarge the recovery area. Another strong argument for that was the

FIGURE 6.1 Environment where the remains were found by the police. Note the ripped plastic bags. Purportedly the white ones were inside the large black waste sack. In this phase the human remains were already put together in one place.

obvious animal bite marks evident in several bones. It was necessary to know what were the animals in that place and to know about their habits. Scavenging is usually followed by scattering, and the search for bones is also a search for the scavengers. As, with time, the number of recovered bones decreases and the searching area for them increases (Cattaneo and Gibelli, 2017), time was a key factor for the resolution of the case. From the pictures taken by the police, it became evident that the local fauna had scattered the remains that were inside the plastic bags (Fig. 6.1).

The first assemblage of bones included the complete skull, three forearm bones, the two humeri, and two incomplete scapulae.

Two weeks later, the police came back with another set of bones. In effect, additional remains were recovered in the surrounding areas, namely bones of the lower limbs, five femur fragments, two portions of tibiae, a fibula diaphysis, an incomplete pelvic bone, a hand phalange, and a first metatarsal. The recovery continued to be quite incomplete since a large number of bones were missing. Among them, ribs and vertebrae, sternum, left pelvic bone, sacrum, hyoid, and foot and hand bones (except for one first metatarsal).

The postmortem examination was then undertaken in two phases. The initial goals were threefold: how many individuals correspond to the remains, identification of the victim(s), and the cause of the bone damage.

Minimum Number of Individuals

There was no duplication of skeletal elements, and the different long bone portions fitted to each other and allowed the reconstruction of part of the femora as well as part of the tibia. Parts of the same bone, like the femora, were reconstructed with several portions, which displayed different colors. Undoubtedly, the remains correspond to only one individual whose skeleton was poorly represented; only about 6% (13 out of 206) of the total bones were recovered.

FIGURE 6.2 Posterior views of both femurs with cuts more or less parallel in the proximal thirds and distal ones. Note the different colors of each portion, which suggest that these bone portions decomposed already separated from each other.

Taphonomic Alterations

At this point, the taphonomic critique was relevant since it is determinant for the evaluation of the other main goals. While some bone portions were brown, others from the same bone were much whitened and with green areas due to contact with vegetation (Fig. 6.2). It became clear that the several bone portions skeletonized already separated from each other, and that each of them had its own taphonomic microenvironment. Bite marks were perceivable in all the recovered bones and will be discussed further. Additionally, the fact that only 6% of the skeletal material was recovered reinforces the hypothesis of animal activity. Besides, plant action was also perceptible since thin plant roots were not only involving the bones but also inside their medullary cavity.

Identification

The general factors of identification were then assessed. Right os coxa, although incomplete, was consistent with a male, and the morphology of the skull also corroborated that estimation; age at death was inferred from what was left of the auricular surface, degenerative changes, and teeth. Ancestry was evaluated on the basis of both metric and

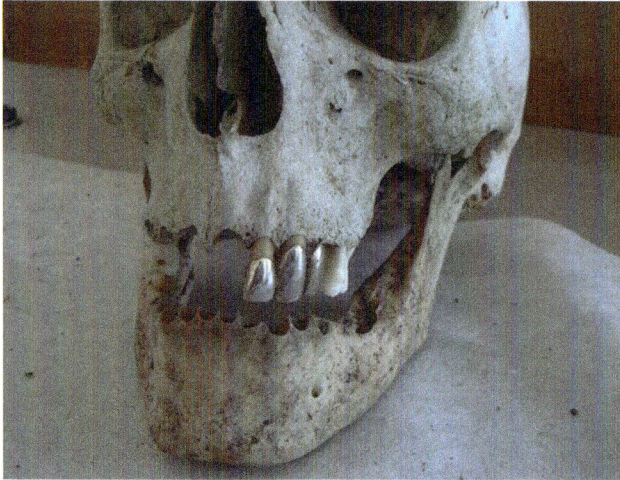

FIGURE 6.3   Detail of the anterior view of the skull where the three silver teeth are striking. Note also the extensive postmortem tooth loss, the antemortem tooth loss of tooth 36, as well as the different colors of the mandible and the remaining skull (much whiter). The different chromatic alterations are due to different decomposition microenvironments and indicate that the mandible was separated from the rest of the skull in an early phase of decomposition.

nonmetric traits of the face. Stature was estimated based on the 1st metatarsal length (Cordeiro et al., 2009). In all, the biological profile points to an adult male, more than 40 and less than 60 years of age; European, with a height of 170—180 mm.

At that time, we asked the police about missing persons in that area. Although there was not a probable victim for this specific case, after a search, it was found there was a Ukrainian individual who had been missing for two years. Fortunately, attempts to identify the body revealed a dental prosthesis with three teeth made up of a silver ligament (Fig. 6.3). In effect, notwithstanding the severe postmortem tooth loss, among the 10 in situ teeth, the silver and shining teeth immediately stood out and were revealed to be paramount (Fig. 6.3). Luckily, in the required photos of that missing individual, he was smiling, and silver teeth were obvious. Since the individual had no direct ascendants or descendants, only his wife, she was asked to provide the antemortem odontogram, which was sent from Ukraine and dated from 3 years before the year her husband went missing. The dental record had reference to a dental prosthesis in teeth 22, 23, and 24. In all, a convincing match was achieved, and a positive identification was reached. Furthermore, it was possible to confirm dental treatment to another two teeth and antemortem tooth loss of other two. It has to be mentioned that genetic identification was not possible since there were no direct ascendants or descendants, or close relatives to compare with.

Altogether, not only was the biological profile in agreement with that of the victim, but also dental alterations worked as paramount identity factors.

Postmortem Interval Estimation

The circumstance that the remains were kept inside plastic waste sacks is known to compromise postmortem interval estimation (PMI), namely the trend is to an underestimation (Scholl and Moffart, 2017). Yet, it seems that the sacks were ripped by the fauna when the remains were still fresh, which means that decomposition mainly happened at an open-air site.

FIGURE 6.4 Sawed left femur. Several points should be noticed. The thin roots inside the medullary cavity were useful for PMI.
The color of the cut surfaces matched the surrounding bone, indicating that the damage did occur before the bone was exposed to decomposition.
The cut marks exhibit a serrated pattern suggesting a toothed tool. Note also the breakaway spurs.

The fact the bones were completely dry and displayed thin plant roots, which were already well developed inside the medullary cavity of the long bones (Fig. 6.4), made us suspect that the postmortem interval was greater than 1 year. No other dating estimate method was done.

Trauma Interpretation

The next step was the trauma interpretation, which is the main focus of this article. Animal bite marks were all over the bones and affected 12 out of the 13 recovered bones (only the hand phalange was not affected) (Fig. 6.5). Damage was consistent with carnivore and rodent action. Both the mastoid processes and the occipital condyles were destroyed by the fauna as well as the mandibular condyles; as previously mentioned, the bones were clearly scattered by the fauna, which tore the plastic garbage bags when the remains were still fresh. But, besides the necrophagous fauna action, there were uniform and linear cut marks, which, upon initial macroscopic inspection, seemed to have been performed by a sharp instrument. The striations were the first clue. Both upper and lower limb fragmented bones displayed visible cuts in addition to animal bite marks. Several portions of the same bone could be matched at the cut mark lines (Fig. 6.2). It became obvious that we were dealing with a dismemberment case.

In what concerns the detail of bone cuts, they exhibit smooth cut surfaces and straight edges (Figs. 6.4, 6.6, and 6.7), which are known to be common in dismemberment cases (Symes et al., 2010). No cut marks were observed close to the joints.

Both humeri were severed at their distal ends (Fig. 6.6). Regarding the proximal ends, the left one displayed a sharp cut whereas the right one was destroyed by the fauna.

Both bones of the right forearm were cut at their distal ends. The ulna also presented a bite mark to the same distal extremity. Regarding the proximal ends, they were both gnawed, and the same applies to both extremities of the left radius diaphysis. Moreover, as already referred to, all of the diaphysis displayed very thin plant roots involving them.

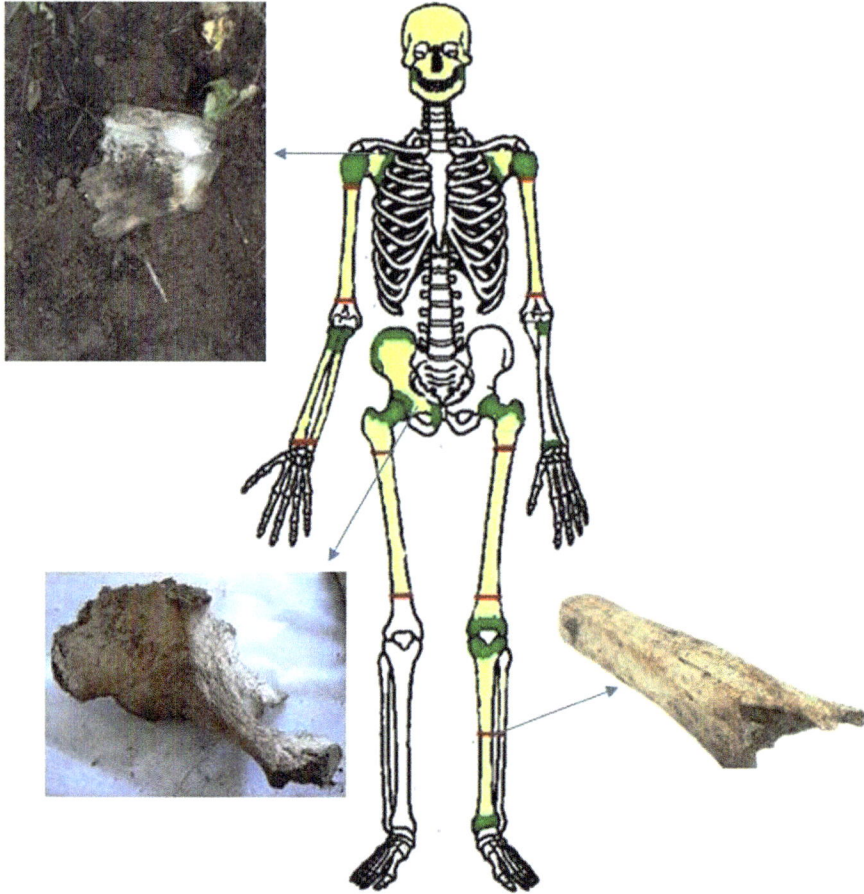

FIGURE 6.5   Schematic view of the case. In yellow: recovered bones. In green: bite marks; in red: cut marks; in white: nonrecovered bones. Some of the bones displaying bite marks are also displayed, namely the right os coxae, the left tibia, and one of the scapulae when it was found at the recovery scene.

Finally, the bodies of the scapulae were destroyed by gnawing. We cannot be completely sure whether some bite marks did not destroy the evidence of some more cut marks or disguised them, namely at the proximal ends of the forearm bones.

Concerning the femora, three portions of the left one and two of the right one could be matched at the cut marks (Fig. 6.2). The only recovered tibia, the left one, was represented by the diaphysis, which was severed at the midshaft. In all, 10 cuts were registered all in long bones.

In the distal portion of the left femur, in its posterior lateral side, two false starts were evident with a squared cross-section (Fig. 6.8). Besides giving an indication about where the cuts had been initiated, they are also informative about the sequence of the events.

FIGURE 6.6 Severed distal epiphysis of both humeri displaying clear dismemberment cuts. These cuts were characterized by their uniformity.

FIGURE 6.7 Some of the human remains discussed in this article with a close-up of the cross-sectional views of the proximal end of the left femur and distal end of the right one.

Once the main goals were achieved, secondary ones were assessed. Again we followed the suggestions of Symes et al. (2002).

Tool Identification

Unequivocally, we were dealing with sharp force trauma, that is, "a narrowly focused, dynamic, slow loaded, compressive force with a sharp object that produces damage to hard tissue in the form of an incision (broad or narrow)" (Symes et al., 2002). But, what type of sharp tool?

For the interpretation of the cuts, we followed Symes' recommendations (Symes et al., 1998, 2002, 2010, 2012) and those of Smith et al. (2003). Besides, he provided his own opinion

FIGURE 6.8 Severed distal end of the femur displaying two false starts. The cross-section of the false starts is wide and square, which is purportedly due to the set of teeth.

on the present case. In addition, we are now using (but not at the time the case was done) the research of Nogueira et al. (2016) since it includes experimental research about saw marks, including hand ones, in bones.

All the cuts were fairly clean and transverse (Figs. 6.4, 6.6, and 6.7). It looks like the hands had been cut on purpose since the cuts are above the wrists (Fig. 6.5). This fact could be informative for the motif underneath the dismemberment; it could eventually reflect the desire to hide the identity of the victim since it precluded fingerprinting. However, the fact that the face is not mutilated, retaining the dental prosthesis (Fig. 6.3), is against that idea.

In general, the cuts were more consistent with transection via sawing. There were no superficial cuts with the exception of two (Fig. 6.9) in the posterior surface, which look like two failed attempts to start the cuts.

It is acknowledged that sharp force trauma in bone may allow assessing the tool that was used to make the defect and how that tool was used (Rainwater, 2015). Consequently, to find the class of tool that had been used, the bone cut edges were fully examined by SEM analysis at the University of Oporto. This analysis provided a more detailed view of the striae in the kerf (Fig. 6.10), which are well known to be associated with sawing with a toothed blade (Reichs, 1998; Symes et al., 2010). Furthermore, those cut edges were also analyzed with a magnifying glass (Fig. 6.11). Parallel striations were the most striking feature and were also considered diagnostic of a saw (Fig. 6.11). Microscopic examination of the cut marks revealed, as well, the presence of recognizable striations, that is, scanning electron microscopy confirmed that the patterned marks were incised striations to the bone.

Both analyses revealed that a saw was the most probable tool involved with the bone sectioning, with the final steps of bone separation being performed manually (Fig. 6.4). Breakaway spurs indeed were visible in the tibia and femur cuts. Breakaway spurs are very well defined by Nogueira et al. (2016: 1) as "projections of the bone that indicate the blade exit due to the pressure exerted," that is, they indicate the direction of the cuts, in this case from the posterior to anterior side of the bones (Fig. 6.4). Nevertheless, we rather

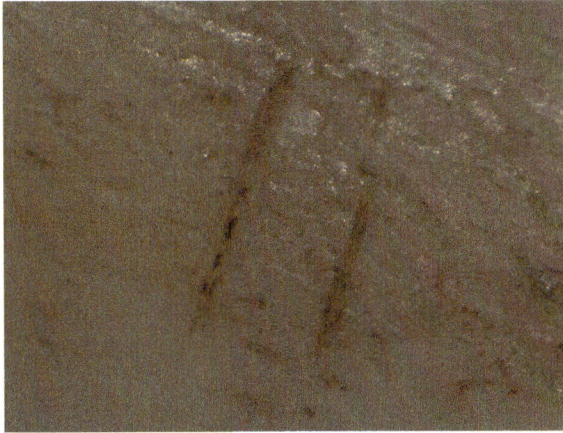

FIGURE 6.9 Two aborted attempts to saw the bone.

FIGURE 6.10 Image taken from the SEM analysis. As saws are used with a continuous or reciprocating action the striae left follow a direction parallel to the kerf floor (Reichs, 1998).

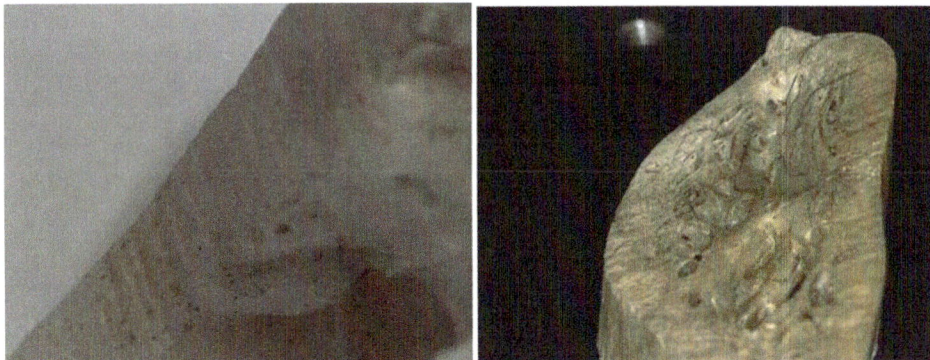

FIGURE 6.11 Two close-ups of the cross-sectional views of the midshaft of the tibia obtained with a magnifying glass. Note the parallel striae, the serrated cut pattern, and the breakaway spur (right).

point to the class of tool without specifying which one, although hand saw was highly probable (Symes et al., 2010).

Body Position and Sequence

Cut mark diagnoses were reinforced through further examination of complete cut surfaces and false starts. The location of the false starts and the symmetry of the damage (Figs. 6.2, 6.5, and 6.6) on even bones allowed us to hypothesize about the body position versus perpetrator position. Initial cuts are commonly accompanied by false starts (Symes et al., 2002). Since the false starts, indicative of the initiation of a cut, were located on the posterior part of the bone, most probably, the victim was face down, and the limbs were cut more or less simultaneously with the legs extended and parallel (Fig. 6.12). The legs were detached from the trunk approximately in the proximal thirds of the femora. Indicators of direction of saw progress center on the false start and breakaway spur.

Modus operandi and the number of perpetrators are frequent questions raised by the courts and were, therefore, approached. The distribution of the cuts is more consistent with what Reichs (1998) designate as limb bisection since the limbs were cut through, that is, transection of bone via sawing, without joint disarticulation (Rainwater, 2015). Generally, it is recognized that dismembering a body is difficult and requires both time and effort (Quatrehomme, 2007). Notwithstanding the fact that only about 6% of the bones were recovered, all the cuts could have been performed by the same perpetrator.

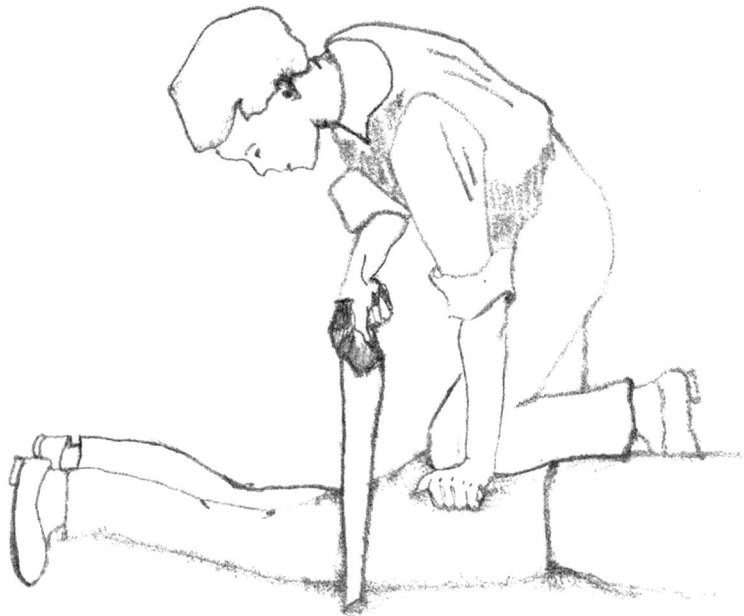

FIGURE 6.12   Reconstruction of the most probable modus operandi, that is the position of the perpetrator versus the victim, inferred on the basis of the cuts analysis. Source: *Drawing by R. Lira.*

When Was the Trauma Inflicted?

The next question was to survey when the cuts were made. Not only did different portions of the same bone display different chromatic alterations, but also the color of the cut surfaces matched the surrounding one (Fig. 6.4). These are two strong indications that the damage occurred before decomposition.

Cause of Death

Since the remains are entirely skeletonized and incomplete, and there is an absence of any type of cranial injury, the cause of death could not be assessed. Moreover, the vast majority of the bones were not recovered (Fig. 6.5). From the forensic anthropology perspective, the only thing that can be stated is that he didn't die from cranial injuries. As dismemberment is not usually chosen as a method of murder, although the cuts were done with the bone still fresh, most probably the victim was already dead. That is, immediately after death, the perpetrator cut the victim.

Motive/Criminal Behavior

Additional clues that may assist the investigation and may even be beneficial in a court of law can still be assessed through anthropological analysis.

It is generally understood that dismemberment may be the product of making a body more easily transportable, attempting to hinder the identification of the remains (Rainwater, 2015: 223). On the other hand, the relationship between dismemberment and psychiatric disorders is not completely clear (Porta et al., 2016; Rajset al., 2017). Obviously, the contribution of forensic anthropology to assess the motives of dismemberment is limited. Nevertheless, we argue that the field can provide clues that once crossed with other forensic disciplines could be very valuable. This case is a good example of that, as we will now justify. Once the victim was identified, it was easy to access the killer. There was another Ukrainian individual, known to be very violent, who was already in jail for another crime. He was the son-in-law of the victim (though the killer's wife was the daughter of the victim's wife only, and thus not the victim's descendant) and while in prison he boasted to have eaten his own father-in-law. Purportedly, he was in prison for other crimes. He had killed his boss, and he was also suspect to have killed another person in Ukraine, 4 years before.

The individual was submitted to a psychiatric exam at INMLCF, and he was diagnosed as a psychopath and potential killer. Indeed, if he was a professional killer, we argue that besides hindering the hands to preclude fingerprinting, he would also have destroyed the skull where the shining teeth were paramount to identification.

In Portugal this type of case is indeed rare since in 20 years of qualified forensic anthropology it is the only one where dry bones were a proof of dismemberment (there are a few other cases of mutilated and dismembered fresh bodies). It is then worthwhile to tell what happened by that time. For unknown reasons, it became known that animal bite marks were found in the skeletal remains. Immediately, daily press crossed that information with the proud confession of the killer/homicidal and titled news, such as "The first case of cannibalism in Portugal was recorded" and "Psychopath killer ate his father in law in his house." These were sensational news stories that were later denied and clarified saying that the bite marks were indeed animal ones but, on the other hand, they show the interest that the general public has in these types of unusual cases and how easy it is to turn them into both fantastic and untrue stories.

The story was that the killer took advantage of the absence of his wife, who was divorcing from him, to kill his father-in-law. He confessed that he dismembered the body with a saw and put the remains inside plastic bags. In a way, some of the conclusions from the forensic anthropology expertise were confirmed. It has to be noted that postmortem interval was also confirmed since the homicide occurred 2 years before the discovery and that all the parameters of the biological profile were in agreement with those of the victim.

LESSONS LEARNED FROM THIS CASE

Based on about a dozen dry bones it was possible to retrieve a lot of information, which allowed for the identification of the victim and the determination of a case of dismemberment. Though among them were the ones that most likely bear the evidence of dismemberment (Hackman and Black, 2017), a part of the modus operandi remains unknown, like the way the separation of the head was performed. Nevertheless, it was possible to assess the class of the tool used to perform the cuts, and to know that the cuts were done with the body still fresh, meaning that the damage occurred before decomposition. Additional forensic information was diagnosed through characteristics of criminal behavior. The body position during dismemberment (face down) versus perpetrator position was proposed as well as the nonprofessional nature of the perpetrator. This case illustrates additional information that allows interpretation and knowledge of the victim's body position during dismemberment. Besides, the taphonomic critique was essential to the case interpretation and to clarify any preliminary doubts. Interdisciplinarity, perseverance, and interagency cooperation (Saul et al., 2005), namely the work of the police officers, forensic anthropology, forensic psychiatry, and the experts on SEM analysis was also very relevant. It has to be mentioned that at the time of this case, a decade ago, there was not yet a forensic odontologist available at the INMLCF. This case highlights the importance of a good and complete recovery of human remains that should be performed by forensic anthropologists, which was not the case. We believe that many other bones could have been found with an exhaustive recovery process and this could have allowed assessment of additional information like the cause of death or the use of other tools. As dismemberments performed by an inexperienced assailant could involve more than one tool (Reichs, 1998) we suspected that this could have been the case but the absence of other bones precludes the retrieval of more information. Fortunately, some practices have been considerably improved since the time of this case and we believe that if another case like it occurs, a better recovery, the analysis of the kerf size, and the use of more complementary examinations, such as histology, would result in better outcomes. As mentioned, this is the only case involving completely dry bones the author has done in 20 years of forensic anthropology practice in Portugal. It has to be noted that in Portugal, like in the United Kingdom (Hackman and Black, 2017), there is no official requirement for forensic anthropology in a dismemberment case. This, in a way, precludes having a real notion of the frequency of dismemberments in the pathology service. For sure, a few other cases involving fresh bodies have occurred, though, in only some of them was there forensic anthropological assistance. Nevertheless, despite some increase in violent behavior, some of which performed by foreign nationals like in the present case, we argue that, in Portugal, as far as dismemberments are concerned, the absence of evidence corresponds to evidence of absence.

Acknowledgments

Agostinho Santos for the help in the contact with the University of Oporto to SEM analysis; Sónia Codinha and Luísa Eiras for the assistance on the practical analysis of the case; Steve Symes for providing recommendations and opinion on the case. Renato Lira for the drawing, Melina Calmon for providing language help.

References

Cattaneo, C., Gibelli, D., 2017. Animal effects on bones. In: Houck, M. (Ed.), Forensic Anthropology. Advanced Forensic Sciences Series. Elsevier, Amsterdam, pp. 31—35.

Cordeiro, C., Munoz-Barus, J., Wasterlain, S., Cunha, E., Vieira, D., 2009. Predicting stature from metatarsal length in a Portuguese population. Forensic Sci. Int. 193 (1—3), . Available from: https://doi.org/10.1016/j.forsciint.2009.09.017131.e1-131.e4.

Hackman, L., Black, S., 2017. The role of forensic anthropology in cases of dismemberment. In: Black, S., Rutty, G., Hainsworth, S., Thomson, G. (Eds.), Criminal Dismemberments, Forensic and Investigation Analysis. CRC Press, Boca Raton, FL.

Nogueira, L., Quatrehomme, G., Rallon, C., Adalian, P., Alunni, V., 2016. Saw marks in bones: a study of 170 experimental false start lesions. Forensic Sci. Int. 268, 123—130. Available from: https://doi.org/10.1016/j.forsciint.2016.09.018. Epub 2016 Sep 28.

Quatrehomme, G., 2007. A strange case of dismemberment. In: Brickely, M., Ferllini, R. (Eds.), Forensic Anthropology. Case Studies From Europe. Charles C Thomas, Springfield, pp. 99—119.

Porta, D., Amadasi, A., Capella, A., Mazzarelli, D., Magli, F., Gibelli, D., et al., 2016. Dismemberment and disarticulation. A forensic anthropological approach. J. Forensic Legal Med. 38, 50—57.

Rainwater, C., 2015. Three modes of dismemberments: disarticulation around the joints, transection of bone via chopping and transection of bone via sawing. In: Passalacqua, N., Rainwater, C. (Eds.), Skeletal Trauma Analysis. Case Studies in Context. Wiley Blackwell, Chichester West Sussex, pp. 222—245.

Rajs, J., Lundstrom, M., Broberg, M., Lidberg, L., Linquist, O., 2017. Criminal mutilation of the human body in Sweden—a thirty year medico-legal and psychiatric study. J. Forensic Sci. 43 (3), 563—580. 1998 May.

Reichs, K., 1998. Postmortem dismemberment: recovery, analysis and interpretation. In: Reichs, K. (Ed.), Forensic Osteology: Advances in the Identification of Human Remains. Charles C Thomas, Springfield, IL, pp. 353—388.

Saul, F., Saul, J., Symes, S., 2005. The lady in the box. AAFS, Proceedings, H31.

Scholl, K., Moffart, C., 2017. Plastic waste sacks alter the rate of decomposition of dismembered bodies within. Int. J. Legal Med 1311, 141—1147. Available from: https://doi.org/10.1007/s00414-017-1535-4.

Smith, O.C., Pope, E.J., Symes, S., 2003. Look until you see: identification of trauma in skeletal material, in hard evidence: case studies. In: Steadman, D.W. (Ed.), Forensic Anthropology. Prentice Hall, Upper Saddle River, NJ, pp. 138—154.

Symes, S., Berryman, H., Smith, O.C., 1998. Saw marks in bone: introduction and examination of residual kerf contour. In: Reichs, K. (Ed.), Forensic Osteology: Advances in the Identification of Human Remains. Charles C Thomas, Springfield, pp. 389—409.

Symes, S., Williams, J., Murray, E., Hoffman, J., Holland, T., Saul, T., et al., 2002. Taphonomic context of sharp force trauma in suspected cases of human mutilation and dismemberment. In: Haglund, W., Sorg, M. (Eds.), Advances in Forensic Taphonomy. CRC Press, Boca Raton, FL, pp. 403—434.

Symes, S., Chapman, E., Rainwater, C., Cabo, L., Myster, S., 2010. Knife and saw toolmark analysis in bone: a manual designed for the examination of criminal mutilation and dismemberment. Document No. 232227.

Symes, S., L'Abbé, Chapm, E., Chapmann, E., Wolf, I., Dirkmaat, D., 2012. Interpreting traumatic injury to bone in medico legal investigations. In: Dirkmaat, D. (Ed.), A Companion to Forensic Anthropology. Wiley-Blackwell, Chichester, pp. 340–389.

Further Reading

Skeletal trauma analysis. In: Passalacqua, N., Rainwater, C. (Eds.), Case Studies in Context. Wiley Blackwell, Chichester West Sussex.

Symes, S., Kroman, A., Myster, S., Rainwater, C., 2006. Anthropological saw mark analysis on bone: what is the potential of dismemberment interpretation? In: AAFS Proceedings, H48.

The Potential of Histological Analysis in Dismemberment Cases

Tania Delabarde[1] and Bertrand Ludes[1,2]

[1]Forensic Institute of Paris, Paris, France [2]Faculty of Medicine, University
Paris-Descartes, Paris, France

INTRODUCTION

Dismemberment cases are complex to investigate. The corpse represents the most compelling evidence of a crime for the murderer, and consequently, dismemberment patterns are of particular importance as the actions and instruments used could be correlated with the perpetrator's intentions (Reichs, 1998; Black et al., 2017). Localized dismemberments involve the separation of some parts of the body and are commonly associated with hindered identifications, easing transport, or body disposal, while generalized dismemberments involve cuts to all aspects of the body and are more often correlated with specific intentions (i.e., decapitation/dismemberment of the victim to terrify societies, in psychiatric illness, or hiding evidence in sexual homicides) (Konopka et al., 2007; Symes et al., 2002; Dogan et al., 2010). Specific capacities of the perpetrator (knowledge of anatomy, use of specific implement) may also be determined based on the analysis of cut mark (Delabarde and Ludes, 2010).

In sharp force injuries, the possibility of determining class characteristics of the suspected implement is mainly associated with macroscopic examination of cutaneous injuries patterns (Spitz and Fisher, 1993; Ambade and Godbole, 2006; Schmidt and Pollak, 2006), bone analysis (Symes et al., 2002; Thompson and Inglis, 2009; Symes et al., 2012), and sometimes additional means such as clothing analysis (Sitiene et al., 2004). Some studies report the possibility to link objects or weapons to the microtraces left behind with scanning electron microscopy in combination with energy-dispersive X-ray spectrometry (SEM/EDS) technique (Vermeij et al., 2012; Bai et al., 2007; Pechníková et al., 2012; Gibelli et al., 2012; Capuani et al., 2014) or the opportunity to determine the uniqueness of tool marks on bone with environmental scanning electron microscopy (ESEM) analysis (Saville et al., 2007).

The transfer of materials between victim and perpetrator was first reported by Locard in the 19th century (Levy, 2008). Based on his principle "every contact leaves a trace" and on the potential of histological analysis that is routinely used in forensic context to detect the presence of iron and copper in electrical burn marks on the skin (Jacobsen, 1997), detect gunshot residue (Gibelli et al., 2010) and fragments resulting from penetrating injuries related to exploding devices (Maggio, et al., 2008), as well as confirm the presence of foreign surgical material in tumors (Duband et al., 2012), we published a preliminary study to demonstrate that histological examination of bone and soft tissue around a penetrating injury (sharp force trauma) could not only provide evidence of the offending implement but also on the environment where victim remained at some point (Delabarde et al., 2017).

METHODOLOGY

A standard autopsy protocol with special attention to the careful use of scalpels in the dissection of the severed body parts is recommended to avoid creating artifactual lesions or contamination of bone section plans. All injuries should be described, photographed, and examined macroscopically prior to further examination. Bone segments and cutaneous incised wounds are systematically retained after autopsy to be firstly examined with a stereomicroscope (ZEISS, Stemi 400-C) to evaluate the presence of exogenous particles.

Bone Histology

We are mainly processing decalcified bone and soft tissues samples. Undecalcified bone samples are used to confirm or complete initial results as acid solutions used in decalcification could potentially dissolve foreign particles. We also recommend the sampling of cutaneous tissue located around the bone sharp injuries as exogenous particles may be present in soft tissue and absent in hard tissue.

Decalcified Bone Sections

Because of its simplicity, decalcified technique is routinely used in forensic cases for bone samples as the removal of calcium deposits simplifies the embedding procedure and cutting (De La Grandmaison et al. 2010; Bancroft and Gamble, 2008). The first important technical step is the fixation. Bone tissues are fixed in 10% phosphate-buffered neutral formalin (NBF), pH 7.2 for approximately 3 weeks (the time is correlate with the sample size). Bone samples are then decalcified in Kristensen's solution (Kristensen, 1948). Decalcification time is variable (e.g., 28 days for a tibia section, 15 days for a humeral section, and 8 days for a vertebra).

To accelerate the process, some products referred to as "rapid decalcifiers" can be used as well as the microwave technique (Cunningham et al., 2001); nevertheless these techniques require strong experience to avoid any problem related to the harmful effect of fast-acting decalcification (An and Martin, 2003). After completion of decalcification, bones are thoroughly rinsed in running tap water for approximately 2 hours. Bone sections are then dehydrated through increasing graded series of ethylic alcohol, cleared in xylene, and embedded in paraffin wax 62°C−64°C (Peel-a-way paraffin embedding wax, Ref: 19304-01, EMS, Philadelphia). Paraffin with a high melting point is retained to provide a more solid matrix to the bone and consequently an easier sectioning.

Cutaneous Samples

Soft tissues are also fixed in 10% neutral phosphate-buffered formalin (NBF), pH 7.2 (Microm Microtech, France) for approximately 2 weeks. Sections are dehydrated through increasing graded series of ethylic alcohol, cleared in xylene, and embedded in paraffin wax 54°C−57°C (Tissue Tek III, Ref 4511, Sakura Finetek).

Mineralized Bone Sections

Despite being technically challenging, undecalcified bone samples offer a great panel of analytical possibilities in histopathology as this technique preserves the structural architecture of bone showing both the mineralized and cellular components and allows a better preservation of the exogenous particles as decalcification implies the use of acid solutions (Goldschlager et al., 2010; Malluche and Faugere, 1986).

Fixation is used to preserve microscopic bone structural details and is the first step in the adequate preparation of nondemineralized bone samples for sectioning. We use ethanol, a relatively weak fixative that does not remove calcium from bone within several weeks of exposure. Ethanol penetrates quickly into small samples of bones while big samples should be divided to allow thorough tissue penetration (An and Martin, 2003). Another fixation method with the combination of both ethanol and formalin is reported to be very efficient, allowing the staining properties of collagen (Beebe, 2000; Chappard, 2015).

Before embedding bone samples in plastic monomer, it is necessary to dehydrate them by using graded concentrations of ethanol (from 70° to 100°) to remove all the water contents within the sample and then clear them in xylene. For embedding of bone, we prefer the use of methyl metacrylate (MMA) as it produces a harder plastic that provides an optimal support for cortical and trabecular bone. In addition, other plastic monomers, such as glycolmethacrylate could be problematic during cutting of samples that remain embedded for prolonged periods (Malluche and Faugere, 1986). Vacuum is used to achieve better infiltration and prevent air-bubble formation. Once polymerized, the blocks are removed from their glass molds and then ground on a polisher machine to be flattened in a plane parallel to the sample core (An and Martin, 2003).

Cutting/Staining/Examination

Motorized microtome with different knives is used for the sectioning of undecalcified bone embedded in MMA and samples in paraffin blocks (An and Martin, 2003; Malluche and Faugere, 1986). Serial sections of 3 μm in thickness of soft tissues and 5−6 μm in thickness of bone tissues in paraffin blocks are cut and then stained with classical histological stains:hematoxylin and eosin (H&E) to assess the general morphology and Perls' Prussian blue reaction with fast nuclear red as counter stain for the demonstration of ferric iron (Perls, 1867). For decalcified bone samples, we recommend halving them in two segments: one stained with Perls' reaction prior to decalcification and the second decalcified without Perls' treatment. This methodology aims to avoid any possibility of iron dissolution in the acidic solution used for decalcification (Vigliani, 2003; Kottke-Marchant and Davis, 2012). We used Picro sirius red (PS) (Junqueira et al., 1979) using Sirius red F3B (C.I. 35782) as a dye for the study of collagen networks and if relevant safranin O/fast green FCF (SO/FG) in place of safranin O/Astra blue for the demonstration of lignin in woody material (Srebotnik and Messner, 1994). For mineralized bone specimens, it is necessary to use stains with a molecular weight (e.g., Toluidine blue) and that allow optimal penetration of the tissue (An and Martin, 2003). For detection of aluminum and iron, Perls' Prussian blue reaction and Modified Gomori stain are recommended for mineralized bone samples (Malluche and Faugere, 1986). All stained slides are examined with a light/polarized microscope (Axioscope A1, Zeiss, Germany) connected to a 3CCD 2M pixels camera (AT-200 GE, JAI, Copenhagen, Denmark) and are scanned at $100 \times$ magnification using the Histolab software (Microvision Instruments, Lisses, France).

HISTOLOGICAL ANALYSIS IN FORENSIC DISMEMBERMENT CASES

The injury mechanism of sharp force trauma (especially in dismemberment cases) typically involves a strong exchange between the tissue and the causative agent, which potentially increases the quantity of residual particles that can be left. Histochemical methods are simple and widely used to detect a number of component like iron, aluminum, lead, and copper with classical stain techniques (Bancroft and Gamble, 2008; An and Martin, 2003; Goldschlager et al., 2010 ; Malluche and Faugere, 1986; Perls, 1867; Vigliani, 2003).

In addition, complete sections of body parts offered open wounds that may retain some exogenous particles from the environment where victims remained. The presence of several inorganic and organic foreign particles can be determined through histology: mineral, synthetic, and plastic exogenous particles could be observed because of birefringent properties detected under polarized light and organic particles like wood or fungi could be determined with specific staining (An and Martin, 2003; Goldschlager et al., 2010; Malluche and Faugere, 1986; Perls, 1867; Vigliani, 2003).

Case 1

The remains of a putrefied dismembered body of a young female that had been disposed of in four plastic garbage bags were exhumed from a house basement. Only lower limbs sustained dismemberment injuries with the complete separation of legs and feet recovered in eight fragments (four fragments from each limb). During autopsy, a stab wound to the chest was evidenced in the precordial region associated with a transmural wound on the anterior aspect of right ventricle with a residual hemopericardium of

150 mL. These findings were consistent with the cause of death determined as massive hemorrhage related to heart stab wound. No macroscopic evidence of hemorrhage was observed in cutaneous wound margins from severed body parts and dismemberment was suspected to be postmortem. The presence of blue exogenous particles was evidenced macroscopically and confirmed by the stereomicroscope observation at the level of the cortical and trabecular bone on 14 complete section walls with the exception of the superior section of the left femur (Fig. 7.1). In addition, brown particles were detected during stereomicroscope examination of cutaneous tissue surrounding tibiae complete proximal sections.

Despite our concern, blue particles were not dissolved either in acidic solution (formic acid) used for decalcification or in solvents, such as ethanol and xylene used for dehydration and clearing of both decalcified and undecalcified bone samples. Under microscopic observation, the blue discoloration appeared as fine black particles along the cut wall of the tibia at the level of the trabecular bone (Fig. 7.2). The Perls' reaction performed prior to decalcification was positive, indicating the presence of ferric particles at the level of the trabecular bone. They appeared as fine blue particles and were always in association with the black particles (Fig. 7.3).

The cutaneous layer covering the tibia also showed macroscopically the presence of a diffuse blue discoloration along the cutting edge and a light brown exogenous particle measuring 1 × 1.5 mm was found embedded in the epidermis. On the transverse section of the skin, amorphous fine black particles where found at the level of cutting edges. At higher magnification on H&E staining, these particles showed the same features as the ones described along the cutting wall of the bone. The Perls' reaction at this level did not demonstrate any fine ferric particles among the black ones. Only some bone flakes, the larger one measuring 450 × 100 μm, were positively stained. The ferric particles were

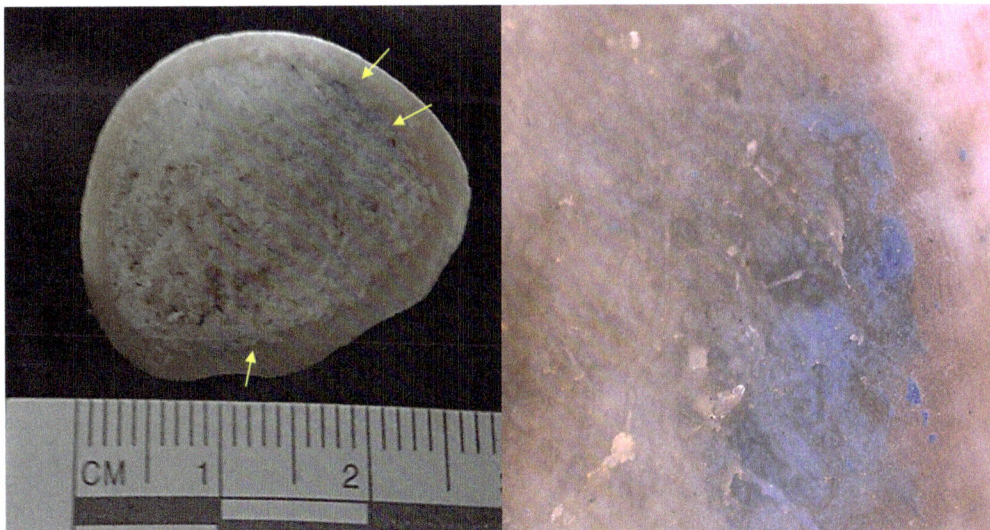

FIGURE 7.1   Complete section of left proximal tibia exhibiting exogenous blue particles (*yellow arrows*; Case 1).

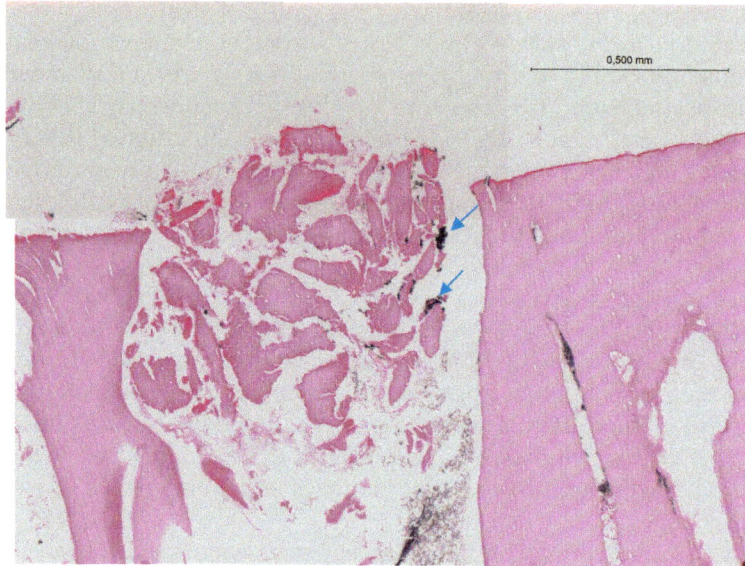

FIGURE 7.2   Tibia decalcified bone sample, stained with H&E showing the presence of black amorphous particles *(blue arrows)* corresponding to the blue discolored area along the cutting wall (Case 1).

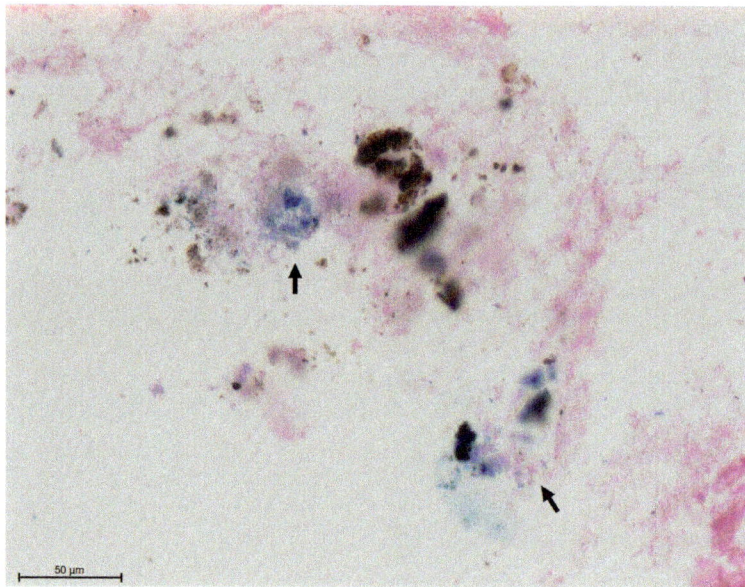

FIGURE 7.3   Tibia sample stained with Perls' before decalcification showing the presence of ferric iron (*black arrows*) embedded in the black amorphous particles (Case 1).

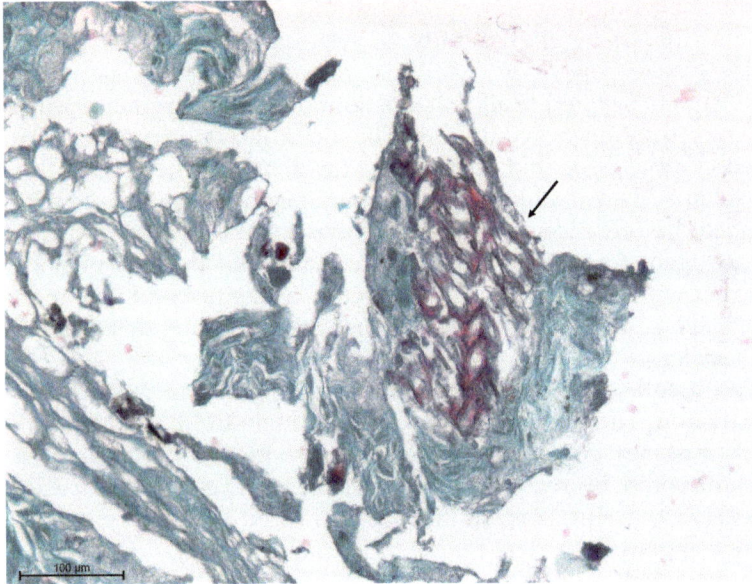

FIGURE 7.4 Foreign wood-like particle found in the dermis of the tibia skin, red staining of the lignin confirming the woody nature of this foreign particle (SO/FG staining) (Case 1).

only retained in the trabecular meshwork of the bone and were absent on the cutaneous cut margins. This could be possibly explained by the difference of density between the bone and the skin, the blade of the saw leaving ferric debris when in contact with hard material rather than when in contact with soft tissue.

The light brown exogenous particle appeared at a microscopic level as wood-like fragment on H&E staining. The Safranin O/Fast green staining demonstrated the presence of lignin within the observed fragment, confirming its woody nature (Fig. 7.4). This finding could be related to the fact that the body was hidden below wooden pallets 24 hours before being dismembered according to perpetrator testimony. Additionally, no evidence of wood component was found in the analysis of soil recovered from the grave.

Histological analysis from Case 1 revealed the presence of lignin particles related to body disposal (wooden pallets) and confirmed the presence of exogenous particles from a saw blade (dismemberment). The characteristics of the kerf walls exhibiting fine and nonuniform striae and kerf floors measuring 1 mm width with square bottom suggested the use of a manual saw (hand saw). Blue particles identified on cortical and trabecular bone were suspected to be paint residue from the saw blade. A hand saw with blue paint blade was recovered at the scene and DNA analysis confirmed the use of this implement by the perpetrator.

Cases 2 and 3

Two cases of criminal decapitation are presented to illustrate complementary histological findings on victims that sustained different state of preservation. In both cases, autopsy findings (e.g., large circumferential injury sharp-edged on the cutaneous tissue at the wound margins and incised bone trauma with loss of fragments) were consistent with the use of a bladed instrument to sever the head from the trunk. The force applied by perpetrators to the blade while severing the head, passing through multiple layers of soft and hard tissue is potentially increasing the quantity of residual particles left by the implement.

Case 2 is a well preserved human severed head that was found on a factory fence while the rest of the body was recovered in a nearby building. The victim was determined to be an adult male that sustained complete separation from head to trunk at the level of the fourth and fifth cervical vertebrae. The examination of cut margins and bone sample with the stereomicroscope evidenced the presence of two different types of exogenous particles: brown homogenous particles and multicolor fibers with synthetic like morphology (Fig. 7.5). The presence of lignin within the cutaneous fragment was confirmed by its morphology at higher magnification and with the Safranin O/Fast green staining determining the woody nature of these particles.

The Perls' reaction was positive both on bone and cutaneous tissue and cut margins revealing the presence of ferric iron. The distribution of the iron differs from the pattern of tissue distribution expected after an acute hemorrhage. We suggested that the iron revealed by the Perls' reaction could be related to the presence of exogenous particles from an iron-content blade. In fact, a long blade knife was recovered by investigators at the scene; the composition of the blade was determined to be stainless steel, which therefore contained iron (Stephenson, 1997).

In addition, a number of birefringent exogenous particles were also found under polarizing light along the cutting edges of the skin (Fig. 7.6). Their morphological characteristics are consistent with plastic/synthetic elements initially observed with the stereomicroscope. Complementary chemical analyses were requested to determine the exact composition. Results were lately communicated to authors and the presence of thermoplastic polymer resin fibers was confirmed originating from a blanket recovered in the perpetrators' van.

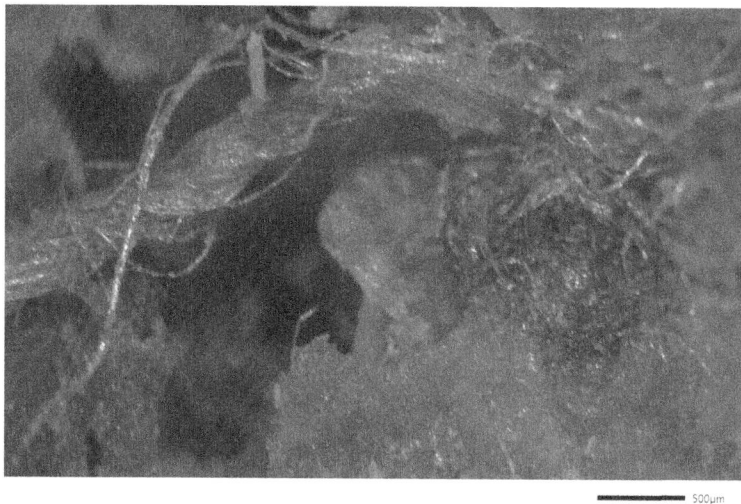

FIGURE 7.5   Multicolor fibers with synthetic like morphology under stereomicroscope (Case 2).

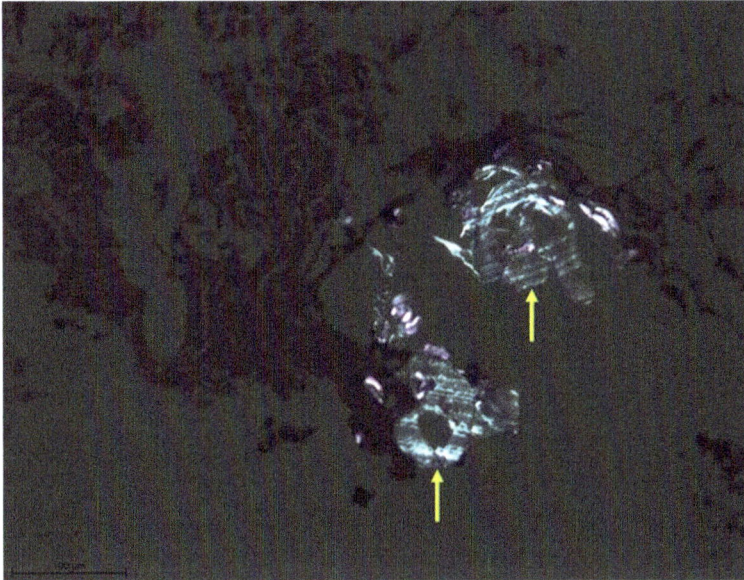

FIGURE 7.6 Birefringent particles (*yellow arrows*), compatible with synthetic/plastic fibers along the cut margin (HE, polarization) (Case 2).

The second beheaded victim is a partially skeletonized body of an adult male that was exhumed from a shallow grave. The head was completely severed from the trunk at the level of the second and third cervical vertebrae. Although Case 3 was putrefied, the main structures of the skin, such as the dermis, hypodermis, and aponeurosis were still recognizable on the histology section. The cut margin appeared as shredded. The Perls' reaction was positive revealing the presence of ferric iron in this area both in mineralized bone samples and decalcified bone (Fig. 7.7). The blue staining corresponding to the iron is limited to the cutaneous fibers of the exposed dermis. The same Perls' positive reaction was observed along the cutting edge of the vertebra. Once again, the blue staining is limited to the cut margin of the vertebra and the exposed trabecular bone as well as the adjacent soft tissue. The pattern of tissue distribution of the iron was different from Case 2 previously described indicating an acute hemorrhage occurring after the sharp force trauma, the hemoglobin being leached insitu from autolyzed red blood cells. The distribution of iron would have been limited to the cutting edges if originated by the use of an iron-content blade to perpetrate the dismemberment.

The comparison between slides from Cases 1, 2, and 3 allow to observe different patterns of tissue distribution of iron suggesting that histological analysis could potentially distinguish ferric iron resulted from hemorrhage and iron from metal exogenous particles based on the distribution of iron in the examined tissue. In medical and dental research, histological techniquesare routinely used to detect and study the impact of metallic and plastic foreign particles related to implants using microscopical techniques and classical stains (including the Perls' reaction) (Jacobsen, 1997; Gibelli et al., 2010; Maggio et al., 2008; Srebotnik and Messner, 1994; Bauer and Zang, 2016).

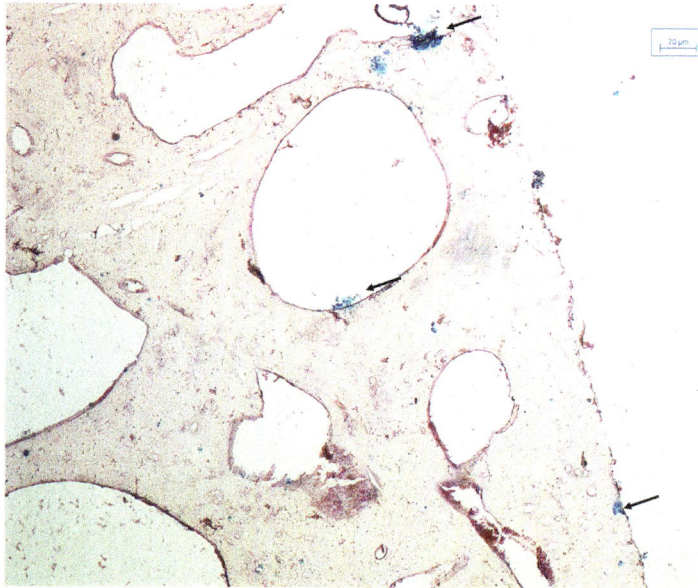

FIGURE 7.7   Positive Perls' reaction (exogenous particles) on undecalcified bone sample from second vertebra (Case 2).

TABLE 7.1   Results of the Detection of Exogenous Particles by Cases and Histological Techniques

Case	Type of Exogenous Particles Detected	Histological Techniques	Contact Agent
1	Wood	Safranin O/Fast green staining	Environment (wooden pallets)
	Painting residue associated with iron particles	HE and Perls' reaction	Hand saw with a blue painted blade
2	Iron particles	HE and Perls' reaction	Iron-contentblade
	Wood	Safranin O/Fast green staining	Environment (wood chips from the factory)
	Plastic/synthetic elements	Polarizing light	Blanket (thermoplastic polymer resin fibers)
3	Silica crystals	Polarizing light	Sandy environment

Numerous birefringent exogenous particles were also found under polarizing light along the cutting edges of the skin and the vertebra from Case 3 and appeared to have a crystal-like morphology. Such morphology is consistent with silica that could be related to a sandy environment. Geological morphological analysis of a soil sample from the exhumation site excluded the presence of sand in the composition of grave soil. Therefore, the presence of silica was suspected to relate to another location where the victim had been killed. It is likely that sand crystals were retained by coagulation during bleeding following decapitation.

Table 7.1 summarizes the results from the three cases. Soft tissue and bone samples from sharp force injuries should be microscopically examined as the offending implement may have left debris in wounds or evidence of the environment where the victim remained at or around the time of death. The detection of exogenous particles could be performed only with routine histology (decalcified paraffin samples), but taking into consideration that decalcification may dissolve some particles, the use of mineralized histological technique could therefore enhance and confirm initial findings.

CONCLUSION

The identification of exogenous particles through histological analysis is a simple, cost effective, and easily repeatable technique. The main limitation of histology in the identification of exogenous particles is the quantification of elements and the determination of their physicochemical characteristics. The histochemical methods are widely used to detect a number of components, such as iron, aluminum, lead, and copper by classical stain techniques. Yet, most types of steel from tools and knives contain other components, such as vanadium, molybdenum, tungsten, silicon, manganese, and nickel (Junqueira et al., 1979). Histochemical findings are complementary and may need to be combined with macroscopical findings during examination of the remains and other techniques, such as scanning electron microscopy/energy-dispersive X-ray analysis (SEM-EDXA) or inductively coupled plasma mass spectrometry (ICP-MS), to identify the chemical composition of exogenous particles and to reach a conclusion with a stronger probative value.

In addition, histology could evidence the presence of several inorganic and organic foreign particles: mineral, synthetic, and plastic exogenous particles could be observed because of birefringent properties detected under polarized light and organic particles like wood or fungi could be determined with specific staining. The identification of exogenous particles that provide some information about both the implement used and the environment where the victim had been at some point could be key for the investigation to reconstruct circumstances surrounding death and find a link to the perpetrators.

Acknowledgments

We are grateful to Catherine Cannet, Annie Llorens and Brigitte Bakrouh, histologists, for their technical work and advice.

References

Ambade, V.N., Godbole, H.V., 2006. Comparison of wound patterns in homicide by blunt and sharp force. Forensic Sci. Int. 156, 166−170.

An, Y.H., Martin, K.L. (Eds.), 2003. Handbook of Histology Methods for Bone and Cartilage. Humana Press, New Jersey.

Bai, R., Wan, L., Li, H., Zhang, Z., Ma, Z., 2007. Identify the injury implements by SEM/EDX and ICP-AES. Forensic Sci. Int. 166 (1), 8−13.

Bancroft, J.D., Gamble, M. (Eds.), 2008. Theory and Practice of Histological Techniques. Elsevier Health Sciences.

Bauer, T.W., Zang, Y., 2016. Implants and implant reactions. Diagn. Histopathol. 22 (10), 384−396.

Beebe, K., 2000. Alcohol/xylene: the unlikely fixative/dehhydrant/clearant. J. Histotechnol. 23, 45−50.

Black, S., Rutty, G., Hainsworth, S.V. (Eds.), 2017. Criminal Dismemberment: Forensic and Investigative Analysis. CRC Press.

Capuani, C., Guilbeau-Frugier, C., Delisle, M.B., Rougé, D., Telmon, N., 2014. Epifluorescence analysis of hacksaw marks on bone: highlighting unique individual characteristics. Forensic Sci. Int. 241, 195−202.

Chappard, D., 2015. Technical aspects: how do we best prepare bone samples for proper histological analysis? In: Heymann, D. (Ed.), Bone Cancer, second edition. pp. 111−120.

Cunningham, C.D., Schulte, B.A., Bianchi, L.M., Weber, P.C., Schmiedt, B.N., 2001. Microwave decalcification of human temporal bones. Laryngoscope 111, 278−282.

Delabarde, T., Ludes, B., 2010. Missing in Amazonian jungle: a case report of skeletal evidence for dismemberment. J. Forensic Sci. 55 (4), 1105−1110.

Delabarde, T., Cannet, C., Raul, J.S., Géraut, A., Taccoen, M., Ludes, B., 2017. Bone and soft tissue histology: a new approach to determine characteristics of offending instrument in sharp force injuries. Int. J. Legal Med. 1−11.

De La Grandmaison, G.L., Charlier, P., Durigon, M., 2010. Usefulness of systematic histological examination in routine forensic autopsy. J. Forensic Sci. 55 (1), 85−88.

Dogan, K.H., Demirci, S., Deniz, I., Erkol, Z., 2010. Decapitation and dismemberment of the corpse: a matricide case. J. Forensic Sci. 55 (2), 542−545.

Duband, S., Govin, A., Dumollard, J.M., Forest, F., Basset, T., Péoc'h, M., 2012. Laryngeal teflonoma identified by Fourier-transform infrared microspectroscopy after forensic autopsy: an interesting tool for foreign material identification in forensic cases. Forensic Sci. Int. 214 (1), e26−e29.

Gibelli, D., Brandone, A., Andreola, S., Porta, D., Giudici, E., Grandi, M.A., et al., 2010. Macroscopic, microscopic, and chemical assessment of gunshot lesions on decomposed pig skin. J. Forensic Sci. 55 (4), 1092−1097.

Gibelli, D., Mazzarelli, D., Porta, D., Rizzi, A., Cattaneo, C., 2012. Detection of metal residues on bone using SEM-EDS—Part II: sharp force injury. Forensic Sci. Int. 223 (1), 91−96.

Goldschlager, T., Abdelkader, A., Kerr, J., Boundy, I., Jenkin, G., 2010. Undecalcified bone preparation for histology, histomorphometry and fluorochrome analysis. J. Vis. Exp. (35), 1707. Advance online publication.

Jacobsen, H., 1997. Electrically induced deposition of metal on the human skin. Forensic Sci. Int. 90 (1), 85−92.

Junqueira, L.C., Bignolas, G., Brentani, R.R., 1979. Picrosirius staining plus polarization microscopy, a specific method for collagen detection in tissue sections. Histochem. J. 11 (4), 447−455.

Konopka, T., Strona, M., Bolechala, F., Kunz, J., 2007. Corpse dismemberment in the material collected by the Department of Forensic Medicine, Cracow, Poland. Leg. Med. Tokyo 9 (1), 1−13.

Kottke-Marchant, K., Davis, B., 2012. Laboratory Hematology Practice, first ed. Wiley Blackwell, Hoboken.

Kristensen, H.K., 1948. An improved method of decalcification. Stain Technol. 23 (3), 151−154.

Levy, A., 2008. La police scientifique - La technologie de pointe au service des enquêteurs. Hachette, Paris, p. 25.

Maggio, K.L., Kalasinsky, V.F., Lewin-Smith, M.R., Mullick, F.G., 2008. Wound fragments from cutaneous sites of US Military personnel deployed in Operation Iraqi Freedom: clinical aspects and pathologic characterizations. Dermatol. Surg. 34 (4), 475−482.

Malluche, H.H., Faugere, M.C., 1986. Atlas of Mineralized Bone Histology. Karger, New York.

Pechníková, M., Porta, D., Mazzarelli, D., Rizzi, A., Drozdová, E., Gibelli, D., et al., 2012. Detection of metal residues on bone using SEM−EDS. Part I: blunt force injury. Forensic Sci. Int. 223 (1), 87−90.

Perls, M., 1867. Nachweis von Eisenoxyd in geweissen Pigmentation. VirchowsArchivfürPathologischeAnatomie und Physiologie und fürKlinischeMedizin 39, 42.

Reichs, K.J., 1998. Postmortem dismemberment: recovery, analysis and interpretation. In: Reichs, K.J. (Ed.), Forensic Osteology, Advances in the Identification of Human Remains. Charles C. Thomas, Springfield, IL, pp. 353−398.

Saville, P.A., Hainsworth, S.V., Rutty, G.N., 2007. Cutting crime: the analysis of the "uniqueness" of saw marks on bone. Int. J. Legal Med. 121 (5), 349−357.

Schmidt, U., Pollak, S., 2006. Sharp force injuries in clinical forensic medicine—findings in victims and perpetrators. Forensic Sci. Int. 159 (2), 113−118.

Sitiene, R., Varnaite, J., Zakaras, A., 2004. Complex investigation of body and clothing injuries during the identification of the assault instrument. Forensic Sci. Int. 146, S59–S60.

Spitz, W.U., Fisher, R.S., 1993. Medicolegal Investigation of Death: Guidelines for the Application of Pathology to Crime Investigation, third ed. Ch. Thomas, Illinois.

Srebotnik, E., Messner, K., 1994. A simple method that uses differential staining and light microscopy to assess the selectivity of wood delignification by white rot fungi. Appl. Environ. Microbiol. 60 (4), 1383–1386.

Stephenson, D., 1997. Metal Cutting Theory and Practice, second ed. CRC Press, Boca Raton.

Symes, S.A., Williams, J.A., Murray, E.A., Hoffman, J.M., Holland, T.D., Saul, J.M., et al., 2002. Taphonomic context of sharp-force trauma in suspected cases of human mutilation and dismemberment. Advances in Forensic Taphonomy: Method, Theory, and Archaeological Perspectives. CRC Press, pp. 403–434.

Symes, S.A., Ericka, N., L'Abbé, E.N.C., Wolff, I., Dirkmaat, D.C., 2012. Bone in medicolegal investigations, A Companion to Forensic Anthropology, 10. Wiley-Blackwell, p. 340.

Thompson, T.J.U., Inglis, J., 2009. Differentiation of serrated and non-serrated blades from stab marks in bone. Int. J. Legal Med. 123 (2), 129–135.

Vermeij, E.J., Zoon, P.D., Chang, S.B.C.G., Keereweer, I., Pieterman, R., Gerretsen, R.R.R., 2012. Analysis of microtraces in invasive traumas using SEM/EDS. Forensic Sci. Int. 214 (1), 96–104.

Vigliani, R., 2003. Demonstration of trivalent iron in decalcified bone marrow specimens. Comparative study of standard Perls stain on sections and the Perls pre-reaction on fragments. Pathologica 95 (3), 140–145.

Further Reading

Symes, S.A., Chapman, E.N., Rainwater, C.W., Cabo, L.L., Myster, S.M., 2010. Knife and Saw Toolmark Analysis in Bone: A Manual Designed for the Examination of Criminal Mutilation and Dismemberment. Mercyhurst College.

Dismemberment and Toolmark Analysis on Bone: A Microscopic Analysis of the Walls of Cut Marks

Alberto Amadasi[1], Debora Mazzarelli[1], Caterina Oneto[1], Annalisa Cappella[1], Andrea Gentilomo[2] and Cristina Cattaneo[1]

[1]LABANOF (Laboratory of forensic anthropology and odontology), Department of Biomedical Science for Health, University of Milan, Milan, Italy [2]Institute of Legal Medicine, University of Milan, Milan, Italy

The term *dismemberment* means to divide into parts or cut into pieces and refers to a voluntary criminal act, which in many occasions follows a murder in order to dispose of the "body" of evidence. Therefore, accidental events are excluded from this definition. With the aim of concealing, remains are usually sealed in wrappings or containers and hidden in places where the perpetrator believes it will be more difficult to discover them (Scholl and Moffatt, 2017).

In such cases, the issues of identification, estimation of the postmortem interval, and reconstruction of the cause and manner of death may be very challenging (Reichs, 1998; Hyma and Rao, 1991): anatomy is subverted, body parts can be missing, signs of injuries may be hidden, and environment (e.g., inside plastic waste bags) can severely alter the rate of decomposition (Dirkmaat et al., 2008).

Concerning the aims and reasons behind the crime (Rajs et al., 1998; Konopka et al., 2007; Konopka et al., 2006; Di Nunno et al., 2006; Koops et al., 1986), different types of dismemberment have been classified. What is nowadays widely accepted is a division in four categories, where the issue of dismemberment was investigated from a psychological perspective, with an effort to interpret the actions of the perpetrator (Rajs et al., 1998;

Konopka et al., 2007; Konopka et al., 2006; Di Nunno et al., 2006; Koops et al., 1986). This led to the identification of the following four categories: the so-called "defensive mutilation" (most frequent) in which the body is hacked in many pieces aiming at easier transport and concealment. The second category is "offensive mutilation," which occurs when the dismemberment relies upon impulsive and aggressive actions against the corpse, the removal of body parts is performed as a demonstrative act. On the other hand, "aggressive mutilation" (frequently decapitation) is represented as the severing of body parts which is the direct cause of death (Türk et al., 2004; Dogan et al., 2010). The last category is "necromaniac mutilation," which occurs when parts of a corpse are severed and preserved for personal sexual pleasure of the perpetrator.

Another classification (Salfati, 2000) distinguishes between "expressive" and "instrumental" mutilations; in the former, the victim is used as a symbolic tool to satisfy the psychological needs of the perpetrator; in the latter case the main aim of the perpetrator is to gain some kind of advantage (e.g., economic benefit).

Very few studies are available concerning the relationship between dismemberment and psychiatric disease. Rajs et al. (1998) described a link between aggressive and defensive mutilations and alcohol/drug addiction, previous psychiatric and criminal records, as well as sexual crimes, anxiety, schizophrenia, or drug addiction, which are frequently present along with previous criminal records. To our knowledge, more precise indications useful for the identification of the offender have never been assessed.

Dismemberment is in most cases performed with sharp objects (hand saws, chainsaws, or different types of knives) (Reichs 1998; Dirkmaat et al., 2008; Salfati, 2000; Delabarde and Ludes, 2010). Specific signs on bone may be detected and linked to such tools. In fact, the analysis of cut and saw marks on the bone can enable the identification of the areas of severing as well as the tools used (Madea and Driever, 2000; Reuhl and Bratzke, 1999; Saville et al., 2007; Bailey et al., 2011).

However, the interpretation of cut marks on bone is still an enormous challenge, although several authors have dealt with this topic from different points of view (macroscopic, microscopic, radiologic, morphologic, metric) (Symes, 1992, 1998, 2002; Cerutti et al., 2014, Gaudio et al., 2014) and despite the fact that many analytical tools (such as optic and scanning microscopy) have been applied to this issue (Bartelink et al., 2001; Alunni-Perret et al., 2005; Cerutti et al., 2016; Gibelli et al., 2012), the available scientific research is still insufficient and many variables come into play in the analysis of cut marks. However, some morphological and metric features in bone can be related to wounding tools, such as knives, saws, or axes. Knife marks are generally thin (less thick or equal to the blade size), have a V-shaped cross-section, and the walls are mostly smooth or with microscopic striations placed perpendicular to the floor of the cut. Saw marks are generally wide (with a greater thickness than the blade size), have a square or U-shape in cross-section, and striations are present along the walls and are well visible and parallel to the floor of the cut. Chop marks are most often wide, with V- or U-shaped cross-sections, and walls appear smooth or with microscopic striations, perpendicular to the floor of the cut. These are the general characteristics provided by the scientific community, but they have however to be critically considered, in particular in case of dismemberments where some of them can be influenced by the dynamics (e.g., the "moving" motion of the wounding tool). In addition, the type of lesion (partial or total) can strongly influence the possibility of identifying the class characteristics of the wounding tool. It is worth noting that bone has some elasticity and may thus deform, so any groove tends to close when the blade is removed and the space between the two walls is reduced with respect to the width of the blade. Nevertheless, hard tissues are more capable of recording and preserving the impression of this and may often be the only evidence when decomposition has led to skeletal remains.

Previous works have focused on the interpretation in general of sharp force trauma in bone to define kerf characteristics (Symes et al., 2007; Freas, 2010), origin of different cut marks (Saville et al., 2007; Alunni-Perret et al., 2005), and pattern of dismemberment (Konopka et al., 2006, 2007; Di Nunno et al., 2006; Koops et al., 1986). The systematic analysis of blade marks is based upon the fact that bones have the ability to retain characteristic features of the wounding weapon. This can be used to provide assistance toward a correct assessment of the main features of the weapon. Indeed, the analyses of cut marks in bone may yield much information on the class characteristics of the blade used and therefore a class assessment may enable forensic pathologists and anthropologists to link cut marks and weapons. Nevertheless, still very little data exist on the identification of individualizing characteristics of different blades (Freas, 2010; Shaw et al., 2011; Thompson and Inglis, 2009). Among these, many studies focused on marks left by saws in cases of dismemberment observed in forensic practice (Konopka et al., 2006, 2007; Di Nunno et al., 2006; Koops et al., 1986), but they do not provide information on whether or not it is possible to identify a unique blade based on the characteristics visible on a bone mark. In addition, the issue concerning the identification of which class of instruments have been used in dismemberment cases needs to take into consideration that dismemberment actions can be usually performed by using a saw (which obviously can cut bones more easily), but it is also not rare to use different types of knives (Porta et al., 2016). In addition, saw marks are the type of lesions mostly studied and reported in literature for dismemberment cases while just a few studies have investigated signs left by other classes of tools (Porta et al., 2016; Symes et al., 2007; Cerutti et al., 2016). Finally, besides the fact that bone marks caused by saws are well known, their metric and morphologic features (microscopically and macroscopically) can be considered also more easily interpretable, in particular if observable within compact bone instead of spongy bone. Accordingly, there is still the need to develop new research ensuring knowledge for the interpretation of bone marks caused from tools different from saws, which can shed light on characteristics considered as specific of some classes of knives. This might be very helpful for the interpretation of dismemberment cases where several tools are used by the murderer, as the case presented below.

CASE REPORT

We wish to present a case that challenged us with a dismemberment performed by different knives, where specific questions were raised concerning the mechanism, and literature was insufficient, which led to a project devised within the expertise to answer these specific questions. This is also an example of how sometimes judicial authorities need to wait for specific trials for experts to supply results or at least hypotheses. The case of dismemberment here presented concerns a body of a 76-year-old male: the body parts were found in several plastic bags discovered within a water canal in Milan in 2010. Remains, still well preserved, were found soon after the homicide was perpetrated thanks to the confession of the murderer who only confirmed his guilt and the place where the homicide occurred. Soon after the confession, during the police search, three different kitchen knives and a walking stick (which had on top a metal portion depicting a horse) were found and sequestered. The three kitchen knives consisted of two linear-edged knives and a serrated-edged bread knife. All the tools were suspected to have been involved in the death and dismemberment since they showed blood stains.

Autopsy Findings and Cause of Death

The autopsy analysis revealed the following findings: the body was severed in six parts (thorax and abdomen, upper limbs, lower limbs, and head) and only at the head multiple irregular blunt force injuries (a total of 28 lesions, only some correlated also to bone fractures) were visible and considered vital given the presence of blood extravasations within soft tissues (Fig. 8.1). Signs of vital reaction (blood extravasation) were found also within the soft tissue margins at the throat dismemberment edges (Fig. 8.2), while the other soft tissue margins of the other dismembered parts of the body did not show any vital reaction.

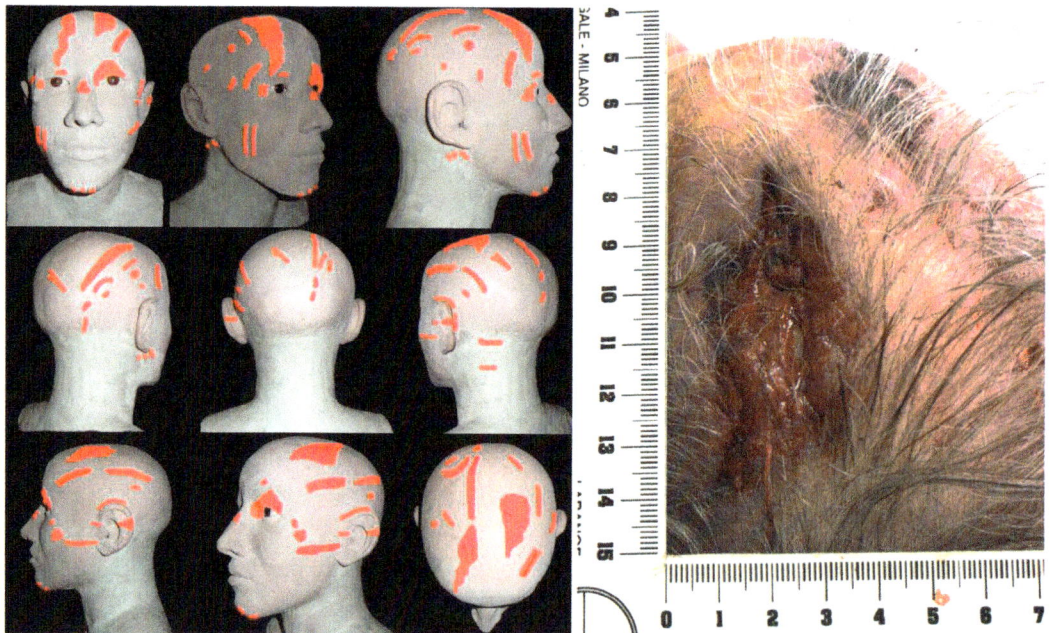

FIGURE 8.1   Left: representation of all the 28 lesions found at the head during the autopsy. Right: image of a skin laceration with clear blood extravasation (i.e., hemorrhagic infiltration).

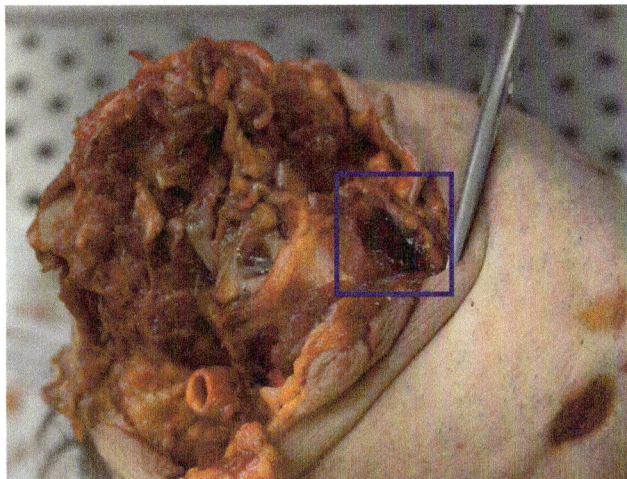

FIGURE 8.2 Image of the cervical edges of cutting showing a small area with vital reaction (blood infiltration).

Death was related to head injuries perpetrated with a blunt object, followed by dismemberment and hiding of the different parts. The autopsy could not provide by itself any suggestions of the tools used for the blunt injury and the dismemberment. Therefore, the sampling of both the edges of the cutting (bone and soft tissue) lesions and the blunt force injuries to the head were performed to apply further analysis intended for correctly interpreting the types of tools used.

Blunt Injury Analysis

Among the suspected tools there was the presence of a blunt object (the sequestered walking stick) (Fig. 8.3), which was supposed to be the one causing all the 28 head blunt force lesions. Indeed, one of the questions the autopsy should have answered was the compatibility between those lesions and the suspected object. The autopsy could not provide insight based just on the lesion morphology and so an anthropological analysis requiring SEM-EDX was carried out to search for metallic residues that might provide additional details. Previous studies in literatures have already demonstrated the possibility to detect metallic residues on bone following blunt force injury that lacerated the soft tissues (Pechnìkova et al., 2012).

This analysis, in fact, highlighted the presence of gray metal stains on some bone samples (Fig. 8.3), which kicked off a series of chemical investigations with SEM-EDX to detect metallic residues left by the blunt object. The SEM-EDX analysis, in fact, could provide a useful chemical profile defining the nature of all metal particles, which were mostly represented by tin residues (Sn), the same chemical component of the superior metal part of the sequestered walking stick (Fig. 8.4).

In this case, the chemical compatibility in addition to the blood stain on the sequestered blunt object demonstrated the link between the head lesions and the walking stick.

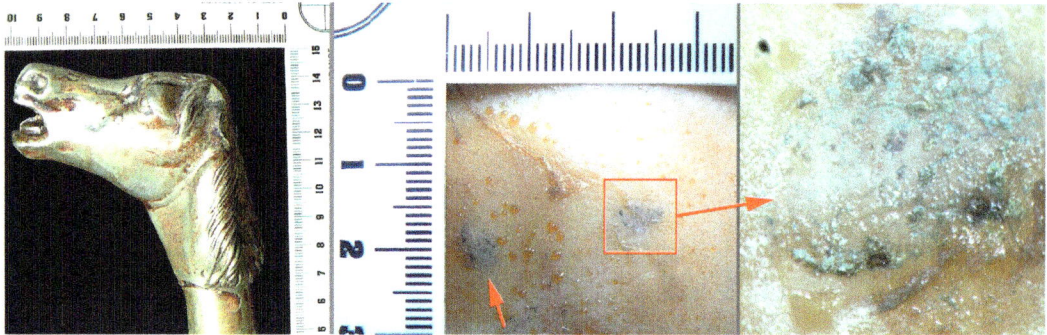

FIGURE 8.3   Left image: A detail of the superior part of the walking stick presumed to have provoked all the lesions of the head. Central image: presence of gray metal stains on the bone skull surface. Right image: a detail of the previous image acquired by the stereomicroscope (6 ×).

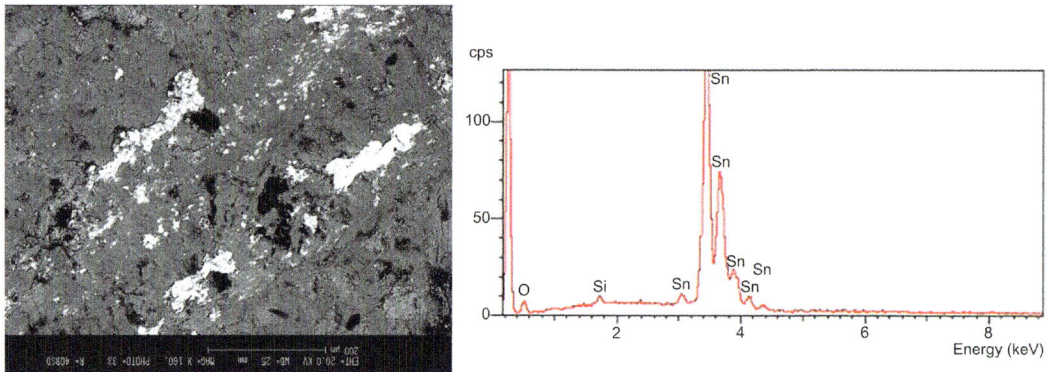

FIGURE 8.4   SEM-EDX microphotograph and spectra of tin traces detected on skull surface.

Dismemberment Analysis

The presumed cutting weapons and the edges of cutting were analyzed by using different techniques: a detailed macroscopic investigation and a microscopic analysis carried out by both the stereomicroscope and the SEM-EDX. All the analyses were conducted with the intent to provide a morphological and metric description and thus a chemical pattern highlighting the presence of metallic residues potentially linkable with the presumed knives. Depending on the body traits analyzed, the macroscopic and stereomicroscopic analysis allowed to notice two main morphologic injury patterns distributed differently: the cervical trait and the right humerus were characterized differently than all the other districts (the left humerus and both femurs). The latter showed a typical pattern presenting parallel striations with a repeated corrugated pattern (Fig. 8.5), while the right humerus and the cervical traits displayed only parallel striations with some irregularity without any specific outline.

FIGURE 8.5   Stereomicroscopic image of the parallel striations with a repeated corrugated pattern found at right femur edges.

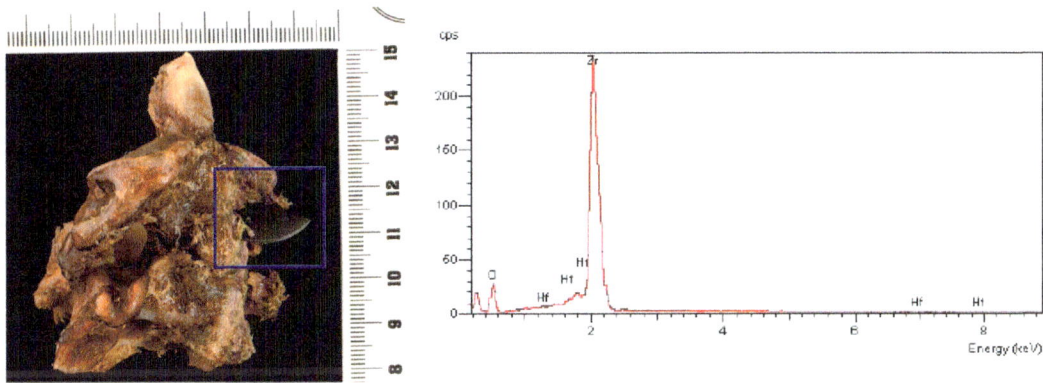

FIGURE 8.6   Image of the splinter embedded in the cervical vertebra (left) and SEM-EDX spectra of the cervical margins of the cut representing hafnium and zirconium.

For what concerns the cut marks found in the cervical vertebrae the morphological pattern demonstrated the use of a blade with a linear edge, also supported by the detection of residues of hafnium and zirconium (component of one of the ceramic knives), as was further proven by the same analysis on the blade. In addition, the finding of a splinter embedded in the second cervical vertebra was also considered as a confirmation: it was reported as surely belonging to one of the two linear-edged ceramic knives, namely the one with the tip of the blade broken (Fig. 8.6).

The morphological pattern of the cut marks on the left humerus and both femora were instead compatible with a serrated-edged blade tool class and SEM-EDX analysis detected residues of iron and chrome (Fig. 8.7): the bread knife showed the same composition confirming its morphological, metric, and chemical compatibility with the edges of cutting.

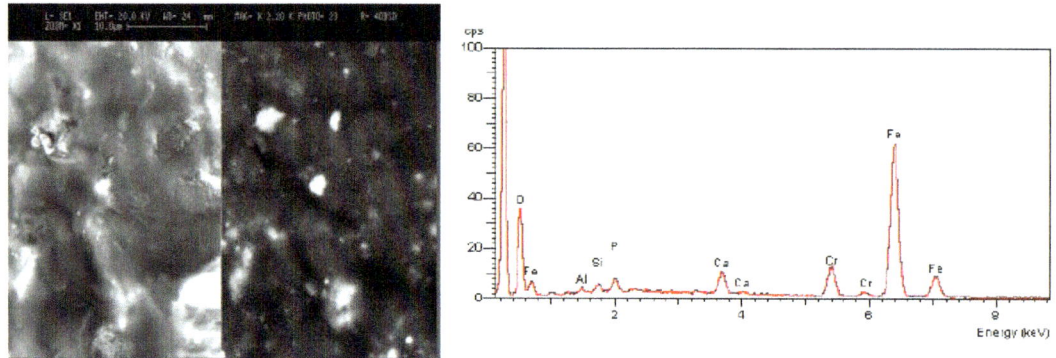

FIGURE 8.7   SEM-EDX microphotograph (left) and spectra (right) of the iron and chrome residues found at both femora and at the left humerus.

The same does not apply for the right humerus cut marks. Its morphological pattern was similar to that found at the cervical edges—hence possibly compatible with a smooth blade tool class—but the metallic residues detected by SEM-EDX analysis were related to all the three "suspected" knives. Indeed, the detected residues found on the edges consisted of hafnium in combination with zirconium and iron in pairing with chrome and so were compatible respectively with one of the ceramic knives and with the serrated-edged bread knife. It follows that the right humeral edges (Fig. 8.8) turned out to be the classical example of cut marks with an ambiguous mode of production and from which many issues still arise on the comprehension and identification of cut marks.

Many hypotheses should be taken into consideration in such a scenario: for example, the use of different kinds of tools to produce and finish one lesion can lead to the presence of unusual morphological patterns and/or the alteration of the morphology left initially from the tool used as the first one. And again, the repeated use of a tool like the serrated blade can leave a mark that is similar to that correlated with smooth blades (or vice versa) because of the many passages, that is, the "to and from motion."

The precise reconstruction of the manner of homicide and dismemberment through anthropological analysis and identification of specific instruments shed light on the whole scenario of the crime (Fig. 8.9).

However, since the use of two different classes of knife (a smooth blade and serrated blade) had been suspected, there was a problem in identifying the type of instrument, which led to two precise questions:

1. How much time is needed to cut soft tissues and bone with those two types of blade?
2. Can patterns between marks on bone and the knife still be matched? In other words, can a match still be obtained after the blade has worn out due to the repeated contact between the blade and bone? How does the repeated back and forth movement affect this comparison?

The only systematic studies on this topic have been performed by Symes (Symes, 1992) whose observations are at present the main sources of information for forensic

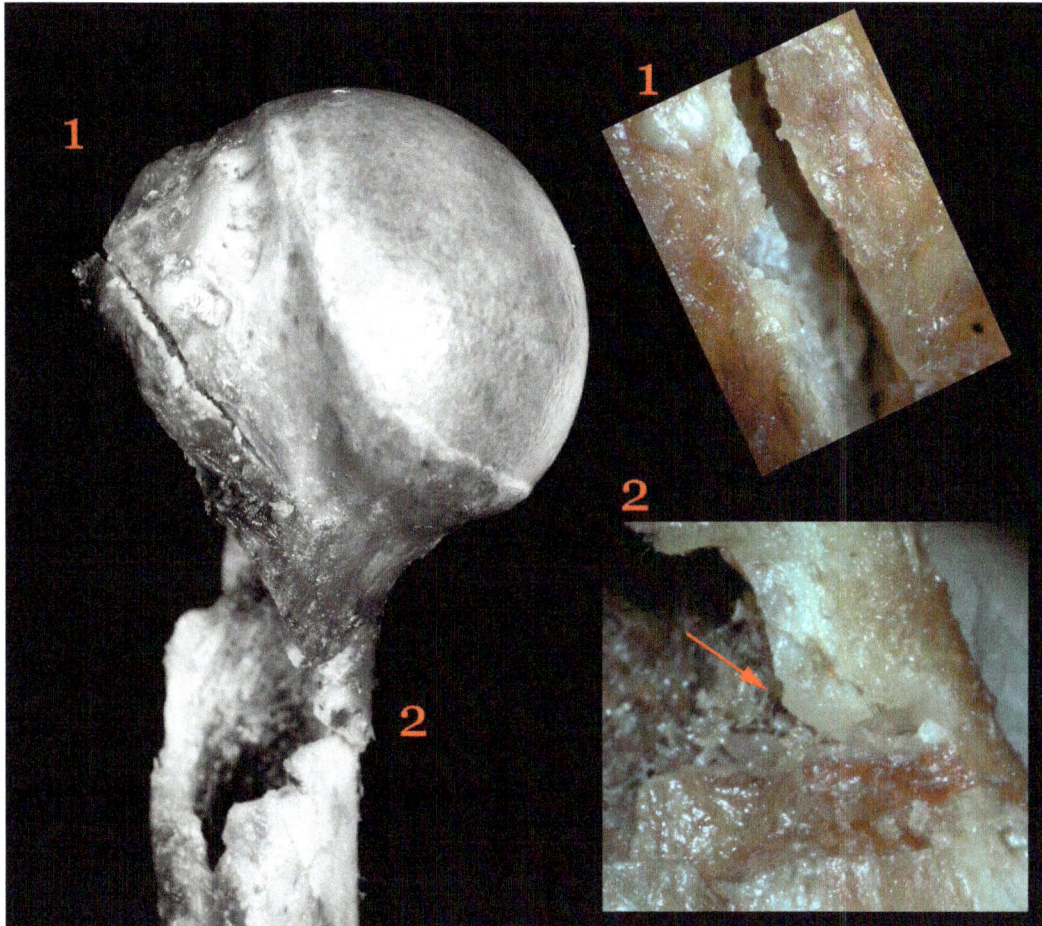

FIGURE 8.8 Right humerus with details of the edges of the cutting (1 and 2) with a very complex morphological pattern.

anthropology in the field of toolmark analysis on bone (Dirkmaat et al., 2008; Symes, 2012; Bartelink et al., 2001; Symes et al., 1995, 2007; Alunni-Perret et al., 2005).

Judicial Experimental Study for Cut Marks Interpretation

Therefore, the present study arose from the need to compare characteristic features observed on kerf walls of wounding sharp weapons and hence add information to existing cut mark analyses. For this the microscopic pattern of different types of blades was compared with the pattern left by these tools on the wall of the cut marks and lesions produced by different sharp instruments were compared with the aim of evaluating differences and similarities. Previous studies already stated that, even if cut marks are

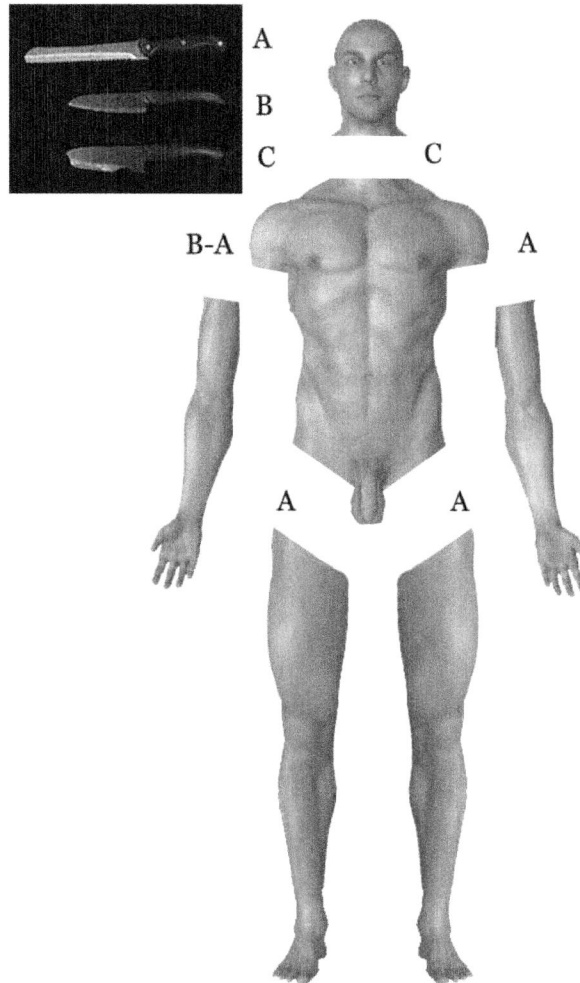

FIGURE 8.9   Illustration of the manner of dismemberment and possible correlation between margins of the cut and tools.

visible with the naked eye or with the aid of a stereomicroscope, the method of choice for a thorough analysis of cut marks in bone has now become scanning electron microscopy (SEM). Scanning electron microscopy provides high resolution images of the surface of the sample and has been widely accepted as a standard tool in forensic science and in cut mark analyses (Kooi and Fairgrieve, 2013). Therefore, the experiment was conducted on cut marks on bone samples, both with stereomicroscopy and with SEM, through a comparative analysis of blades and lesions before and after the cutting action. The research was widened with the investigation on whether cut marks can still be recognizable after the tool has already had repeated contact with bone.

The goal of the experiment for this specific case was to verify if the motion of different blades (serrated and non) repeated for minutes or hours can alter the initial morphological appearance of lesions and how, in particular, the striations that typically characterized the mark patterns, which often are the features leading to the recognition of the class of blade.

Materials and Methods

Three blades were used: a serrated blade, a metal saw, and a smooth blade. The characteristics of the blades are summarized in Table 8.1. Pictures of the blades were taken before and after use with SEM (scanning electron microscope) Cambridge Stereoscan 360

TABLE 8.1   Characteristics of the Blades Used for the Study

Blades

1	Serrated blade knife	Thickness of the blade	Grind	Min	0.06 mm
				Max	0.61 mm
			Blade level	Min	0.61 mm
				Max	1.71 mm
		Length of the blade		23 cm	
		Grind shape		Chisel	
		Grind height		1.8 mm	
		Number of teeth per inch		5	
2	Metal saw	Thickness of the blade		0.5 mm	
		Length of the blade		30 cm	
		Grind shape		N/A	
		Grind height		N/A	
		Number of teeth per inch		24	
		Set of teeth		Universal	
3	Smooth blade knife	Thickness of the blade	Grind	Min	0.02 mm
				Max	0.04 mm
			Blade level	Min	0.04 mm
				Max	0.06 mm
		Length of the blade		10 cm	
		Grind shape		Flat	
		Grind height		0.04	
		Number of teeth per inch		—	

with electron gun, vacuum pump, image acquisition software, and EDS spectrometry with detector from 138 eV to 5.9 keV (Oxford Link Pentafet, Oxford, UK).

The samples consisted of human long bones collected according to the Mortuary Police regulations and laws. Bones were stored refrigerated, defrosted, and cleaned. The long bones were cut into samples approximately 3 cm long, for a total of six samples. Moreover, the circular diaphysis was halved to obtain two semicircular samples. Once the blades and the bone samples were prepared a parallel lesion was produced. The term *parallel lesion* refers to lesions created with a repeated movement of the blade (back and forth) conducted on a parallel plane with respect to the floor of the lesion. This kind of lesion differs from other mark types such as the transverse ones, which are instead cut marks produced by a single stroke from top to bottom (Fig. 8.10). In this study, due to the complexity of the topic and also the presence of a multitude of factors that may influence results, only parallel lesions were considered for the case described earlier.

The bone sample was secured in a bench-vice with an appropriate protective device to avoid damage. The bone sample was cut using the blade manually after having measured the anterior–posterior diameter and the compact bone thickness at the anterior shaft surface (the one involved by the cut). The time employed by the operator to completely cut the bone sample was recorded. The operator tried to use a constant amount of energy and to keep the blade with constant inclination. Once the sample was cut, one half of the diaphysis (representing the left wall of the cut) was named "A" while the right half of the diaphysis (representing the other wall of the cut) was called "B" (Fig. 8.10A).

Each of the two sides (the halves called A and B) was observed under a Wild M650 stereomicroscope and photographed at different magnifications: $6\times$, $10\times$, and $16\times$. All the samples were then subjected to survey with SEM.

SEM and Processing of the Results

Blades and bone samples were prepared for the analysis with SEM. Firstly they were coated with graphite as required by standard preparatory procedures. The blades and bone samples were observed at magnifications from $5\times$ to $50\times$. Pictures of blades and bone samples, were overlapped using Adobe Photoshop CS4 to obtain a picture of the

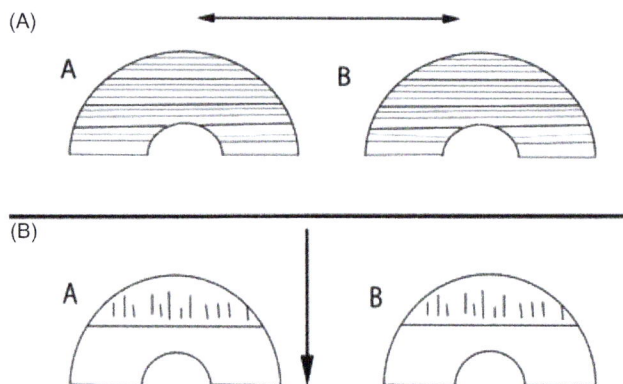

FIGURE 8.10 Scheme of the different type of striations visible on walls. The type of striations, whether (A) parallel or (B) transverse, depend on the manner of production of a cut.

whole surface with better resolution. Then the pictures were compared: the blades before the lesion, the kerf walls, and the blades after the stroke or cutting action. For each type of lesion a form was completed where the following parameters were recorded:

- direction, based on the longitudinal axis of the cut;
- shape;
- number of striations, calculated in an area 3 mm wide;
- striation width: calculated as the average of 5 random striae;
- distance between the striae: calculated as the average of the distance between 5 random striae next to each other;
- relation between the striae (e.g., parallel, criss-crossing);
- appearance of the superior edge;
- presence of chipping;
- shape of the breakaway spur.

Results

Results are divided according to lesions caused by the different type of blades, and summarized in Table 8.2. Fig. 8.11 shows the appearance of the lesions determined by the three blades by using both stereomicroscopy and scanning electron microscopy.

Serrated Blade Knife

About 20 minutes were necessary for the cut to be completed. The femur diameter measured 31 mm at the *linea aspera* while the compact bone thickness measured 6 mm at the anterior shaft surface. Both walls showed a similar pattern of striae: on wall A, the striae were mainly parallel to each other with a linear path, along with some isolated criss-crossing. Some other areas of the cut surface were smoother and without defined striae. Linear and grossly parallel striae were detectable only in small, defined areas of wall B, which appeared smoother. On both walls the presence of "chipping" on the lateral edges was observed both on entrance and exit sides. The top edge of wall A also showed an outward bend. False start kerfs were visible on both halves: more than 20 on side A and 15 on side B. All showed a V-shaped profile and followed the same direction, although they were crossing each other. On the 3-mm line of side A, a total of 38 intersecting striae were detected.

Metal Saw

Less than 5 minutes were necessary for the complete cut of the femur sample whose anterior—posterior diameter and the compact bone thickness at the anterior shaft surface measured respectively 34 mm and 8 mm. No false start kerfs were observed. The striae showed a linear shape and parallel direction, apparently with different depths from the surface. The presence of exit chipping on both walls and a U-shaped breakaway spur were detected. On the 3-mm line there were 27 incident striae on side A and 25 on side B. The two walls, although nonspecular, were similar and showed the same characteristics.

TABLE 8.2   Results Concerning Parallel Lesions Caused From the Three Blade Typology

Parallel Lesions

Features	Wall	Serrated Blade	Metallic Saw	Smooth Blade
Direction of the striae (based on the longitudinal axes of the cut)	A	Grossly parallel	Parallel	Parallel with some bowing
	B	Visible ones are grossly parallel	Parallel	Parallel with some bowing
Striae shape	A	Linear	Linear	Linear and some bowed
	B	Visible ones are linear	Linear	Linear and some bowed
Striae number (on a vertical line of 3 mm)	A	38	27	32
	B	—	25	38
Striae width (average of 5)	A	15.29 μm	14.7 μm	9.02 μm
	B	—	20.23 μm	12.94 μm
Distance between striae (average of 5)	A	33.65 μm	90.19 μm	37.65 μm
	B	—	80.29 μm	45.09 μm
Relation between striae	A	Grossly parallel, with single vertical lines	Parallel	Parallel with single vertical lines
	B		Parallel	Parallel with some criss-crossing
Appearance of the superior edge, superior vision	A	Irregular	Regular	Regular
	B	Irregular	Regular	Regular
Presence of lateral chipping	A	Enter and exit side	Exit side	Enter and exit side
	B	Enter side	Exit side	No
Presence of false starts kerf	A	Yes	No	Yes
	B	Yes	No	Yes
Number of false starts kerf	A	>20	—	12
	B	15	—	8
Appearance of the false starts' floor	A	V-shaped	—	V-shaped
	B	V-shaped	—	V-shaped
Relation between the false start kerfs	A	Criss-crossing	—	Parallel
	B	Grossly parallel and some criss-crossing	—	Parallel
Homogeneity	A	Yes	Yes	Yes
	B	No	Yes	Yes

(Continued)

TABLE 8.2 (Continued)

Parallel Lesions

Features	Wall	Serrated Blade	Metallic Saw	Smooth Blade
Positive breakaway spur		Present	Present	Present
Appearance of the superior surface of the positive breakaway spur		Presence of pleating, grossly broken	U-shaped	V-shaped
Negative breakaway spur		Present	Present	Present
Observations		Presence of smooth areas	Different depth of striae's depth	Smooth areas and different depth of striae

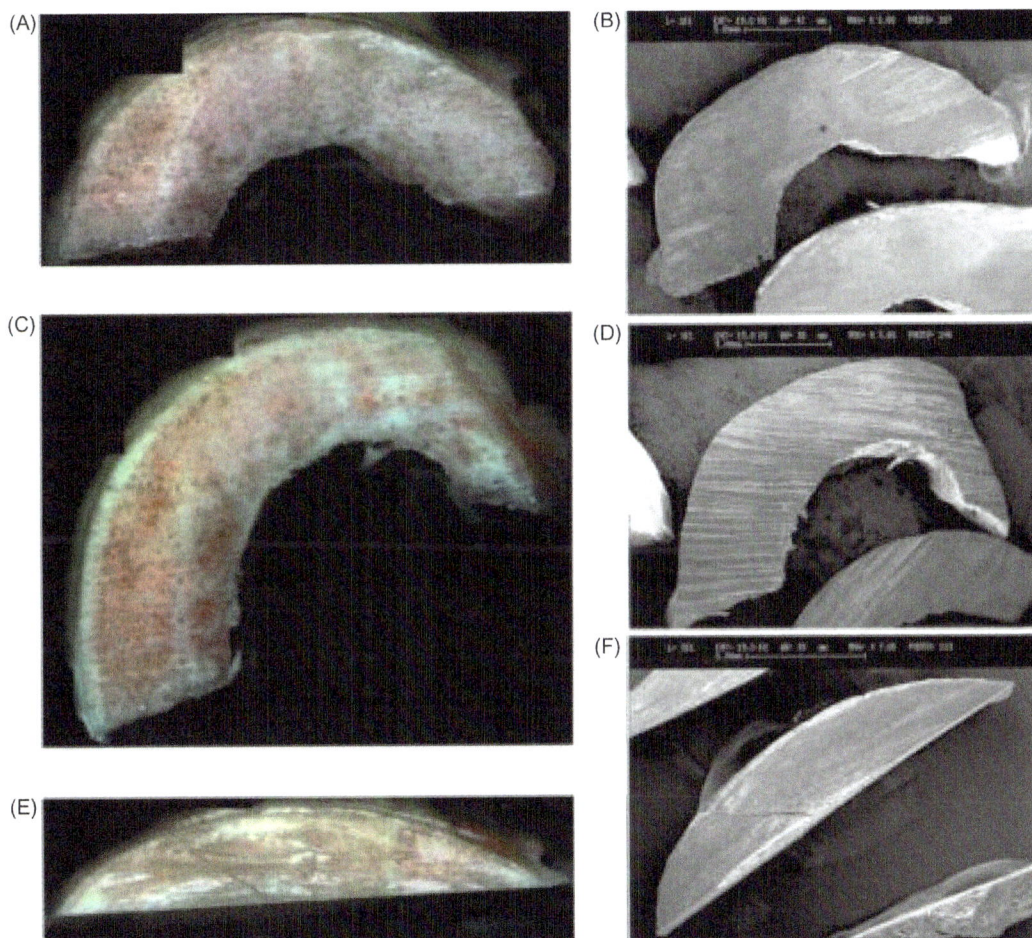

FIGURE 8.11 Serrated blade knife lesion, wall A: (A) stereomicroscopy 10× and (B) SEM 7×; metal saw lesion, wall A: (C) stereomicroscopy 10× and (D) SEM 7×; smooth blade knife lesion, wall A: (E) stereomicroscopy 10× and (F) SEM 7×.

Smooth Blade Knife

About 5 hours were requested for a complete cut and since the sample was still not divided, it was necessary to sample just the bone walls involved by the cut. In this case the anterior–posterior diameter measured 32 mm while the compact bone thickness at the anterior shaft surface resulted to be 7 mm. The striae followed various directions and showed an overall criss-crossing pattern. In single areas some striae showed linear paths, slightly bowed. In general, there was a parallel pattern with isolated transverse lines. On the 3-mm line 32 incident striae on side A and 38 on side B were detected. On side A, exit and entry chipping were observed, while none were detected on the other side. Also V-shaped false start kerfs on both sides (8 on A, 10 on B) were detected. The surfaces showed a smooth appearance and the striae had different depths.

The serrated knife proved to be an effective cutting tool. The striae left by this type of knife were still quite defined but less evident than those left by the saw. The last tool (smooth blade knife) showed the most irregular pattern of striae.

Discussion

The major aim of the present study was to search for evidence on the relation between the marks left on bones by a sharp tool and the features of the wounding weapon, since scarce literature is available on this topic and mainly related only to saw lesions (Symes, 1992, 1998; Symes et al., 1995, 2002, 2007; Bartelink et al., 2001; Alunni-Perret et al., 2005). Moreover, the possibility of identifying cut marks and wear of the instrument is a fascinating challenge, which catalyzed the idea of the study. This type of analysis may be crucial in cases of every sharp lesion as in the case of stab wounds or dismemberment, especially when only skeletal remains are available. Although the study was performed on a small number of samples, it provided interesting results. It was set as a morphological and not quantitative study and focused on a dual comparison: between different injuries in bone, but also on the different features of wounding sharp weapons and their effects on the morphology of bone precedent lesions. In fact, this type of test, with a comparison of the effects of the same weapon on the bone after repeated use, has never been performed. In the present case report, the morphological and dimensional characteristics of the knife did not match perfectly with the bone lesion, thus we wanted to see how the repeated passage of serrated and nonserrated knives could alter morphology of bone lesions.

The purpose of the experiment was to investigate with microscopy whether the passage of a smooth or serrated blade for minutes or hours can distort the lesion and striae.

The lesion features detected for serrated blades may be related to the out and back pulling of the blade. Results showed a minimal difference between the two kerf walls. The higher number of striae, if compared with those left by the saw, can be an indicator of the number of strokes needed to cut the bone. Moreover, the distance between the striae for both knives (serrated and smooth) was less than the saw. These elements showed that more strokes were needed for knives to cut the sample because of their lesser cutting power. Chipping was present both on the entrance and on the exit side of the lesion and occurred where the stroke was due to a single sawing movement. This may be due to the bone spalling as teeth exited the bone (Symes, 1998). The presence of chipping on both sides was probably due to the absence in serrated knives of a front or a back side as in saws. The false start kerfs had a V-shaped incision and their number might indicate that the cutting action was not clear and unique. The pattern created by the saw was indeed typical and distinctive. Therefore, the majority of the characteristics described by Symes (Symes, 1998) were detectable, with the presence of exit chipping on both sides and the same features of the kerf wall on the breakaway spur. False start kerfs were absent, indicating the effectiveness of such tools in cutting bones. Striae of different depths and widths were observable on the surface of the sample, according to the study of Saville et al. (2007) on saws, where different types of striations were detected. The cut with the smooth blade left striae with different directions, as sign of the attempts to proceed along the bone during the cutting action. Vertical single striae were also present as a possible indicator of the back and forth movement. The observation that both exit and entrance chipping were present on the lateral edges might again be related to the explanation given by Symes (1998) for serrated knives. Thus, the results showed that the three blades may leave different types of striae and a thorough analysis may be crucial in identifying the type of sharp tool used.

Therefore, the present study showed that the class characteristics for each sample are at least accessible even after multiple use. Previous literature was confirmed, such as the statements of Alunni-Perret et al. (2005) indicating that lesions might be reproducible if the bone is hit with the same force and inclination. Also the characteristics of saw marks described by Symes (1998) and Reichs (1998) were confirmed. Furthermore, and especially, features that these authors had assigned only to saw lesions were observed also for serrated and smooth blades knives, that is, exit chipping.

As Kooi and Fairgrieve (2013) stated, the study confirmed that SEM is extremely useful for the observation of cut mark characteristics. In case of sharp force injuries, moreover, SEM proved to be useful even in the detection of the metal residues left by the tool (Gibelli et al., 2012). Moreover, the stereomicroscope is an excellent tool for the confirmation of the presence of such elements. Given these considerations, in this study interesting characteristics were observed and specific features related to the different blades were recorded. Furthermore, this piece of research helped create or reinforce hypotheses for the case study.

References

Alunni-Perret, V., Muller-Bolla, M., Laugier, J.P., Lupi-Pégurier, L., Bertrand, M.F., Staccini, P., et al., 2005. Scanning electron microscopy analysis of experimental bone hacking trauma. J. Forensic Sci. 50 (4), 796–801.

Bailey, J.A., Wang, Y., van de Goot, F.R., Gerretsen, R.R., 2011. Statistical analysis of kerf mark measurements in bone. Forensic Sci. Med. Pathol. 7 (1), 53–62.

Bartelink, E.J., Wiersema, J.M., Demaree, R.S., 2001. Quantitative analysis of sharp-force trauma: an application of scanning electron microscopy in forensic anthropology. J. Forensic Sci. 46, 1288–1293.

Cerutti, E., Magli, F., Porta, D., Gibelli, D., Cattaneo, C., 2014. Metrical assessment of cutmarks on bone: Is size important? Legal Med. 16 (4), 208–213.

Cerutti, E., Spagnoli, L., Araujo, N., Gibelli, D., Mazzarelli, D., Cattaneo, C., 2016. Analysis of cutmarks on bone: can light microscopy be of any help? Am. J. Forensic Med. Pathol. 37 (4), 248–254.

Delabarde, T., Ludes, B., 2010. Missing in Amazonian jungle: a case report of skeletal evidence for dismemberment. J. Forensic Sci. 55 (4), 1105–1110.

Di Nunno, N., Costantinides, F., Vacca, M., Di Nunno, C., 2006. Dismemberment: a review of the literature and description of 3 cases. Am. J. Forensic Med. Pathol. 27 (4), 307—312.

Dirkmaat, D.C., Cabo, L.L., Ousley, S.D., Symes, S.A., 2008. New perspectives in forensic anthropology. Am. J. Phys. Anthropol. 47, 33—52.

Dogan, K.H., Demirci, S., Deniz, I., Erkol, Z., 2010. Decapitation and dismemberment of the corpse: a matricide case. J. Forensic Sci. 55 (2), 542—545.

Freas, L.E., 2010. Assessment of wear-related features of the kerf wall from saw marks in bone. J. Forensic Sci. 55, 1561—1569.

Gaudio, D., Di Giancamillo, M., Gibelli, D., Galassi, A., Cerutti, E., Cattaneo, C., 2014. Does cone beam CT actually ameliorate stab wound analysis in bone? Int. J. Legal Med. 128 (1), 151—159.

Gibelli, D., Mazzarelli, D., Porta, D., Rizzi, A., Cattaneo, C., 2012. Detection of metal residues on bone using SEM-EDS-Part II: sharp force injury. Forensic Sci. Int. 223, 91—96.

Hyma, B.A., Rao, V.J., 1991. Evaluation and identification of dismembered human remains. Am. J. Forensic Med. Pathol. 12 (4), 291—299.

Konopka, T., Bolechala, F., Strona, M., 2006. An unusual case of corpse dismemberment. Am. J. Forensic Med. Pathol. 27 (2), 163—165.

Konopka, T., Strona, M., Bolechala, F., Kunz, J., 2007. Corpse dismemberment in the material collected by the Department of Forensic Medicine, Cracow, Poland. Lag. Med. (Tokyo) 9 (1), 1—13.

Kooi, R.J., Fairgrieve, S.I., 2013. SEM and stereomicroscopic analysis of cut marks in fresh and burned bone. J. Forensic Sci. 58, 452—458.

Koops, E., Burwinkel, K., Kleiber, M., Püschel, K., 1986. Criminal dismemberment of the corpse. Acta Med. Leg. Soc. 36 (1), 165—175.

Madea, B., Driever, F., 2000. Cadaver dismemberment by chain saw. Arch. Kriminol. 205 (3—4), 75—81.

Pechnìkova, M., Porta, D., Mazzarelli, D., Rizzi, A., Drozdova, E., Cattaneo, C., 2012. Detection of metal residues on bone using SEM-EDS. Part I: blunt force injury, Forensic Sci. Int. 223. pp. 87—90.

Porta, D., Amadasi, A., Cappella, A., Mazzarelli, D., Magli, F., Gibelli, D., et al., 2016. Dismemberment and disarticulation: a forensic anthropological approach. J. Forensic Legal Med. 38, 50—57.

Rajs, J., Lundstöm, M., Broberg, M., Lidberg, L., Lindquist, O., 1998. Criminal mutilation of the human body in Sweden--a thirty-year medico-legal and forensic psychiatric study. J. Forensic Sci. 43 (3), 563—580.

Reichs, K.J., 1998. Postmortem dismemberment: recovery, analysis and interpretation. In: Reichs, K.J. (Ed.), Forensic Osteology, Advances in the Identification of Human Remains. Charles C. Thomas, Springfield, IL, pp. 353—398.

Reuhl, J., Bratzke, H., 1999. Death caused by a chain saw-homicide, suicide or accident? A case report with a literature review (with 11 illustrations). Forensic Sci. Int. 105 (1), 45—49.

Salfati, C.G., 2000. The nature of expressiveness and instrumentality in homicide: implication for offender profiling. Homicide Stud. 4 (3), 265—293.

Saville, P.A., Hainsworth, S.V., Rutty, G.N., 2007. Cutting crime: the analysis of the "uniqueness" of saw marks on bone. Int. J. Legal Med. 121 (5), 349—357.

Scholl, K., Moffatt, C., 2017. Plastic waste sacks alter the rate of decomposition of dismembered bodies within. Int. J. Legal Med. 131 (4), 1141—1147.

Shaw, K.P., Chung, J.H., Chung, F.C., Tseng, B.Y., Pan, C.H., Yang, K.T., 2011. A method for studying knife tool marks on bone. J. Forensic Sci. 56, 967—971.

Symes, S., 1998. Morphology of saw marks in human bone: introduction and examination of residual kerf contour. In: Reichs, K.J. (Ed.), Forensic Osteology, Advances in the Identification of Human Remains. Charles C Thomas, Springfield, pp. 389—409.

Symes, S.A., 1992. Morphology of saw marks in human bone: identification of class characteristics. PhD dissertation, Department of Anthropology, University of Tennessee, Knoxville.

Symes, S.A., Smith, O.C., Gardner, C.D., Francisco, J.T., Horton, G.A., 1995. Anthropological and pathological analysis of sharp trauma in autopsy [Abstract]. Proc. Am. Acad. Forensic Sci. 5, 177—178.

Symes, S., Williams, J., Murray, E., Hoffman, J., Holland, T., Saul, J., et al., 2002. Taphonomic context of sharp-force trauma in suspected cases of human mutilation and dismemberment. In: Haglund, W., Sorg, M. (Eds.), Advances in Forensic Taphonomy: Method, Theory, and Archaeological Perspectives. CRC Press, Boca Raton, FL, pp. 403—434.

Symes, S.A., Rainwater, C.W., Myster, S.M.T., 2007. Standardizing saw and knife mark analysis on bone [Abstract]. Proc. Am. Acad. Forensic Sci. 13, 336.

Thompson, T.J.U., Inglis, J., 2009. Differentiation of serrated and non-serrated blades from stab marks in bone. Int. J. Legal Med. 123, 129–135.

Türk, E.E., Püschel, K., Tsokos, M., 2004. Features characteristic of homicide in cases of complete decapitation. Am. J. Forensic Med. Pathol. 25 (1), 83–86.

Skeletal Evidence of Sharp-Force Disarticulation and Tissue Flensing in 54 Cases Exhibiting Approximately 4200 Bone Strike Injuries

Carl N. Stephan[1], Jodi M. Caple[1,2], Jen G. Atkins[1,2], Jeffrey J. Lynch[1], Brandon Meikle[1] and Wes Fisk[2]

[1]Laboratory for Human Craniofacial and Skeletal Identification (HuCS-ID Lab), School of Biomedical Sciences, The University of Queensland, Brisbane, QLD, Australia [2]Gross Anatomy Facility, School of Biomedical Sciences, The University of Queensland, Brisbane, QLD, Australia

INTRODUCTION

Sharp-force skeletal trauma inflicted during dismemberment and skeletization holds clear and obvious relevance to homicide investigations. In general terms, however, the literature on straight blade inflicted sharp-force trauma to bone is relatively sparse and that relating to human dismemberment is even narrower (approximately 10 papers total; Table 9.1). This in part is underpinned by the general low frequency of dismemberments in forensic casework, for example, in Sweden about 0.1 cases per million inhabitants and year (Rajs et al., 1998). However, cases of dismemberment may be underestimated (see Chapter 11).

While single forensic cases hold important informative value of dismemberment, disarticulation, decapitation and flensing practice in the forensic context, from a scientific viewpoint, large-scale samples are additionally useful to determine what locations are most prone to bone strike injuries. Large-scale samples also provide the capacity to select exemplar injuries for training and illustration purposes, rather than relying on a limited suite of injury patterns observed in few single cases. So far, only two large-scale investigations on

TABLE 9.1   Literature on Sharp-Force Trauma to Bone, Human Dismemberment, and Human Dismemberment Via Sharp-Force Disarticulation With Skeletal Injury

Assorted Papers on Skeletal Sharp-Force Trauma	Papers Specifically on Human Dismemberment (by # of Cases Reported)			
	1 Case	2−4 Cases	5−6 Cases	20−23 Cases
Alunni et al. (2018); Andrews (2012); Bello et al. (2016); Berg (2008); Bromage and Boyde (1984); Capuani et al. (2013); Cerutti et al. (2014); Chacòn et al. (2008); Crowder et al. (2013); Humphrey et al. (2017); Lewis (2008); Lynn and Fairgrieve (2009); Shaw et al. (2011); Thompson and Inglis (2009)	Delabarde and Ludes (2010)[a] Dogan et al. (2010) Hyma and Rao (1991) Konopka et al. (2006)	Di Nunno et al. (2006) Glaister and Brash (1937)[a] (2 of 2)	Porta et al. (2016)[a] (5 of 6) Reichs (1986)[a] (3 of 6) Symes et al. (2002)[a] (1 of 5)	Konopka et al. (2007) Rajs et al. (1998)

[a]Papers providing skeletal evidence of disarticulation (# of these cases provided in parentheses).

dismemberment appear in the published literature with Konopka et al. (2007) reviewing 23 total cases and Rajs et al. (1998) reviewing 22 cases. Per aforementioned trends, both reviews pay limited attention to the bone and even less to sharp-force trauma. Relating to skeletal evidence of disarticulation, the most comprehensive account to date is by Porta et al. (2016) where details of five cases are given, followed closely by Reichs (1986) who reports three cases.

Here we draw upon another little discussed, yet commonly available, dismemberment sample to provide real-life but larger-scale data: bodies processed and defleshed to support the medical teaching skeleton trade prior to the Indian export ban of 1985 (Banerjie, 1985; Carney, 2011; Hefner et al., 2016; Putka, 1986; Stephan et al., 2017). This trade, colloquially known as the Calcutta Bone Trade, operated from around 1944 (Litten, 1944) to 1985 and at its height, resulted in the shipment of up to 65,000 skeletons from India per year (Anonymous Article, 1989). This trade was collectively extensive (literally hundreds of thousands of skeletons) and allegedly generated $1.4−6.7 million in trade per annum (AFP, 1985; Anonymous Article, 1981, 1985; Corrales, 1987; Fineman, 1991). Given the breadth of this skeleton trade prior to 1985, it is commonplace that well-established anatomy facilities from around the globe hold skeletons derived from India as a result of these historic practices.

The information presented in this chapter is derived from 54 cases (exhibiting approximately 4200 bone strike injuries in total), examined as part of an internal audit on the osteology collection held in the Gross Anatomy Facility of the University of Queensland between 2016 and 2018. The aim of the audit was to inventory and label all osteological elements held within the facility's half skeleton library for traceability. Upon starting the audit, it became apparent that this osteology exhibited large numbers of sharp-force trauma from straight-edged blades (mean of 78 bone strikes per case) that also required documentation. In most cases, this trauma was clearly associated with disarticulation of single bones to produce single osseous elements and in some cases associated flensing. For distribution of trauma numbers per case, see Fig. 9.1.

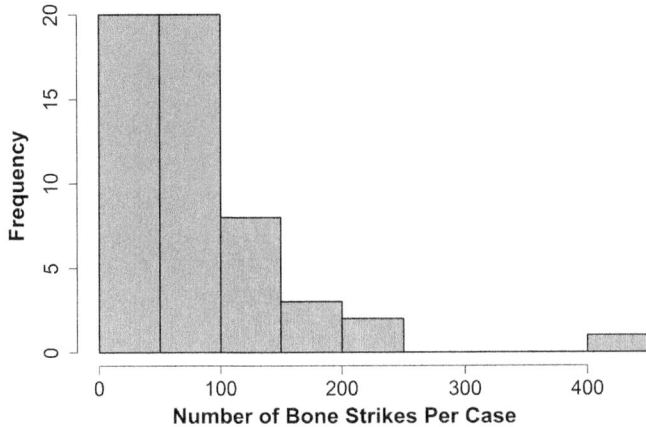

FIGURE 9.1 Histogram of bone strikes per case for the skeletal assemblage reported in this chapter.

Each case is a "half" medical teaching skeleton, which in reality represents elements from multiple individuals, pieced together based on similarities in bone size at the time of their production (by the original bone traders) to give the appearance of a single half skeleton (Stephan et al., 2017). We do not attempt to sort this commingled material here, but rather retain it under its originally grouped case-limited provenance. Often the skeletons are of young individuals (adolescents to young adults), indicated by still fusing epiphyseal lines, such as S1/S2 junctions, iliac crests, and in at least one case, unfused distal epiphyses of the metacarpals (Stephan et al., 2017). Fig. 9.2 provides illustrative examples of two half skeletons and Fig. 9.3 provides an overarching homunculus of total elements present across the assemblage.

As typical for most medical teaching skeletons, there are few written records that accompany the 54 skeletons discussed in this chapter. Thirty-nine cases represent skeletons that have been transferred from members of the public (typically from retiring physicians, surgeons, or their associated family members) to the anatomy facility. The other 15 cases represent skeletons historically present within the facility (first established in 1927). For the transferred skeletons, the evidence that these skeletons are derived from the Calcutta bone trade is in some cases direct (e.g., bone trader labels affixed to the skeletons) and some cases indirect (e.g., medical supplier labels on receipts of past skeleton purchase or labels affixed to the container in which skeletons were delivered; Fig. 9.4). One of the transferred cases (39) derives from France (a common source of medical teaching skeletons prior to the Calcutta bone trade; Fig. 9.4). For the 15 cases historically present in the facility, only indirect association with the Calcutta bone trade exists: four other osteological specimens in the facility hold labels of the medical supplier Adam Rouilly (Fig. 9.4) known for prior onward selling of skeletons to customers from Reknas Ltd—a former large Calcutta bone trading company. Given the intent of bone traders to supply teaching quality specimens that appeared to the untrained eye to be more or less complete and undamaged, the disarticulation and dismemberment activities undertaken are probably best described as produced by semiskilled individuals who held varying degrees of knowledge of arthrology and osteology, primarily as a result of on-the-job training (see Discussion for further comment).

FIGURE 9.2   Two example medical teaching half skeletons. (A) case 33 comprised of commingled elements from at least two (possibly three) individuals; and (B) case 32 comprised of commingled elements from at least two (possibly five) individuals. Scale bands are 100 mm. Source: *Images reproduced from Stephan, C.N., Caple, J.M., Veprek, A., Sievwright, E., Kippers, V., Moss, S., et al., 2017. Complexitites and remedies of unkonwn-provenance osteology. In: G. Strkalj (Ed.), Commemorations and Memorials in Anatomy: Tribute to the Giver. World Scientific, Singapore, pp. 65–95; with permission from World Scientific.*

GENERAL OBSERVATIONS AND TRAUMA IDENTIFICATION

Prior to describing specifics of injury patterns held by this sample and their medicolegal utility, it is worth mentioning some generic observations:

1. Evidence of bone strike trauma associated with dismemberment can be highly varied and difficult to observe in some cases. Identifying the presence of sparse trauma of small size (<1 mm in some cases) requires meticulous examination of the entire

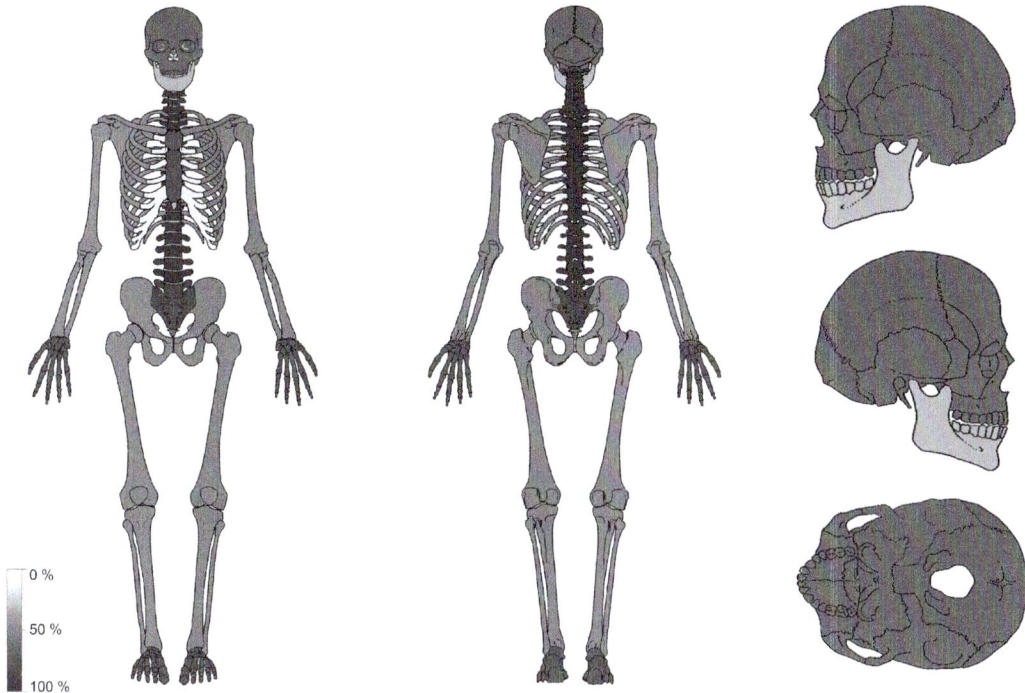

FIGURE 9.3   Percent elements present across 54 cases of the medical teaching skeletons reported in this chapter. The skeleton homunculus is adapted from the JPAC-CIL (now DPAA) Laboratory Manual and has been supplemented with skull outlines from Standards (Buikstra and Ubelaker, 1994).

skeleton, so as not to overlook any instance of dismemberment/disarticulation/ decapitation/flensing (Fig. 9.5). Special attention should be paid to those regions where the trauma is frequently observed (see Fig. 9.8 below for details).

2. Identification of subtle trauma, in our experience, is facilitated by appropriate lighting conditions and facilitated by certain bone positions relative to the light source (Fig. 9.6). For example, it is possible for little or no trauma to be observed in an anterior view with direct illumination, however, the trauma becomes saliently obvious when the element is slightly rotated relative to the light source (Fig. 9.6). This makes it essential to conduct thorough analysis of the elements (especially at zones of high strike frequency) under different light sources, to ensure that no evidence of tissue flensing/dismemberment is overlooked. Analysts should be alert to the possibility that the disarticulation trauma may be large, deep, prominent, and easy to observe, or small, tiny, shallow, infrequent in number, and difficult to detect (compare, e.g., Figs. 9.5C−9.10A).

3. An additional contributing factor to trauma saliency is the location of the injury site. Small incisions are easy to identify on sharply projecting bony ridges, where any shallow cut(s) breaking the bone's natural edge are obvious. Similar small-sized trauma is, however, much more elusive and more difficult to observe on less undulating surfaces, such as plain long bone diaphysis, where the incisions cannot be so easily visualized in a "cross-sectional" format (Fig. 9.7).

FIGURE 9.4   Trade labels associated with historical medical teaching skeletons. (A) Calcutta bone trade label on deep cranial vault surface from case 38; (B) medical supplier label affixed on internal lid of the original container for case 38; (C) medical supplier label on original receipt of purchase for case 32; (D) medical supplier label on superficial cranial vault on case 39; and (E–H) medical supplier labels on other historically acquired osteology in the UQ anatomy rooms. Source: (E–H) Images reproduced from Stephan, C.N., Caple, J.M., Veprek, A., Sievwright, E., Kippers, V., Moss, S., et al., 2017. Complexitites and remedies of unkonwn-provenance osteology. In: G. Strkalj (Ed.), Commemorations and Memorials in Anatomy: Tribute to the Giver. World Scientific, Singapore, pp. 65–95; with permission from World Scientific.

Observations made in this chapter were typically the product of using at least two of three light sources: standard ambient laboratory lighting (4000 K fluorescent lights), mobile Maquet Lucea 50 LED surgical lights (4300 K; Orléans, France) and Kaiser RB 300 copy stand quartz halogen lights (3200 K each, Augsburg, Germany) attached to a Kaiser

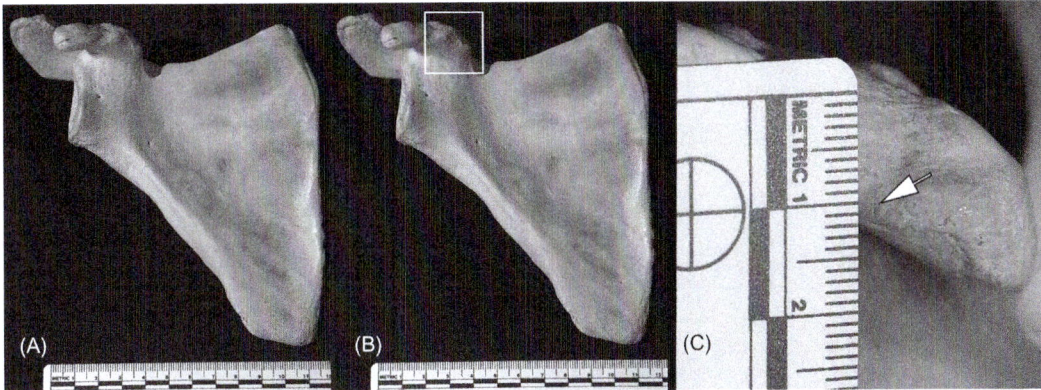

FIGURE 9.5 A deceptively "normal" scapula from a case exhibiting 14 total skeletal injuries of dismemberment—one to the scapula—and illustrating the requirement for detailed examination of all elements to ensure trauma identification. (A) Seemingly uninjured scapula at low magnification; (B) area of interest; and (C) unmistakable 2-mm-long sharp-force incision on the proximal coracoid process not readily apparent in (A) (*white arrow*).

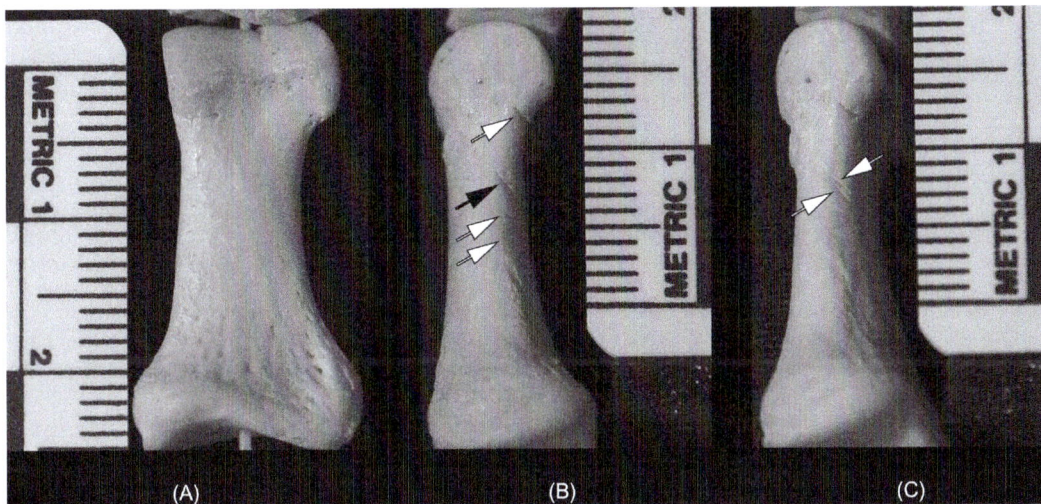

FIGURE 9.6 Demonstration of the potential impact of lighting conditions (here light angle relative to the bone) on trauma counts and morphology on the same proximal phalanx from the 1st digit. (A) anterior view—no trauma evident except perhaps a single distal lateral incision; (B) the same phalanx, illuminated from a more lateral angle, and now clearly illustrating four bone strikes along the lateral margin (*arrows*); and (C) further rotation of the same phalanx, clearly illustrating that the bone strike marked by the *black arrow* in (B) is comprised of two separate incisions not one, making five incisions total along the lateral margin of the phalanx (*white arrows*).

Fototechnik RS1 copy stand (Buchen, Germany). The latter light source formed the basis for photographs presented in this chapter, which included a 150-mm lightning scale by Powder Company or a Forensics Source issued ABFO #2 scale (Jacksonville, FL, USA).

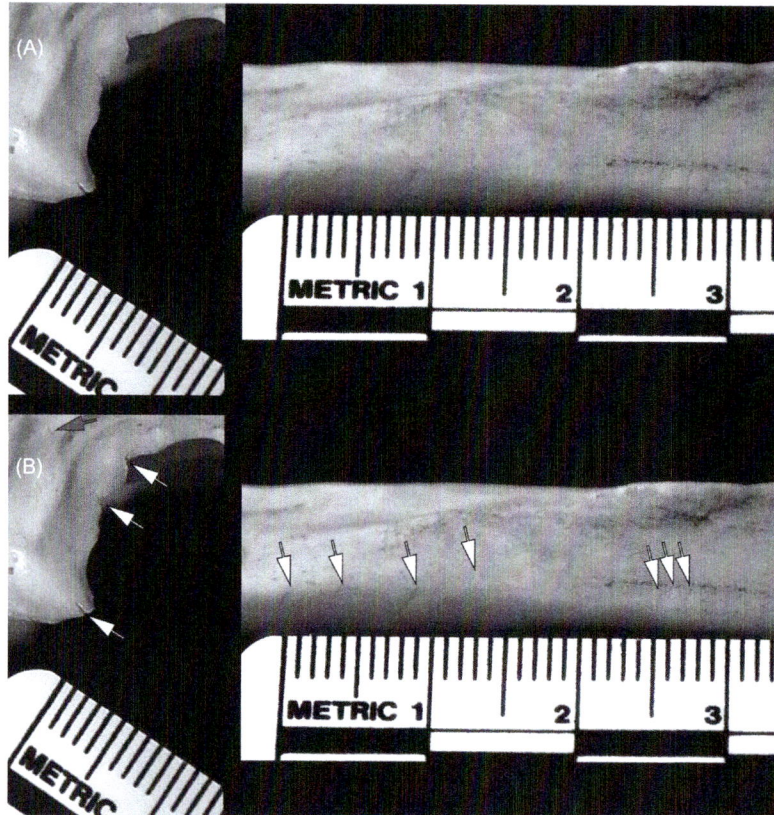

FIGURE 9.7 Illustration of the difference in saliency of small (≤1 mm) disarticulation/flensing trauma depending on skeleton location. (A) left image, lateral pterygoid plate (case 10); right image, posterior proximal ulnar shaft (case 23); (B) the same bone regions with sharp-force trauma highlighted. One millimeter cuts through pronounced ridges/plates of bone are clearly evident, while those along less peaked regions, such as long bone shafts, are shallower and harder to distinguish. The *gray arrow* in (B) marks a shallow V-shaped incision line extending from the injury marked by the middle *white arrow* on the lateral pterygoid plate. Angles of specimens to light sources have been optimized for trauma visualization—see Fig. 9.6 for further details/examples.

Images were acquired using a full-frame 20.2 megapixel Canon 6D camera body fitted with a Canon EF 24–105 mm f/4 L IS USM zoom lens. To ensure subtle features were clearly recorded at angles that best caught the light, the camera was not mounted to the copy stand, but rather was handheld to allow precision and flexibility of position.

OVERARCHING TRAUMA DISTRIBUTION

For the 54 cases reported here, the mean number of trauma per case is 78, with a range from zero (one case only) to 431. There are a total of 4203 injuries across the entire sample. Fig. 9.8 presents the collective distribution of this trauma on a single skeletal homunculus.

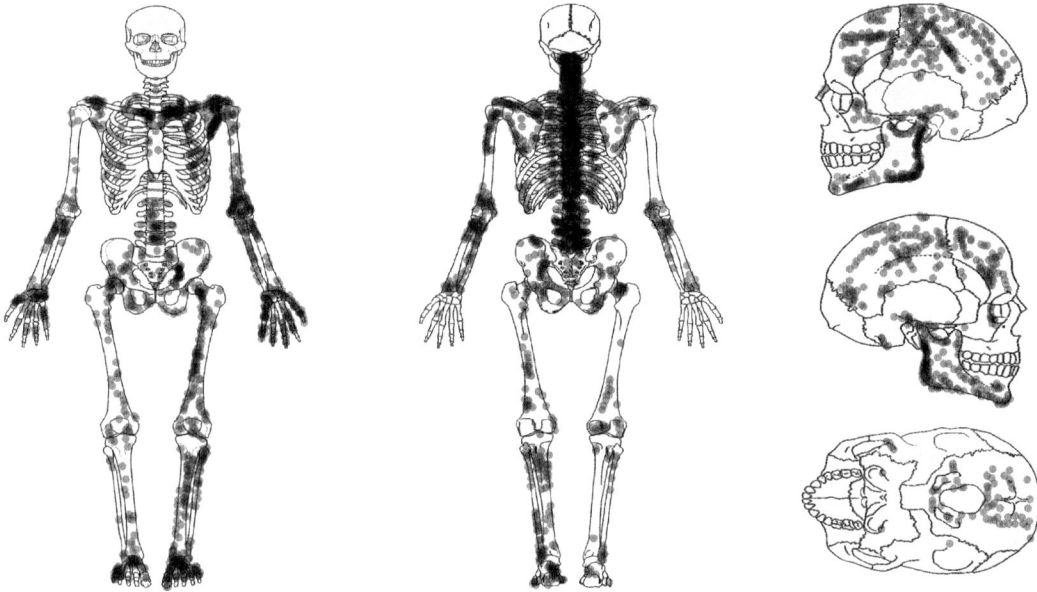

FIGURE 9.8   The distribution of all 4203 bone injuries across the skeleton in the 54 cases of this chapter. Each trauma is plotted as a simple dot (20% opacity) in R (R Core Team, 2013) using the TraumaVision script available at CRANIOFACIALidentification.com. The skeleton homunculus is adapted from the JPAC-CIL (now DPAA) Laboratory Manual and has been supplemented with skull outlines from Standards (Buikstra and Ubelaker, 1994).

Comparison of Figs. 9.3 and 9.8 show that the high frequency of vertebra, hand, and foot elements at least partly explain the high incidence of trauma at these locations. Clavicle and scapula densities are also inflated to a degree because parts of these elements are visible on the homunculus in one view only, consolidating anterior/posterior trauma (pertains to medial clavicle and vertebral scapular margin). The high incidence of trauma to the ramus of the mandible, scapula margins, elbow, greater sciatic notches of os coxae, femoral necks, lesser trochanters, and proximal and distal fibula are notable, due to their high counts irrespective of the corresponding lower osseous element frequency within the assemblage (Fig. 9.3). This suggests that in addition to scapula, clavicle, vertebrae, hands, and feet, these other aforementioned elements should be awarded special attention in any search for signs of sharp-force disarticulation or dismemberment trauma across any skeleton.

EXEMPLAR SKELETAL DISARTICULATION TRAUMA

Mandible

Incisions to the posterior mandibular border were frequently observed, often pronounced and easy to identify (Fig. 9.9). While speculative, in some cases this trauma may have resulted from strikes during decapitation by disarticulation at the cervical vertebrae because

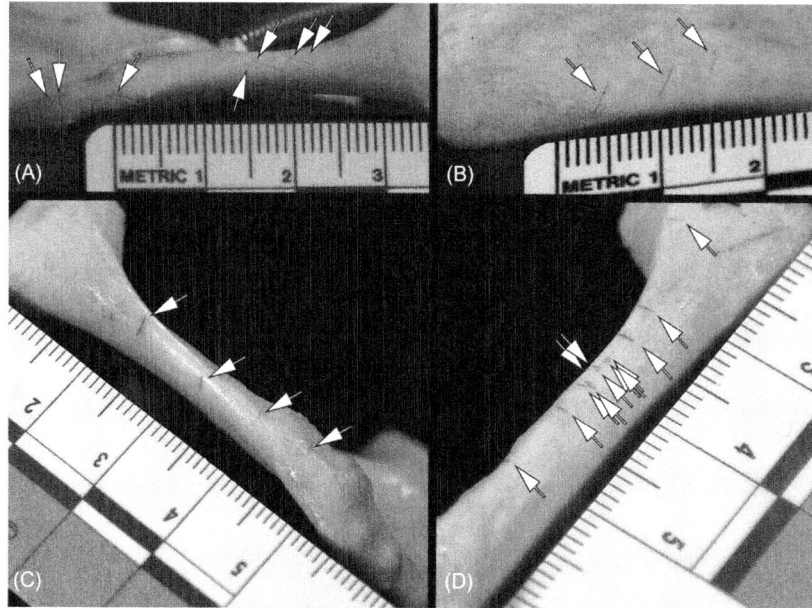

FIGURE 9.9   Illustrative sharp-force trauma (*white arrows*) to the posterior margin of the ramus of the mandible. (A) seven bone strikes on the right ramus of case 15; (B) three incisions on the superficial left ramus of case 24; (C) four bone strikes on the left ramus of case 10; and (D) 13 bone strikes highlighted on the right ramus of case 10.

these vertebrae are in close anatomical proximity to the rami and tucked behind them (for additional information on decapitation, see the section "Exemplar Disarticulation Trauma to Decapitate" below). Often, injuries to the posterior ramus, angle and body of the mandible are multiple (Figs. 9.8 and 9.9). While strikes to the mandibular body have previously been reported (Porta et al., 2016) along with larger blows to the posterior ascending ramus with machetes (Berg, 2008), to our knowledge, the posterior ramus has not previously been identified in the prior literature as a common site of incision injuries associated with dismemberment via disarticulation. The high incidence of this trauma, observed at this location in the current assemblage, suggests value for specific inspection during any skeletal analysis.

Vertebrae

A high density of varied incisions are recorded on the vertebrae in this assemblage, and multiple sequential vertebrae are often involved (e.g., Figs. 9.8 and 9.10). This is not especially surprising, given that the vertebrae are irregular bones interconnected by tough ligamentous tissues and abundant intrinsic back muscles closely related to the bone. In addition to parallel cut marks to the vertebral bodies, similar to that previously reported in the literature (see, e.g., Chacòn et al., 2008; Reichs, 1986), we also observed more

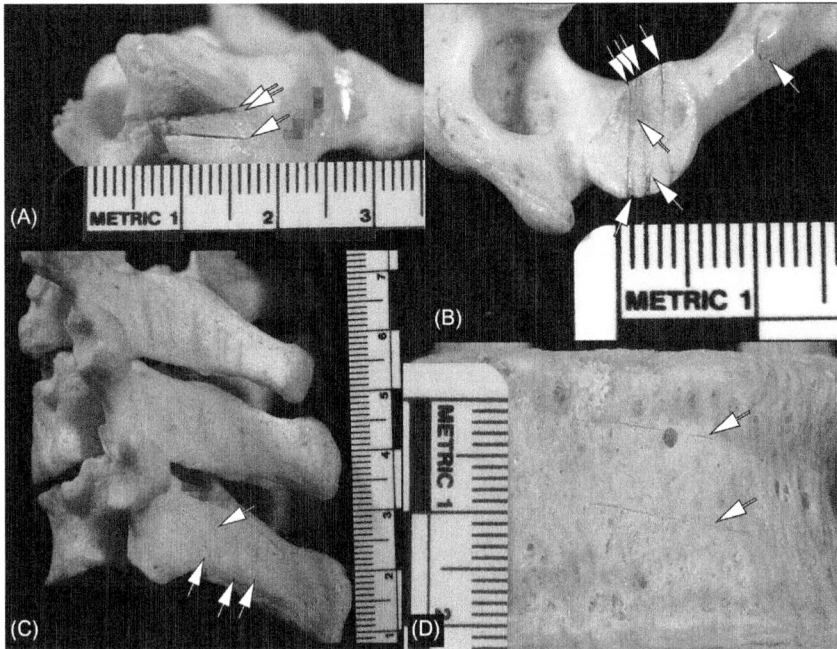

FIGURE 9.10 Illustrative sharp-force trauma (*white arrows*) to the vertebrae. (A) three bone strikes at the left lateral aspect of C3 of case 31; (B) seven bone strikes at the right inferior articular facet of C3 (and one on the posterior arch) in case 23; (C) four bone strikes highlighted on the neural arch (left side) of T3 in case 30 (note multiple other incisions on T1 and T2); and (D) two bone strikes to the anterior body of L5 in case 15. Single cuts that mark elements in multiple places are only indicated once.

irregular vertical incisions down the vertebral column on the neural arches and incisions to the transverse processes and spinous processes (Fig. 9.10). Flensing and disarticulation may both be responsible for these lesions. Decapitation by disarticulation should be considered when damage to the cervical vertebrae and/or occipital condyles is observed (for further details, see Section: Exemplar Disarticulation Trauma to Decapitate).

Scapulae

The coracoid process, spine, and lateral margin of the scapulae were all common bone strike areas (Fig. 9.11). In the prior literature, Reichs (1986) has presented some strikes to the lateral margin of the scapula and proximal to the shoulder joint in a single case. Using the large sample of trauma we observed, we can confirm that the lateral scapular margin is a common strike zone but equally important in this category are the coracoid process and scapular spine (Fig. 9.8). Injuries to the lateral border of the scapula, along its subscapular border, may be indicative of either disarticulation of the upper limb at the scapula—thoracic junction or disarticulation at the glenohumeral joint. We speculate that injuries to the scapular spine, given its posterior position and location far from the

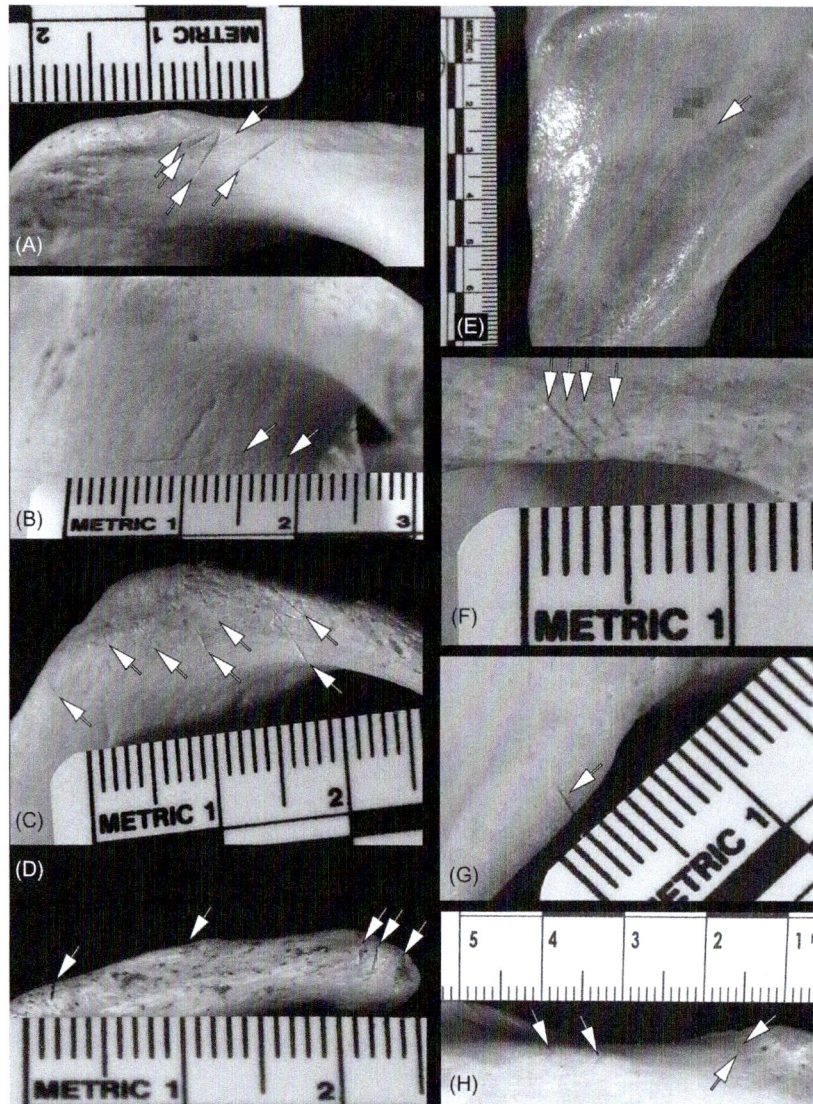

FIGURE 9.11   Illustrative sharp-force trauma (*white arrows*) to the scapulae. (A) five incisions to the inferior aspect of the coracoid process of the left scapula in case 32; (B) two incisions at the junction of coracoid process with the left scapular body of case 7; (C) seven bone strikes to the inferior coracoid process of the left scapula in case 11; and (D) five bone strikes highlighted on the coracoid process of the left scapula in case 13 (note the fracture and missing tip of the coracoid process as a result of the far lateral incision); (E) meandering incision through the infraspinous fossa of the right scapula of case 1; (F) four incisions to the medial spine of the left scapula of case 3; (G) a single deep incision to the lateral margin of the right scapula just below the lateral angle on case 22; and (H) four small incisions along the lateral subscapular margin of the left scapula of case 7.

glenohumeral joint, are more indicative of flensing than disarticulation. (The latter class being more likely associated with marks on the subscapular surface and more proximal to the glenohumeral joint.)

Femora

In this sample, shallow incision marks were often observed on the anterior femoral neck (Fig. 9.12), reflecting other observations from limited cases by Porta et al. (2016) and Reichs (1986). These shallow marks unlikely represent sustained attempt to transect the neck with a blade but instead represent opening of the synovial joint capsule overlying the anterior neck. Note the hip joint capsule extends distally down the anterior femoral neck, thus providing easier, more convenient access to free the femoral head from the acetabulum, in contrast to plunging deep toward the os coxae or trying to work from a posterior aspect toward the capsule. Another prime location for blade strikes to the femur is at the prominent tendinous attachment of iliopsoas muscle to the lesser trochanter (Fig. 9.12).

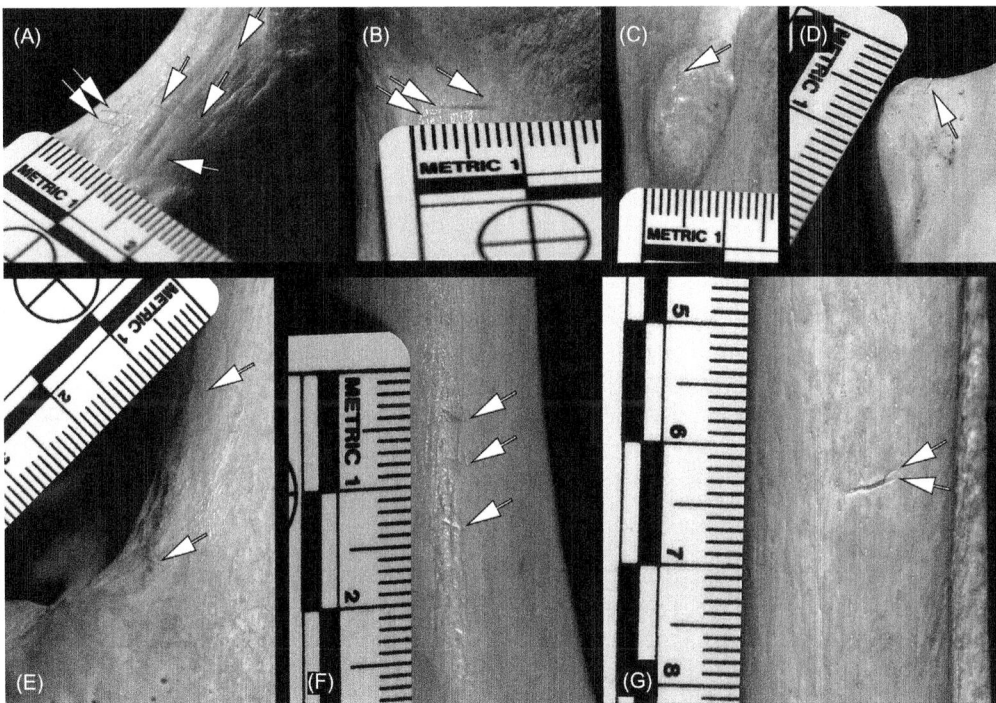

FIGURE 9.12 Illustrative sharp-force trauma (*white arrows*) to femora. (A) six incisions to the anterior femoral neck of case 7; (B) three incisions at the anterior femoral neck of case 55; (C) incision to the lesser trochanter of case 1; (D) incision to the lesser trochanter of case 13; (E) two incisions on the lateral distal femur of case 1; (F) three bone strikes to the anterior distal metaphysis of the right femur of case 1; and (G) two deep almost superimposed incisions to the lateral margin of the left femoral midshaft in case 1.

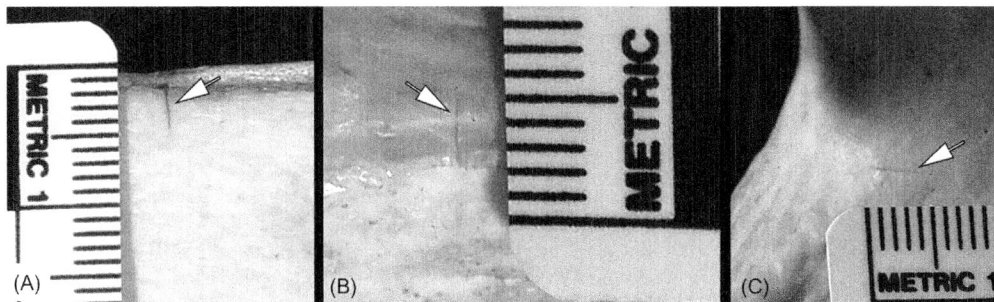

FIGURE 9.13   Illustrative sharp-force trauma (*white arrows*) to the os coxae. (A) bone strike at the apex of the iliac crest in case 14; (B) incision at the arcuate line of the pelvic brim of the left os coxae in case 15; and (C) incision on the margin of the greater sciatic notch in case 15.

Os Coxae

Typically the os coxae in this sample illustrated a limited variety of small (≤5 mm in length) incisions and these were similar in morphology to those already described by Porta et al. (2016) and Reichs (1986). Typically bony prominences or grooves were sites of these injuries, such as greater sciatic notch, iliac crest, pelvic brim, and ischial tuberosity (Fig. 9.13).

EXEMPLAR DISARTICULATION TRAUMA TO DECAPITATE: OCCIPITAL CONDYLES AND ATLAS

Although decapitation by disarticulation may be achieved at any cervical vertebra level (see, e.g., Fig. 9.10B earlier), trauma to the atlas and occipital condyles is especially indicative when present. Here we illustrate several instances of trauma to the atlas (C1; Figs. 9.14 and 9.15) and the occipital condyles (Fig. 9.15). One case is also presented where atypical fusion of the atlas to the occipital bone likely provided an unexpected encounter, as evidenced by a multitude of bone strikes on the anterior aspect of the fused atlas at the approximate level where the atlantooccipital joints would normally be present (Fig. 9.15D).

EXEMPLAR FLENSING TRAUMA: EDGE SHEAR AND MACROSCOPIC BARBS

In addition to V-shaped linear incision wounds that are far from joints, signs of flensing include uniform flat surfaces on the bone and multiple barbs at elevated ridges (supracondylar ridge of the humerus is a classic example; Fig. 9.16). The parallel or oblique use of blades along diaphyses risks running edges too deep and either shearing superficial layers of bone off the cortical surface (leaving uniform flat surfaces termed "edge-shear"), or leaving macroscopic barbs of bone if the honed edge drives deep or impacts elevated surfaces, such as ridges (Fig. 9.16). Of course, there can be a combination of the two

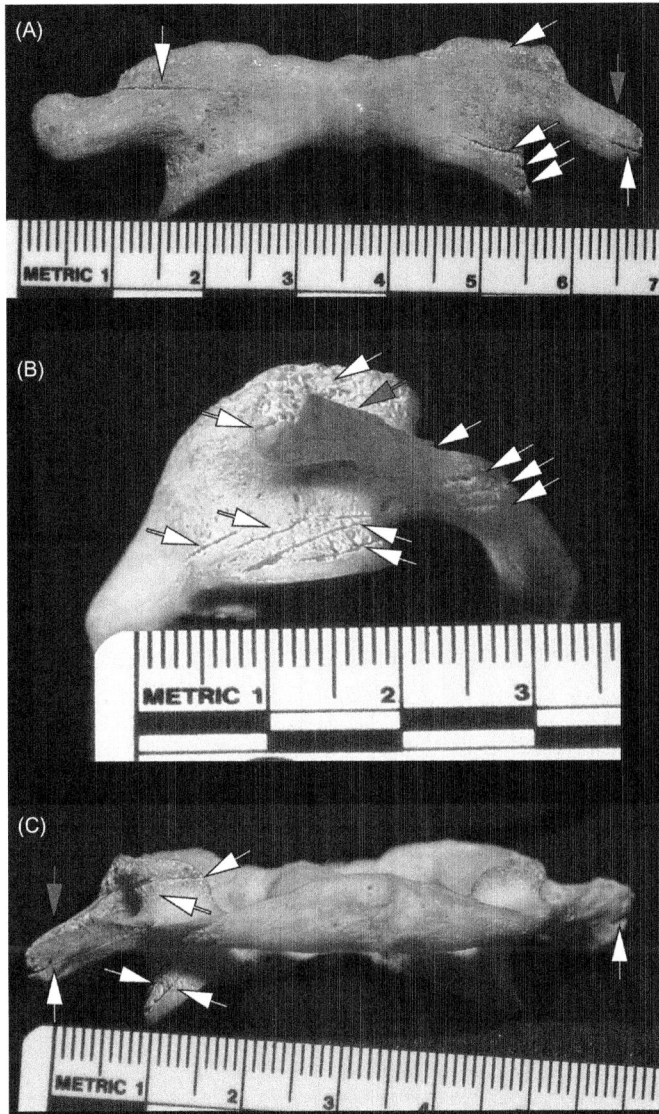

FIGURE 9.14 Extensive sharp-force trauma to atlas of case 5. (A) anterior view exhibiting seven incisions (*arrows*); (B) left lateral oblique view exhibiting 11 incisions, including some visible in anterior view (*arrows*). Multiple trauma from the same bone strike is not highlighted. (C) Posterior view exhibiting seven incisions from this viewing angle (*arrows*). NB. The single sharp-force event that has entirely removed the superior half of the left transverse process of the atlas (*gray arrow* in all panels).

morphologies, where an incomplete edge-shear leaves a barb that is then fractured, for example, by rotation of the blade (Fig. 9.16).These macroscopic barbs have also been described as "peeling" or "shaved" defects (Chacòn et al., 2008) and they should not be confused with small jagged microscopic features of the incision, also termed "barbs" by some authors (Shipman and Rose, 1983). The flat surfaces of edge-shear have not previously been highlighted or commented upon in the literature, yet this trauma morphology represents an important class since it differentiates between (1) blade use approximately parallel to the cortical surface as necessary for flensing of soft tissues from bone, rather

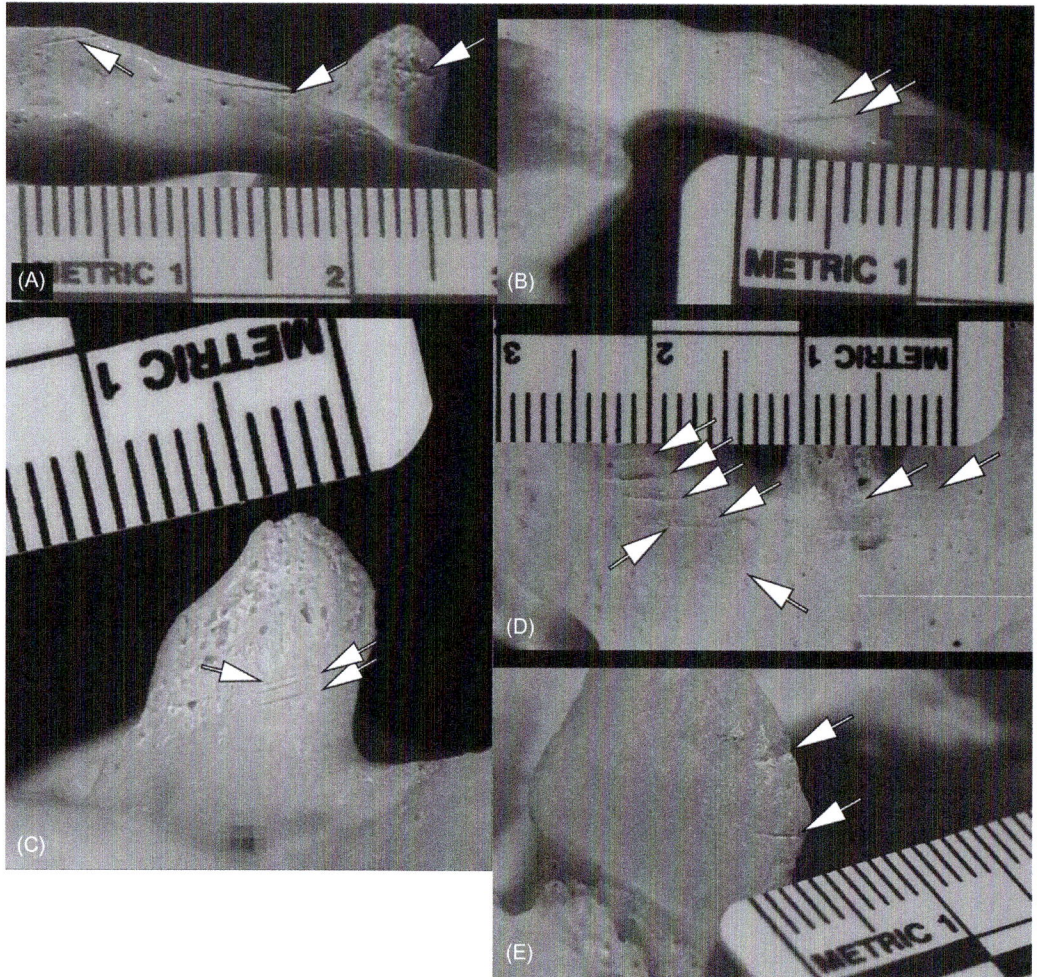

FIGURE 9.15 Illustrative sharp-force trauma (*white arrows*) to the atlas and occipital condyles. (A) three bone strikes at atlantoocciptal junction of case 32; (B) two bone strikes at posterior arch of atlas in case 15; (C) three bone strikes at posterior aspect of right superior articular process of atlas in case 19; (D) eight bone strikes at anterior aspect of fused atlas–occipital bone in case 14 (multiple trauma from the same bone strike is not highlighted); (E) two bone strikes on the posterior margin of the articular surface of the left occipital condyle in case 10.

than (2) simple transection of tissues with the blade more or less perpendicular to the bone surface, which produces otherwise characteristic V-shaped linear incision marks.

To identify the edge-shear a relatively strong and focused examination light should be used to identify the flat reflective surfaces on the bone (Fig. 9.16B)—such as when searching for occlusal wear facets on teeth that have only recently reached occlusion. Attempting to find shallow edge-shear morphology under ambient room lighting, without a strong examination light, is a challenging exercise that risks overlooking this trauma (Fig. 9.16).

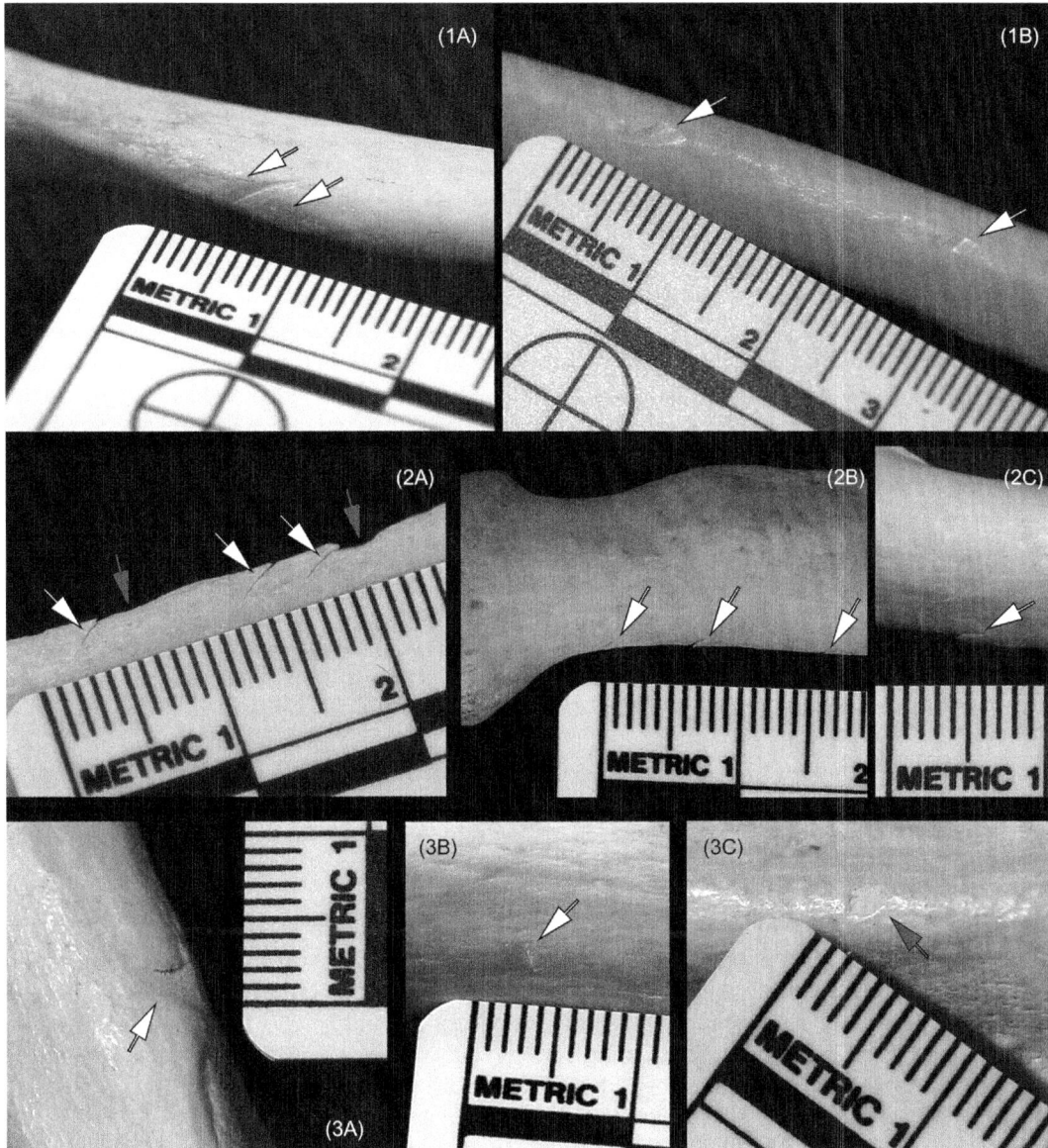

FIGURE 9.16 Sharp-force trauma indicative of flensing (*white arrows*). (1A) full thickness edge-shears on distal ulna of case 2; (1B) full thickness edge-shears on the inferior left rib 5 margin of case 4; (2A) macroscopic barbs on the supracondylar ridge of the distal humerus of case 11 (*gray arrows* indicate regions of edge-shear); (2B) macroscopic barbs on the metaphysis of the proximal radius of case 11; (2C) a single barb on the proximal end of the midshaft of the clavicle of case 55; (3A) a single edge-shear with fractured barb distal to the rhomboid fossa of the clavicle of case 50; (3B) edge-shear with fractured barb on the distal surgical neck of the humerus of case 4; and (3C) a single edge-shear with fractured barb on the left lateral subscapular border in case 18. NB. This injury in (3C) may be an exception, i.e., a consequence of disarticulation at the scapula–thoracic joint, not flensing.

DISCUSSION

The dry bones of medical teaching skeletons provide a unique large-scale source of exemplar straight-edge blade dismemberment and disarticulation trauma, as highlighted by the case reports of this chapter. This enables high-frequency strike zones to be calculated, new trauma characteristics of flensing to be identified, and exemplar trauma to be presented in atlas-like format for training and education purposes. This trauma is clearly, in part, associated with decapitation and flensing as indicated by injury morphologies and their location on the skeleton.

Given that the majority of medical teaching skeletons examined in this assemblage hold indirect ties to the Calcutta bone trade, it is speculative though not unreasonable to classify the trauma as having been inflicted by persons with semiskilled skeletization technique, since these skeletons were produced in factory-like fashion between 1940 and 1985. The label "semiskilled" is justified on the grounds that sharp-force injuries to the human endo-skeleton are the simple consequence of driving too deep with a sharp edge so it is not expert skeletization practice, irrespective of any time pressures in place. The common observation that many sharp-force incisions are commonly found at irregular projecting surfaces (e.g., bony outcrops or notches) suggests unexpected encounters by persons performing the incisions and limited anatomical knowledge. Incisions to the bone are also not necessary when maceration techniques are employed to achieve further skeletization, per the widely known protocols of the Calcutta bone trade (Carney, 2011). Further, periosteum encases all bones of the skeleton, providing a small but important buffer zone before hard-tissue registration of an injury. Consequently, bone strikes can only result from the full penetration through the periosteum and failure to recognize its initial breach prior to encountering bone matrix, or at joints failure to recognize breach of the synovial and joint capsule.

In regards to the sharp-force trauma documented from cases reported here the question may be posed "how relevant is this trauma from historical anatomical teaching skeletons to modern day forensic anthropology casework practice?" Our view is that it is highly informative given that the historical anatomical preparations of skeletons reflect real-life (not laboratory) examples of sharp-force trauma to dismember, disarticulate, and flense. The morphology of a straight-edge sharp-force trauma incision injury on bone is valid, no matter if made in the anatomical skeleton preparation context or the forensic homicide context. The near identical trauma morphology of incision wounds between this study and other reports of dismemberment by disarticulation specifically in the forensic case-work context supports this view (see, e.g., Glaister and Brash, 1937; Porta et al., 2016; Reichs, 1986; Symes et al., 2002). Observations from anatomical cases holds the additional advantage of larger sample sizes, which provides further insight into trauma patterns and a greater array of examples.

The prominence of trauma to medical teaching skeletons, first reported by the senior authors in 2017 (Stephan et al., 2017) but expanded on here in regard to larger samples, is in one sense not surprising given that these skeletons were processed for commercial activities where processing was no doubt conducted under time pressures (Carney, 2011). It is somewhat strange, however, that this trauma has gone entirely unmentioned within the prior mainstream anatomical literature, forensic science literature, and/or media accounts of anatomical skeleton preparations. In most cases, the abundance of trauma to the osseous elements makes it relatively easy to notice. Given that 98% of the 54 cases examined here exhibited sharp-force trauma, we suspect that this result can be generalized to other medical teaching skeletons with confidence. Even the one much older case derived from outside the Calcutta bone trade (France) in this sample exhibited 45 bone strike injuries confirming the broader generality of the findings to anatomical skeleton preparations. The fact that every skeleton so far received from retired surgeons to our anatomy rooms exhibits multiple sharp-force trauma adds further weight to the generalization that medical teaching skeletons are generally not trauma free. In this context it would be interesting to know if other medical teaching skeletons held in other anatomy schools or subject to prior forensic anthropology research (see, e.g., Hefner et al., 2016) exhibit similar trauma patterns when specifically reexamined for sharp-force trauma injuries.

The routine observation of straight-edge sharp-force trauma to medical teaching skeletons presents a number of forensically relevant complexities as Hefner et al. (2016) also allude to. These historical skeletons can become, and we suspect in the future are more likely to become, entangled within forensic investigations. Sharp-force trauma to the bones additionally superimposes another layer of complexity beyond what has previously been recognized. In addition to their informative nature as real-life examples of sharp-force dismemberment and disarticulation, the additional forensic aspects related to the sharp-force trauma warrant attention:

1. Do all anatomy facilities upward report medical teaching skeletons that almost universally possess sharp-force trauma to the coroner's or medical examiner's office? If not, why not?
2. How do anatomy facilities and/or coroners' offices or medical examiners' offices differentiate medical teaching skeletons from other cases of forensic interest and how can anatomy facilities be assured they do not possess (or are actively accepting) material of forensic significance?
3. What processes are (or should be) put in place to encourage retiring medical practitioners or surgeons to transfer medical teaching skeletons to anatomy schools in contrast to disposing of them by other means—such as second or third generation family members who might have inherited the materials scattering and burying anatomical teaching skeletons with sharp-force trauma in covert locations?

Below we present recommendations on each item.

Recommendations to Address Medicolegal Concerns Pertaining to Medical Teaching Skeletons

1. Anatomy schools should maintain strong channels of communication with the legal authorities and regulating bodies so that open dialogue can be held concerning any or all skeletal remains at, or entering, the anatomical facility. Problematic cases that might arise can therefore be readily and easily addressed. Further, all cases should be evaluated by an appropriately qualified forensic anthropologist to help flag any irregularities and visits

should be paid to the anatomy facility by the coroner's or medical examiner's office, to inspect any transferred human skeletal remains at regular intervals. Anatomy technical or academic staff should generally not be making the assessment of how consistent skeletons are (or are not) with medical teaching preparations unless qualified in forensic anthropology/osteology.

In agreement with the local coroner's/medical examiner's office (and any other relevant regulator), a standard record of transfer of medical teaching skeletons from the public domain to the anatomy school should be established. This institution endorsed and controlled form should document the driver's license number of the individual transferring custody of the remains (must be sighted by the accepting school) and must document contact details and address of the person making the transfer, so that if any problems emerge, the police hold all necessary contact information. All transferred material should be photographed as soon as practicable upon delivery and at stages of unpacking to provide a record of examination per normal evidence procedures. Full inventory of elements received in the transfer and any trauma present on the remains should be documented.

2. Authenticity of materials as anatomical teaching skeletons is best provided by the multiple lines of supporting evidence and none alone is conclusive of material being an anatomical preparation:

   a. Osteology is completely dry, not greasy, and free of any musty or decomposition odor.
   b. Osteology does not show signs of soil staining or burial.
   c. Osteology is bleached white, commingled (though duplicate elements may not be present), and typically of a mid-to-older adolescent or young adult.
   d. No other perimortem trauma, except for straight-edge incisions and autopsy saw cut to the cranium are present.
   e. Authentic original receipt of purchase from a medical supplier is present.
   f. Calcutta bone trade label is stamped or affixed to remains (see, e.g., Fig. 9.4).
   g. Authentic original medical supply container accompanies remains (ideally with original medical supplier label affixed to container; see, e.g., Fig. 9.4)—in Australia three common, uniform sized wooden containers were used by medical suppliers and these possess characteristic hinges and latches.
   h. Authentic anatomical hardware (including hooks, loops, screws, springs, drill holes, pins, articulating wires, and latches on the skeleton) is present.
   i. Skulls and infracranial skeleton are consistent with Caucasoid morphology. [In the future, quantitative methods may become available to test skulls for South Asian group affinity per approaches recently attempted by Hefner et al. (2016). At the current time these methods require further development and validation tests.]

Should only one or few of these lines of evidence be present in regards to a transfer, suspicious trauma or other bone characteristic be observed, or the transferee not be willing to supply a contact details or a valid driver's license number, then red flags are immediately raised and law enforcement should be notified.

3. Literally thousands of skeletons exhibiting sharp-force trauma are circulating in the public space as a result of the Calcutta bone trade. These skeletons hold the potential to produce an increasing problem in the medicolegal domain as former "custodians" of the skeletons reach the end of their own lives. Surviving individuals holding these

skeletons should be encouraged to transfer them to appropriate authorities per local law enforcement preferences, rather than independently opting for other disposal methods. Here it is worth noting that the hardware normally accompanying anatomical preparations of skeletons usually only pertains to the skull, hands, and feet of the disarticulated half skeletons. Subsequently, single elements (likely possessing evidence of sharp-force disarticulation) will provide significant challenges in terms of context recognition if the bones become disassociated from the rest of the skeletal set. Retiring medical practitioners should be encouraged to transfer their medical teaching skeletons to a legally authorized institution for human tissues (e.g., authorized anatomy school) such that these human biological tissues are appropriately removed from public circulation, thereby avoiding the aforementioned problems into the future. Anatomy schools should be prepared to handle these transfers per requirements of the regulating bodies and above-outlined guidelines.

References

AFP, 1985. Police Seize Skeletons in Child Murder Inquiry. The Age.

Alunni, V., Nogueira, L., Quatrehomme, G., 2018. Macroscopic and stereomicroscopic comparison of hacking trauma of bones before and after carbonization. Z. Rechtsmed. 132, 643–648.

Andrews, P.P., 2012. How to approach perimortem injury and other modificaitons. Methods Mol. Biol. 915, 191–225.

Anonymous Article, 1981. Sell skeletons. The Montreal Gazette Feb 21, 40.

Anonymous Article, 1985. Human skeleton trade blacklisted by India. The Montreal Gazette Aug 17, A-12.

Anonymous Article, 1989. Calcutta Exports Skeletons. Manila Standard.

Banerjie, I., 1985. Skeleton Exports: Bizarre Trade. India Today.

Bello, S.M., Wallduck, R., Dimitrijević, V., Zivaljević, I., 2016. Cannibalism versus funerary defleshing and disarticulation after a period of decay: comparisons of bone modifications from four prehistoric sites. Am. J. Phys. Anthropol. 161, 722–743.

Berg, G.E., 2008. Probable machete trauma from the Cambodian killing fields. In: Kimmerle, E.H., Baraybar, J.P. (Eds.), Skeletal Trauma: Identification of Injuries Resulting from Human Rights Abuse and Armed Conflict. CRC Press, Boca Raton, pp. 314–319.

Bromage, T.G., Boyde, A., 1984. Microscopic criteria for the determination of directionality of cutmarks on bone. Am. J. Phys. Anthropol. 65, 359–366.

Buikstra, J.E., Ubelaker, D.H. (Eds.), 1994. Standards: For Data Collection from Human Skeletal Remains. Arkansas Archeological Society, Fayetteville, Arkansas.

Capuani, C., Rouquette, J., Payré, B., Moscovici, J., Delisle, M.B., Norbert Telmon, N., et al., 2013. Deciphering the elusive nature of sharp bone trauma using epifluorescence macroscopy: a comparison study multiplexing classical imaging approaches. Z. Rechtsmed. 127, 169–176.

Carney, S., 2011. The Red Market: On the Trail of the Wolds Organ Brokers, Bone Thieves, Blood Farmers, and Child Traffickers. Harper Collins, New York.

Cerutti, E., Magli, F., Porta, D., Gibelli, D., Cattaneo, C., 2014. Metrical assessment of cutmarks on bone: Is size important? Leg. Med. 16, 208–213.

Chacòn, S., Peccerelli, F.A., PaizDiez, L., Fernández, C.R., 2008. Disappearance, torture and murder of nine individuals in a community of Nebaj, Guatemala. In: Kimmerle, E.H., Baraybar, J.P. (Eds.), Skeletal Tramua: Identification of Injuries Resulting from Human Rights Abuse and Armed Conflict. CRC Press, Boca Raton, pp. 263–313.

Corrales, S., 1987. Skeleton Shortage is Giving Medical Schools a Headache. Los Angeles Times.

Crowder, C., Rainwater, C.W., Fridie, J.S., 2013. Microscopic analysis of sharp force trauma in bone and cartilage: a validation study. J. Forensic Sci. 58, 1119–1126.

Delabarde, T., Ludes, B., 2010. Missing in Amazonian jungle: a case report of skeletal evidence for dismemberment. J. Forensic Sci. 55, 1105–1110.

Di Nunno, N., Costantinides, F., Vacca, M., Di Nunno, C., 2006. Dismemberment: a review of the literature and description of 3 cases. Am. J. Forensic Med. Pathol. 27, 307–312.

Dogan, K.H., Demirci, S., Deniz, I., Erkol, Z., 2010. Decapitation and dismemberment of the corpse: a matricide case. J. Forensic Sci. 55, 542–545.

Fineman, M., 1991. Outrage Brings Halt to Calcutta's Human-Skeleton Trade. Los Angeles Times.

Glaister, J., Brash, J.C., 1937. Medico-Legal Aspects of the Ruxton Case. William Wood and Co, Baltimore.

Hefner, J.T., Spatola, B.F., Passalacqua, N.V., Gocha, T.P., 2016. Beyond taphonomy: exploring craniometric variation among anatomical material. J. Forensic Sci. 61, 1440–1449.

Humphrey, C., Kumaratilake, J., Henneberg, M., 2017. Characteristics of bone injuries resulting from knife wounds incised with different forces. J. Forensic Sci. 62, 1445–1451.

Hyma, B.A., Rao, V.J., 1991. Evaluation and identification of dismembered human remains. Am. J. Forensic Med. Pathol. 12, 291–299.

Konopka, T., Bolechala, F., Strona, M., 2006. An unusual case of corpse dismemberment. Am. J. Forensic Med. Pathol. 27, 163–165.

Konopka, T., Strona, M., Bolechala, F., Kunz, J., 2007. Corpse dismemberment in the material collected by the Department of Forensic Medicine, Cracow, Poland. Legal Med. 9, 1–13.

Lewis, J.E., 2008. Identifying sword marks on bone: criteria for distinguishing between cut marks made by different classes of bladed weapons. J. Archaeol. Sci. 35, 2001–2008.

Litten, W., 1944. Bones for sale. Life Magazine. Time Inc, New York, pp. 17–18, 20, 22.

Lynn, K.S., Fairgrieve, S.I., 2009. Macroscopic analysis of axe and hatchet trauma in fleshed and defleshed mammalian long bones. J. Forensic Sci. 54, 786–792.

Porta, D., Amadasi, A., Cappella, A., Mazzarelli, D., Magli, F., Gibelli, D., et al., 2016. Dismemberment and disarticulation: a forensic anthropological approach. J. Forensic Legal Med. 38, 50–57.

Putka, G., 1986. Indian export ban leaves medical schools bone-dry. Wall Street. J. Montreal Gazette A1–A7.

R Core Team., 2013. R: A language and environment for statistical computing. Vienna, Austria: R Foundation for Statistical Computing. Available from: http://www.R-project.org/.

Rajs, J., Lundstrom, M., Broberg, M., Lidberg, L., Lindquist, O., 1998. Criminal mutilation of the human body in Sweden—a thirty-year medico-legal and forensic psychiatric study. J. Forensic Sci. 43, 563–580.

Reichs, K.J., 1986. Postmortem dismemberment: recovery, analysis and interpretation. In: Reichs, K.J. (Ed.), Forensic Osteology. Charles C Thomas, Springfield, pp. 353–388.

Shaw, K.P., Chung, J.H., Chung, F.C., Tseng, B.Y., Pan, C.H., Yang, K.T., et al., 2011. A method for studying knife tool marks on bone. J. Forensic Sci. 56, 967–971.

Shipman, P., Rose, J., 1983. Early hominid hunting, butchering, and carcass-processing behaviors: approaches to the fossil record. J. Anthropol. Archaeol. 2, 57–98.

Stephan, C.N., Caple, J.M., Veprek, A., Sievwright, E., Kippers, V., Moss, S., et al., 2017. Complexities and remedies of unkonwn-provenance osteology. In: Strkalj, G. (Ed.), Commemorations and Memorials in Anatomy: Tribute to the Giver. World Scientific, Singapore, pp. 65–95.

Symes, S.A., Williams, J.A., Murray, E.A., Hoffman, J.M., Holland, T.D., Saul, J.M., et al., 2002. Taphonomic context of sharp-force trauma in supected cases of human mutilation and dismemberment. In: Haglund, W.D., Sorg, M.H. (Eds.), Advances in Forensic Taphonomy: Method, Theory, and Archaeological Perspectives. CRC Press, Boca Raton, pp. 403–434.

Thompson, T.J.U., Inglis, J., 2009. Differentiation of serrated and non-serrated blades from stab marks in bone. Z. Rechtsmed. 123, 129–135.

Intentional Body Dismemberment Following Nonhomicidal Deaths: A Retrospective Study of Body Packer Cases in New York City

Bradley J. Adams[1], Christopher W. Rainwater[1,2,3] and Corinne N. Ambrosi[1,4]

[1]Office of Chief Medical Examiner, New York City, NY, United States [2]Department of Anthropology, Center for the Study of Human Origins, New York University, New York City, NY, United States [3]New York Consortium in Evolutionary Primatology, New York City, NY, United States [4]Department of Forensic Medicine, New York University School of Medicine, New York City, NY, United States

INTRODUCTION

Symes and colleagues (2002) define sharp force trauma (SFT) "as a narrowly focused, dynamic, slow-loaded, compressive force with a sharp object that produces damage to hard tissue in the form of an incision (broad or narrow)." Forensic anthropologists frequently consult on SFT given it often impacts bone or cartilage (Banasr et al., 2003) and these types of cases may make up a significant portion of a forensic anthropologist's casework, especially in a medical examiner's office (Crowder et al., 2013). Similarly, forensic anthropologists embedded in a medical examiner's office are likely to review every dismemberment case the office receives.

Various reasons for postmortem body dismemberment have been suggested but it is generally agreed that dismemberment may be the product of making a body more easily transportable, attempting to hinder the identification of the remains, or as symbolic disregard for the decedent (Black et al., 2017; Hakkanen-Nyholm et al., 2009; Rajs et al., 1998; Symes 1992; Symes et al., 2002). The forensic science literature has numerous classification schemata for these types of cases. For instance, one may reference the state of mind of the perpetrator as being defensive (getting rid of the body), aggressive (rage induced), or offensive (lust or psychosis) (Hakkanen-Nyholm et al., 2009). Typically, forensic anthropologists may simply reference the physical evidence observed at the postmortem examination, identifying three modes of dismemberment: disarticulation around the joints, transection of bone via chopping, and/or transection of bone via sawing (Rainwater 2015).

Regardless of the proposed reasons or classification schemata, most studies of intentional dismemberment associate the act with homicide. An exception to this includes examples when body parts may be retained from cadavers or exhumed corpses as a trophy or fetish. In their study of dismemberment cases in Poland, Konopka and colleagues (2007:1) state: "Apart from rare cases of necrophilia, the victim of dismemberment is always a victim of homicide." Similarly, the study by Rajs and colleagues (1998) of dismemberment cases in Sweden found that, with one exception (dismemberment of an exhumed corpse), all instances of dismemberment in Sweden were associated with known or suspected homicides.

This chapter focuses specifically on two unusual cases of dismemberment in New York City where the manner of death was deemed an accident as opposed to a homicide. Both cases were associated with body packers, or people who ingest packets of illicit drugs or insert them into body cavities for purposes of smuggling. In the two New York City cases we present later, the accidental deaths were followed by postmortem evisceration of the body for retrieval of the drugs, as well as body dismemberment for subsequent disposal of the decedent.

BODY PACKER FATALITIES

Body packers ingest illicit drugs concealed within small packets (Fig. 10.1), often balloons or condoms. In most body packer fatalities, the cause of death is an acute intoxication due to the disruption or leakage of the packaging and gastrointestinal absorption of the illicit drugs (e.g., Gill and Graham 2002; Hutchins et al., 2000; Wetli and Mittlemann 1981; Wetli et al., 1997). As a result, these deaths are commonly ruled as accidents.

FIGURE 10.1   Drug packets recovered from the gastrointestinal tract of two body packer fatalities.

The body packer may ingest numerous packets (e.g., some New York City cases revealed >100 packets at autopsy) representing a large quantity of potentially valuable drugs. In some instances, accomplices of the deceased body packer may remove the intact packets from the gastrointestinal tract. This is accomplished by postmortem cutting of the torso and evisceration to access the concealed drug packets. Wetli and colleagues (1997) detail 10 cases of body packer fatalities in Florida and New York, two of which involve postmortem evisceration of the decedent for retrieval of drugs by an accomplice.

BODY PACKER CASES IN NEW YORK CITY

A list of New York City body packer fatalities was compiled by conducting keyword searches on autopsy reports at the New York City Office of Chief Medical Examiner (OCME) dating from 1990 to 2017. This search augments the previous study of New York City body packer fatalities reported by Gill and Graham (2002). Search terms included *packer*, *smuggling*, and *balloons*. In addition, the OCME's Evidence Unit database was queried for all body packer cases in which the drug packets had been accessioned. After vetting, there were 91 confirmed cases of body packer fatalities within the five boroughs of New York City between 1990 and 2017.

Fig. 10.2 shows that the peak years for body packer fatalities were in the late 1990s and early 2000s, specifically between 1995 and 2003. More recently the number of body packer cases has been very small with only one body packer fatality between 2013 and 2017. Fig. 10.3 shows the number of body packer cases by New York City borough. Not surprisingly, the highest number of cases are in Queens, which is home to two major airports and

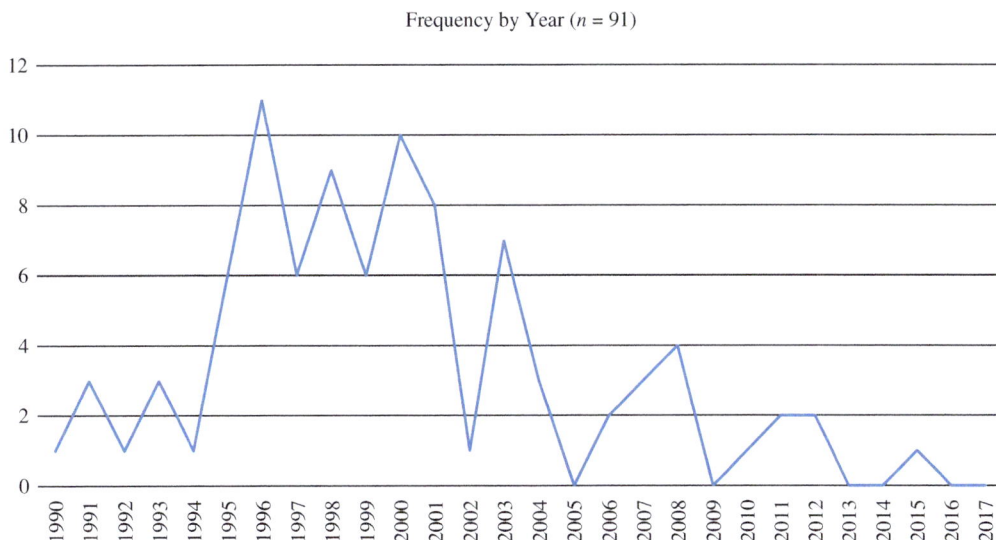

FIGURE 10.2   Frequency of body packer fatalities in NYC between 1990 and 2017.

1990-2017 by Borough (*n* = 91)

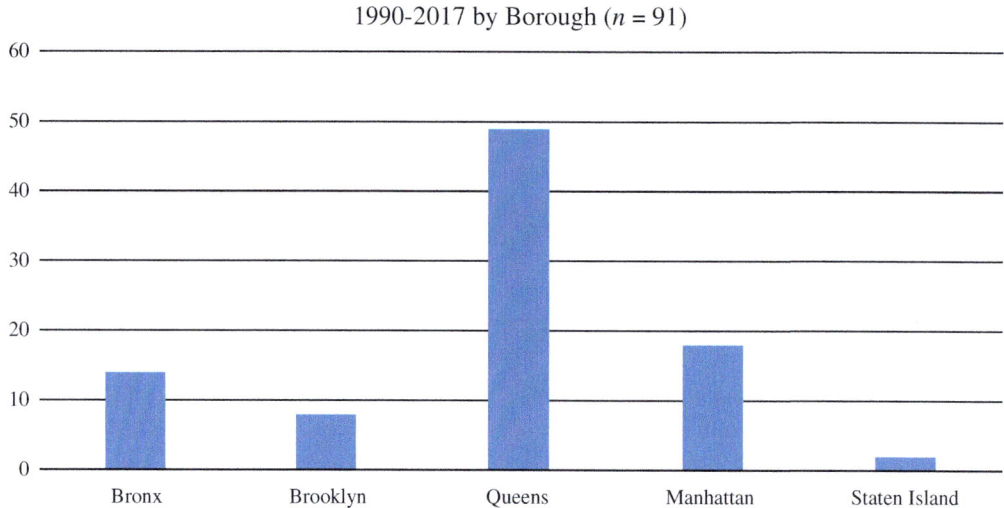

FIGURE 10.3   Frequency of body packer fatalities by NYC borough.

numerous hotels serving the New York City area. Most of the decedents were male (*n* = 75), compared with only 16 females.

Of the 91 New York City cases, six were found to have postmortem body mutilation (6/91, 6.6%). Four of the six only involved incision of the abdomen, but two cases (2/91, 2.2%) also included postmortem body dismemberment. Clearly the abdominal incisions were created for evisceration to access the smuggled drugs, while the two cases with additional body dismemberment appear to have been associated with subsequent disposal of the body. The motive for the postmortem dismemberment in these two NYC body packer cases conforms to the motive observed in many homicide cases (transport/concealment/disposal of the body), but the manner of death in these body packer fatalities was certified as an accident.

While prior publications have described body packer cases in which there has been postmortem evisceration of the decedent for removal of the drugs (e.g., Wetli et al., 1997), no other body packer studies were found that mention postmortem dismemberment. The two NYC body packer fatalities involving postmortem dismemberment are detailed below.

CASE EXAMPLES

Case 1

On June 5, 1996, three black plastic bags were discovered on the street next to a cemetery in Queens, New York. Inside the bags were dismembered human body parts. At autopsy, the remains were determined to be those of a white or Hispanic female,

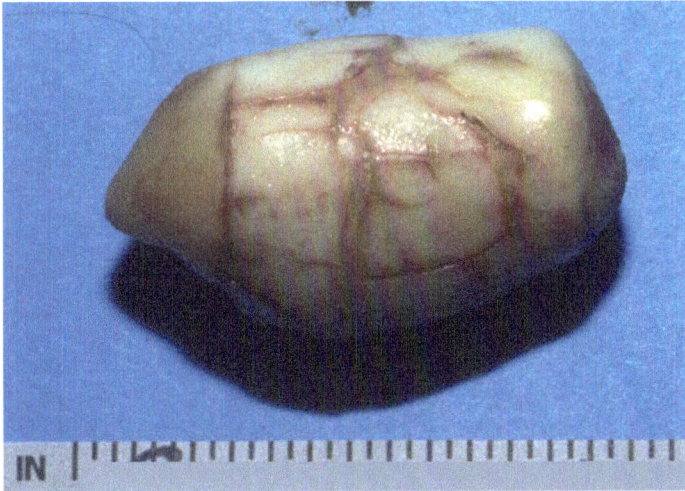

FIGURE 10.4 One of the drug packets recovered from the body during autopsy.

approximately 62″ tall, weighing 142 pounds, and estimated to be approximately 50 years old. The body parts were well-preserved with only minimal postmortem changes associated with very early decomposition. All body parts were recovered from within the bags. In addition, three drug packets were recovered with the body parts, all of them consistent with drug packets used by body packers (Fig. 10.4).

The three plastic bags recovered from the street included the following items:

- Bag 1: Head/upper torso/arms, a short-sleeve t-shirt was still on the torso.
- Bag 2: Lower torso/thighs.
- Bag 3: Lower legs/feet, also a bag with intestines. Two empty beverage bottles were also in this bag.

The body was dismembered at the second lumbar vertebra and at the knees. There were a total of three dismemberment cuts resulting in a total of four separate body parts (Fig. 10.5). The dismemberment was achieved by disarticulation through the joints with a knife. There was also an additional midline cut on the anterior surface of the torso that extended from the xiphoid to the pubis (Fig. 10.5). It appears that the anterior cut to the torso was made to remove the intestines for retrieval of the drug packets concealed within the body (three packets were missed and were subsequently found at autopsy).

No hemorrhage was noted at any of the cut locations at autopsy, indicating that all the observed cuts to the body occurred postmortem. No perimortem trauma was observed anywhere on the body. The toxicology findings showed high levels of drugs. Based on the toxicology findings and the lack of any perimortem injuries, the medical examiner certified the case as an accidental death due to drug overdose. The postmortem dismemberment of the individual was for retrieval of the drug packets concealed within the decedent's body, as well as for ease of subsequent body transport and disposal.

The decedent was subsequently identified as a 53-year-old Hispanic female.

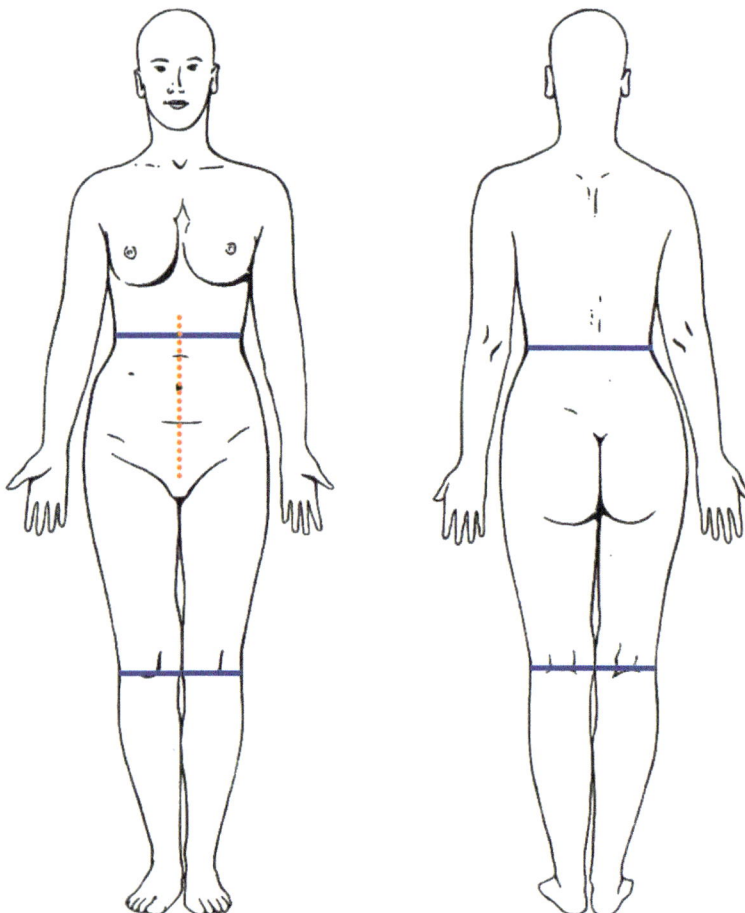

FIGURE 10.5 Body diagram showing location of incisions (*dotted line*) and dismemberment cuts (*solid lines*).

Case 2

On October 8, 1999, human body parts were discovered on the sidewalk in front of an industrial complex in Queens, New York. The body parts were in three separate containers: a black nylon duffle bag, a white nylon duffle bag, and a black canvas luggage-type bag (Fig. 10.6). The body parts had been put inside green plastic bags prior to their placement in the outer containers. Clothing, jewelry, and miscellaneous items were also found in the bags in association with the body parts. The body parts were unclad.

The three bags recovered from the street included the following items:

- Bag 1: Numerous clothing items, head, left upper extremity (complete arm), right forearm, right upper arm, left lower leg/foot, and left thigh.
- Bag 2: Numerous clothing items, upper portion of torso, right lower leg/foot, right thigh.
- Bag 3: Numerous clothing items, mop head, hack saw label, scouring pads, middle portion of torso, pelvis/buttocks.

FIGURE 10.6 Three bags found outside of an industrial complex.

At autopsy, 11 body parts were recovered (Fig. 10.7). The body was that of a large-framed male, likely white or Hispanic, approximately 72″ tall, weighing approximately 220 pounds, and estimated to be approximately 30 years of age. The body parts were well-preserved with slight postmortem changes associated with early decomposition. The body parts recovered within the bags represented a complete body. In addition, within the small intestine lumen was a firm yellow packet with crimped edges weighing 9.4 g and a disrupted packet consisting of only the flexible outer wrapper (Fig. 10.8). The retrieved packets were consistent with drug packets used by body packers.

A total of 10 dismemberment locations were present that resulted in 11 body parts (Fig. 10.7). The head was removed at the neck, both arms were removed at the shoulders, the right arm was also separated at the elbow (the left arm was not), the legs were removed at the hips and transected at the knees, and the torso was separated into three portions. The dismemberment sites showed a combination of transection (sawing through bones) and disarticulation (separation of body parts at joints).

In addition to the dismemberment sites, there were also incised areas on the anterior surface of the body. There was a wedge-shaped incision on the anterior upper torso in the midline, there was an incision on the right side of the middle torso, and there were vertical incisions along the midline of the middle and lower portions of the torso exposing the liver and intestines (Fig. 10.7). The sternum was also cut vertically in the midline.

No hemorrhage was noted at any of the cut locations at autopsy, indicating that all the observed cuts to the body occurred postmortem. No perimortem trauma was observed anywhere on the body. The toxicology findings showed the presence of drugs. Based on the toxicology findings and the lack of any perimortem injuries, the medical examiner certified the case as an accidental death due to drug overdose. The postmortem dismemberment of the individual was for retrieval of the drug packets concealed within the decedent's body (one intact packet was missed), as well as for ease of subsequent body transport and disposal.

The individual was subsequently identified as a 32-year-old white male.

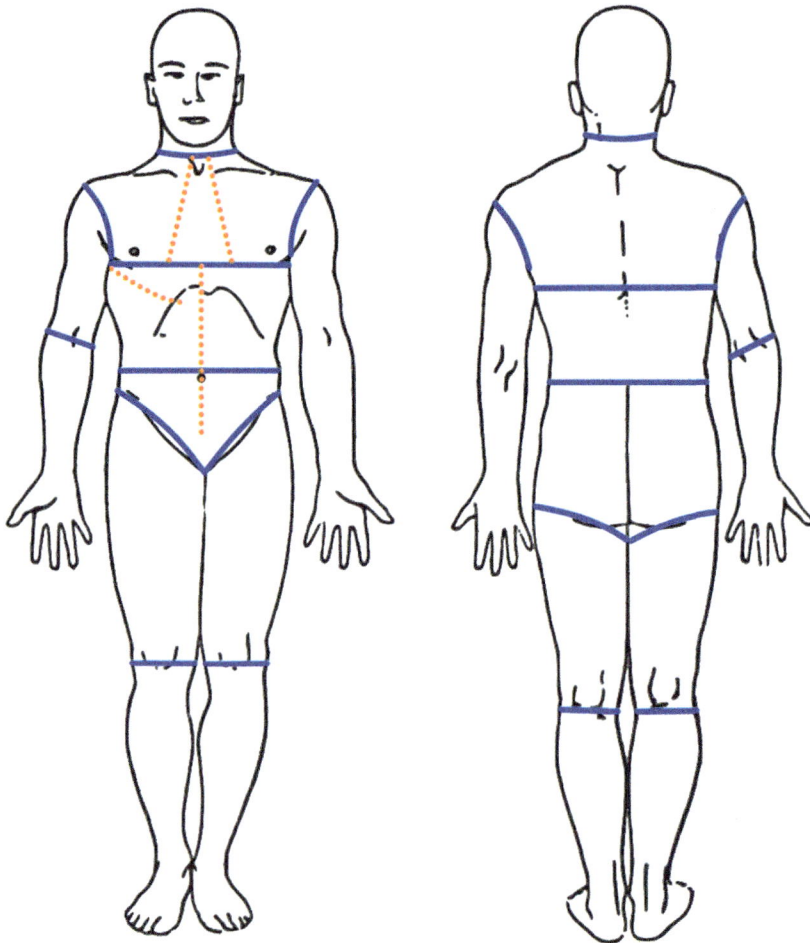

FIGURE 10.7 Body diagram showing location of incisions (*dotted lines*) and dismemberment cuts (*solid lines*).

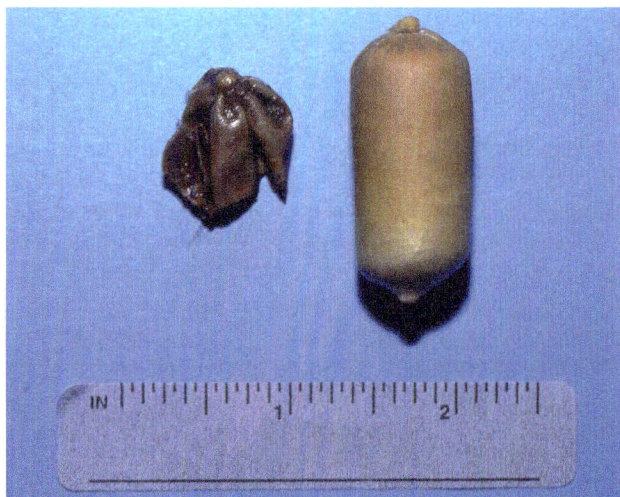

FIGURE 10.8 Disrupted and intact drug packets recovered during autopsy.

SUMMARY AND CONCLUSION

Most cases of intentional dismemberment are associated with homicides. The cases presented herein illustrate an unusual combination of *accidental* death followed by postmortem dismemberment. Both cases are body packer fatalities. The most common cause of death in body packers is an acute intoxication due to disruption/leakage of the ingested packets and gastrointestinal absorption of the illicit drugs, resulting in an accidental death. Of the 91 body packer fatalities that occurred in New York City between 1990 and 2017, two included body dismemberment. Both cases included postmortem incisions to the anterior torso to remove the drugs and additional dismemberment of the torso and extremities for body disposal. A review of all dismemberment cases in New York City in a similar time frame showed that complete cuts through the torso were uncommon findings. Only five dismemberment cases had cuts through the torso and two were the body packer cases described earlier. Overall, accidental deaths of body packers with associated postmortem dismemberment represent an unusual occurrence (only two cases in a 28-year period in New York City), but practitioners should be aware of the possibility.

References

Banasr, A., de la Grandmaison, G.L., Durigon, M., 2003. Frequency of bone/cartilage lesions in stab and incised wounds fatalities. Forensic Sci. Int. 131 (2–3), 131–133.

Black, S., et al., (Eds.), 2017. Criminal Dismemberment: Forensic and Investigative Analysis. CRC Press, Boca Raton.

Crowder, C., Rainwater, C.W., Fridie, J.S., 2013. Microscopic analysis of sharp force trauma in bone and cartilage: a validation study. J. Forensic Sci. 58 (5), 1119–1126.

Gill, J.R., Graham, S.M., 2002. Ten years of "body packers" in New York City: 50 deaths. J. Forensic Sci. 47 (4), 843–846.

Hakkanen-Nyholm, H., et al., 2009. Homicides with mutilation of the victim's body. J. Forensic Sci. 54 (4), 933–937.

Hutchins, K.D., et al., 2000. Heroin body packing: three fatal cases of intestinal perforation. J. Forensic Sci. 45 (1), 42–47.

Konopka, T., et al., 2007. Corpse dismemberment in the material collected by the Department of Forensic Medicine, Krakow, Poland. Legal Med. 9 (1), 1–13.

Rainwater, C.W., 2015. Three modes of dismemberment: disarticulation around the joints, transection of bone via chopping, and transection of bone via sawing. In: Passalacqua, N.V., Rainwater, C.W. (Eds.), Skeletal Trauma Analysis: Case Studies in Context. Wiley Blackwell, West Sussex, pp. 222–245.

Rajs, J., et al., 1998. Criminal mutilation of the human body in Sweden—a thirty-year medico-legal and forensic psychiatric study. J. Forensic Sci. 43 (3), 563–580.

Symes, S.A., 1992. Morphology of Saw Marks in Human Bone: Identification of Class Characteristics Dissertation, Anthropology. University of Tennessee.

Symes, S.A., et al., 2002. Taphonomic context of sharp-force trauma in suspected cases of human mutilation and dismemberment. In: Haglund, W.D., Sorg, M.H. (Eds.), Advances in Forensic Taphonomy. CRC Press, Boca Raton, pp. 403–434.

Wetli, C.V., Mittlemann, R.E., 1981. The "body packer syndrome"-toxicity following ingestion of illicit drugs packaged for transportation. J. Forensic Sci. 26 (3), 492–500.

Wetli, C.V., Rao, A., Rao, V.J., 1997. Fatal heroin body packing. Am. J. Forensic Med. Pathol. 18 (3), 312–318.

Toolmark Identification on Bone: Best Practice

Ann H. Ross[1] and Deborah Radisch[2]

[1]Department of Biological Sciences, North Carolina State University, Raleigh, NC, United States [2]North Carolina Office of the Chief Medical Examiner, Raleigh, NC, United States

INTRODUCTION

The dismemberment of homicide victims has been attributed to the following reasons: for ease of transportation, to hinder identification, and abhorrence or disregard for the victim (Reichs, 1998; Dogan et al., 2010; Rutty and Hainsworth, 2014; Symes et al., 1992) with each of the three displaying a different pattern of mutilation based on the motive (see Chapter 12). Thus, a primary purpose of dismemberment examination is to distinguish the type and class of tool(s) used to sever the body parts as well as the pattern of disarticulation. This should begin with a gross examination of the false starts and cut cross-sections (Reichs, 1998).

A variety of instruments have been recorded in the postmortem dismemberment of a body including saws, knives, chopping instruments, such as a hatchet, ax, etc., and in our experience even a shovel. Toolmarks are the marks left on a softer substrate by a harder material when used to cut or strike, which leave an imprint of the tool on the softer surface, or striations left by the edge of the tool when cutting or sawing (Rutty and Hainsworth, 2014). According to Thomson and Black (2017) the definition of toolmark analysis is imprecise but overall refers to the detection, enhancement, comparison, and evaluation of marks or indentations left behind on a softer substrate after contact with a tool and/or implement. Witness marks, marks left on the bone by saws used in the dismemberment, appertain to the size, shape, width, and set of the saw teeth as well as the sawing action of the instrument operator (Hainsworth, 2017). Generally, publications detailing dismemberment, disarticulation, and mutilation cases state that disposal of a homicide victim by dismemberment is a rare occurrence (Spitz, 2006; Rutty and Hainsworth, 2014; Dogan et al., 2010; Di Nunno et al., 2006). However, since 2011 until the present, the NC Human Identification & Forensic Analysis Laboratory at North Carolina

State University has worked 12 cases of dismemberment and mutilation including one cold case reexamination from 1998. Only Quatrehomme (2007) has stated that postmortem dismemberment of the body is not a rare occurrence, which is evident by the recent breadth of literature published on dismemberments (e.g., Black et al., 2017). These types of cases are most likely underestimated as they are generally folded into various cause and manner of death categories that do not allow for the correct estimation of actual dismemberment counts.

At present, forensic anthropological examination of sharp force trauma consists of determining the class of weapon used (Crowder et al., 2013). However, matching the morphology of a defect to a specific weapon is generally delegated to the toolmark examiner even though morphological comparisons are well within the toolkit of the forensic anthropologist. The focus of this chapter is to detail the identification protocols used in toolmark comparisons in dismemberment and disarticulation cases from a forensic anthropological perspective.

BRIEF GENERAL CHARACTERISTICS OF SAWS/BLADES

Because of the vast varieties of saws, Quatrehomme (2015) finds it useful to first differentiate between hand and mechanical (electric) saws and states that in cases of dismemberments hand saws are a more common tool than mechanical saws but acknowledges that mechanical saws, particularly portable mechanical saws, are becoming much more prevalent in cases of dismemberment in France. Hand saws tend to leave straight, uneven striations due to the sawing action, while power or mechanical saws with straight blades, such as a reciprocating saw, leave straight, regular marks (Maples, 1986). Per contra, Quatrehomme (2015) notes that mechanical table saws such as circular saws leave curved marks (Maples, 1986), and band saws are rarely used in dismemberments. Maples (1986) reported that in Florida, hacksaws were the most commonly used tool in all but one case where the bones were severed and the body was not disarticulated. Two important parameters of hand saws are points per inch (PPI) or teeth per inch (TPI), which is always one less than PPI (Hainsworth, 2017). When measuring the teeth, you measure from gullet to gullet, and count only the number of full teeth in one inch. On the other hand, PPI is a measure of only the peaks or points of the teeth and *not* the full tooth including the left and right face. Because PPI only measures the points and not the full teeth, there will always be one less tooth than there are points. So a 6-PPI saw and 5-TPI saw are the same (Fig. 11.1). The second parameter is tooth set or the way the teeth are bent to the side, which widens the kerf (or the slit mark made by a saw) to prevent it from getting stuck (Saville et al., 2007). The most common tooth set is alternating set (Hainsworth, 2017). For a more thorough discussion of saw construction see Symes et al. (1998) and Quatrehomme (2015).

TOOLMARKS ON BONE

Toolmark examiners can readily identify and match marks made on wood, metals, and polymers (Petraco, 2010). However, marks on bone are more challenging and should be left to the forensic anthropologists as bone experts. Marks left on trabecular bone are difficult, if not impossible to distinguish, as the trabeculae fracture in response to applied force

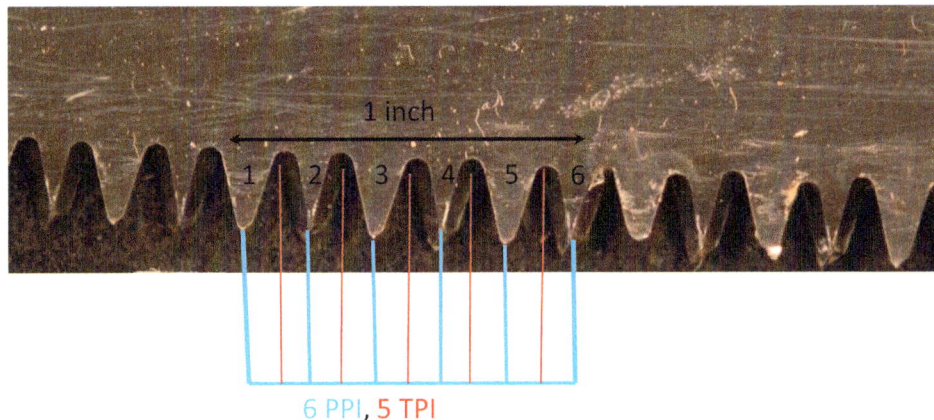

FIGURE 11.1   Example of how to count PPI versus TPI.

from the saw. Marks on cortical bone are more readily distinguished. Thus, on cortical bone, kerf walls and floors can be used to determine the size, set, shape, power, and direction of the cut (Symes et al., 2010). Kerf width in false starts or persistence marks is never the exact width as the tool but always greater (Hainsworth, 2017).

Two types of saw characteristics can be gleaned from bone: individual and class. Individual characteristics are random imperfections along the cutting edge that leave striations on the bone or substrate. Class characteristics, such as TPI, PPI, set type (e.g., raker, etc.), saw design (e.g., crosscut, universal, and rip saw) are similarities that will place the tool within or eliminate it from a group (Bailey et al., 2011; Nogueira et al., 2016). For example, a fine tooth saw blade such as a 32-TPI blade will be closer together than a course saw blade such as a 7-TPI blade.

VALIDATION OF TOOLMARKS: IS IT POSSIBLE?

Numerous studies have attempted to validate toolmark analysis through various measures and statistical methodologies (Bachrach et al., 2010; Bailey et al., 2011; Capuani et al., 2014; Cerutti et al., 2014; Crowder et al., 2013; Nogueira et al., 2016; Puentes and Cardoso, 2013; Wang, 2016). Wang (2016) tested three types of saws on dry cow proxies using a handheld device to take images from the same viewing position at 25 × magnification and concluded that morphological and microscopic appearance using eight criteria could be used to differentiate the three types of saws. Another recent study by Capuani and colleagues (2014) showed that the class, subclass, type of saw, as well as the specific saw used could be determined using fluorescence analysis. Bailey and coworkers (2011) reported that 70%–90% of saws could be eliminated based on kerf width alone using a cumulative logit model. Love and colleagues (2013) also validated microscopic saw marks and found that minimum kerf width was the most informative variable that differed significantly between the four types of saws tested. However, they were unable to validate most of the variables identified as informative class characteristics by Symes et al. (1992, 2010) as they were unable to replicate them in their study. Nonetheless, Thomson and Black (2017) maintain that toolmark examination and analysis is still subjective and opinion based that places heavy reliance on the examiner's training and experience.

LABORATORY TOOLMARK EXAMINATION PROTOCOLS

There are two distinct evaluations undertaken during the examination of toolmarks on bone in a trauma examination. This chapter will focus on dismemberment and disarticulation cases: class (for an unknown) and individual (if there is a comparative tool from the crime scene to be tested) (Houck, 1998).

In cases where there is no suspect implement, only class characteristics can be determined based on the pattern observed on kerfs (e.g., minimum kerf width) and cross-sectional cut surfaces. If testing an actual instrument found at a crime scene it is imperative that the law enforcement agency in charge first examine the instrument for trace, DNA, etc. before beginning the anthropological examination. To identify toolmarks left on bone, test marks should be made with the suspect instrument on the same type of skeletal element (e.g., long bone, vertebrae, etc.) to account for cortical and trabecular bone composition. To replicate a real case scenario, the analog elements should be fleshed. For example, if cut marks are found on neck vertebrae then analog fleshed vertebrae should be used to conduct the test marks in order to simulate the case scenario. We generally use domestic pig (*Sus scrofa*), which are obtained from the NC State Swine Farm, as a human analog for our test cuts. The NC Human Identification & Forensic Analysis Laboratory at NC State has been requested to match suspect implements by either employing the actual implement found at the crime scene or by acquiring an instrument using the information from a store purchase receipt listing a particular instrument. Obviously the approach to an examination is dependent upon the equipment available to a particular laboratory, which can lead to different outcomes (Baldwin et al., 2013). For example, the acquisition of a Keyence VHX 1000 digital microscope in late 2011 by our laboratory has allowed for more detailed comparisons between scene (i.e., from victim) and test marks than was possible prior to the acquisition of this equipment. In addition, sometimes it is necessary to cast the tool in question with a material such as Mikrosil for comparison to witness marks. Fig. 11.2 presents the workflow for trauma analysis in dismemberment cases. The interpretation and evaluation (e.g., submission of report) are critical components of any forensic anthropological examination and caution must be exercised to not overstep one's professional bounds. Because toolmark analysis has a strong subjective component, it is impossible to definitively state that "this tool made this mark" as questions of variability have not been answered to date. Thus, standard weighted designations similar to those used for personal identification (e.g., tentative, presumptive, and positive) are recommended when comparing witness marks with test marks: elimination, consistent/correspondent, and inconclusive.

Marks With Striations

Case 1

A nasty custody battle concluded with the murder and dismemberment of Laura Ackerson. The dismembered remains of Laura Ackerson were found in a creek in Texas 2

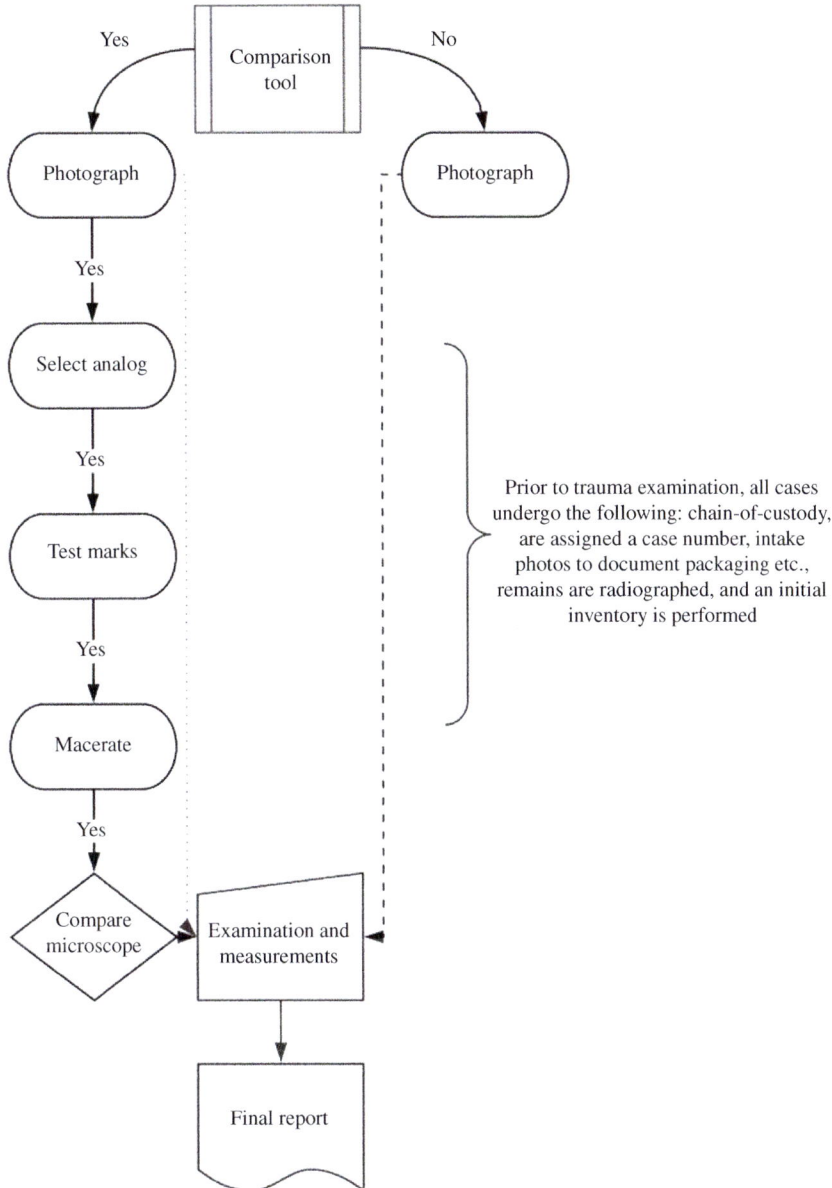

FIGURE 11.2 Workflow for toolmark comparisons on bone.

weeks after her disappearance from Kinston, NC. The victim had been dismembered in Raleigh, placed in a cooler, and transported in a rented U-Haul truck by her ex-boyfriend Grant Hayes and his wife Amanda Hayes, to Amanda Hayes' sister's house in Texas.

The police investigation revealed that a reciprocating SKIL saw (Fig. 11.3), an all-purpose saw blade, and a wood saw blade were purchased by Grant Hayes at a local

FIGURE 11.3   An example of the reciprocating SKIL saw tested.

general merchandise store. These same tools were purchased by the State since the actual saw used by Grant Hayes in the dismemberment of Laura Ackerson was never recovered. These were provided to our laboratory for comparison with Ms. Ackerson's remains (left femoral shaft). Test cuts were made on a fleshed pig analog using both blades at different saw speeds. After maceration, test cuts (or marks) and those found on the victim (witness marks) were microscopically examined utilizing a digital microscope and images were saved. The archived test and witness marks were then compared using the split-screen function on the Keyence VHX 1000, which can be utilized as a comparison scope. The comparison using the Z20 lens at 100% magnification with the ALL PURPOSE blade was not consistent with the striations observed on the victim's remains (Fig. 11.4). The comparison made with the WOOD/FAST blade using the Z20 lens at 100% magnification was consistent with the striations observed on the victim's remains (Fig. 11.5).

Hacking Marks, Corto-contundente

The classification of *corto-contundente* wounds is defined in both the Spanish and Portuguese medicolegal literature as those that are produced by a heavy weapon with a sharp or cutting edge, such as axes, heavy knives, machetes, shovels, aircraft and boat propellers, etc. (Di Maio and Dana, 2003). The literal translation of *corto-contundente* is *incised-blunt*, which is a more precise descriptor of these types of injuries. Generally, injuries include the following characteristics: broad, irregular, sinuous, and rarely distinct (Lossetti and Patito, 2000).

Case 2

In early 2016, the perpetrator called 911 and told the responding officers that he feared something terrible had happened to his wife. The victim had bite marks throughout her body, genital wounds, and her head and arms were partially disarticulated. Several tools were found at the scene including a kitchen knife found under her body, a straightedge shovel, and a baseball bat. The County Sheriff's Office provided the knife and shovel found at the crime scene for comparison with the witness marks. Test cuts were made on fleshed pig neck and leg analogs. It took several attempts with the shovel to resolve how it

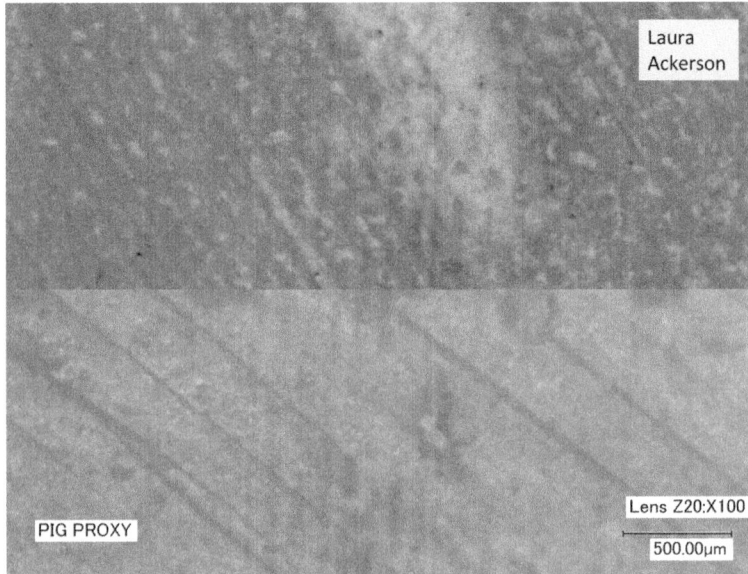

FIGURE 11.4 Comparison of all-purpose blade to witness mark at same magnification.

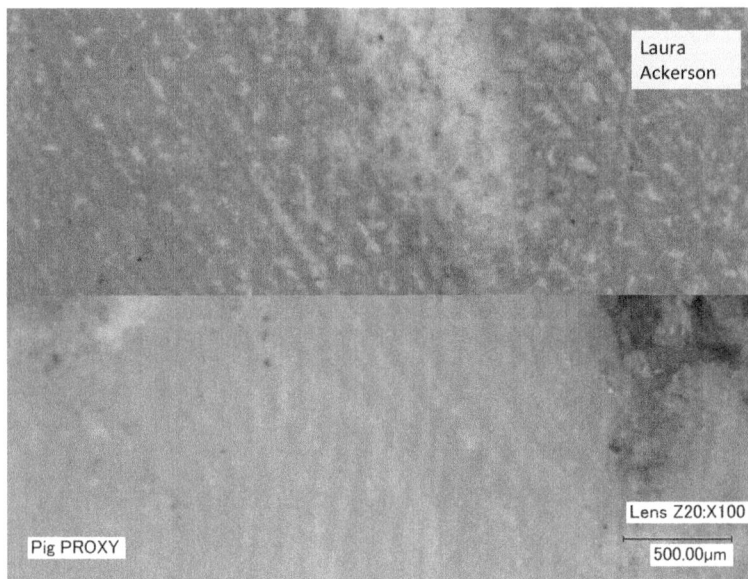

FIGURE 11.5 Correspondence between witness and test mark using the wood/fast blade.

was wielded to be able to disarticulate a body with ease and based on the multiple test attempts it was concluded that the shovel had to be held with the blade and cutting edge facing medially allowing one to strike down with force (Fig. 11.6). After maceration these were microscopically compared. Fig. 11.7 presents the comparison of the knife utilized for the test cut and shows that it has a straightedge that does not correspond to the witness mark. The shovel produced a more sinuous mark, which corresponded to the witness

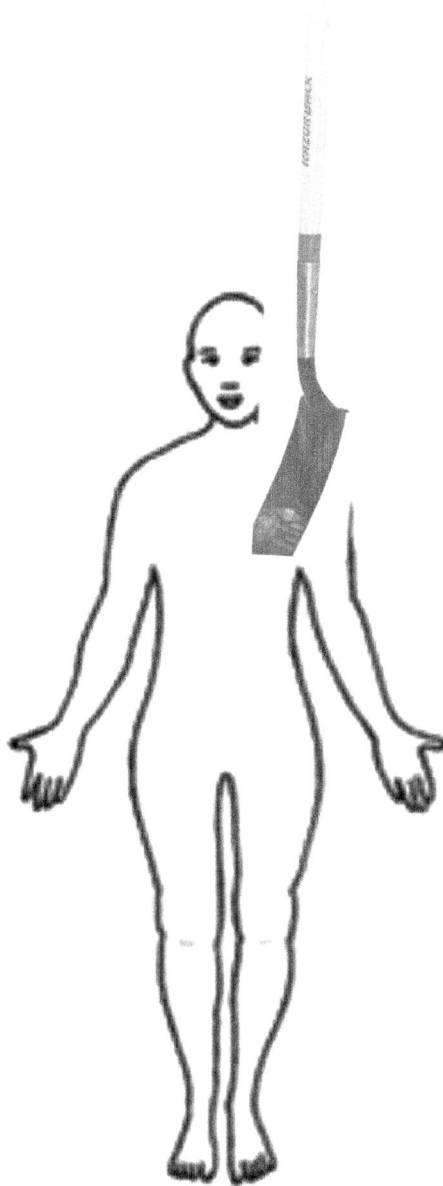

FIGURE 11.6   Diagram illustrating how shovel had to be held to be able to disarticulate the body.

mark observed on the anterior aspect of the fifth cervical vertebral body (Fig. 11.7). Sharp force injuries resulting in blunt force fractures or *corto-contundente* wounds are generally characterized by sharp edges, smooth walls, and bone loss are illustrated in Figs. 11.8–11.10.

FIGURE 11.7 Comparison of knife found at the scene and pattern on victim.

FIGURE 11.8 Comparison of shovel and witness marks showing corresponding morphology.

Case 3

On Christmas Eve 2014, a 2-year-old toddler was reported missing. His fragmentary remains were found on December 26, 2014 in a lake. His remains showed evidence of burning with blunt and sharp force trauma. His father, charged with first degree murder, pled guilty to a reduced second degree charge and was sentenced to 31 years in prison. His mother was also charged in connection with the crime.

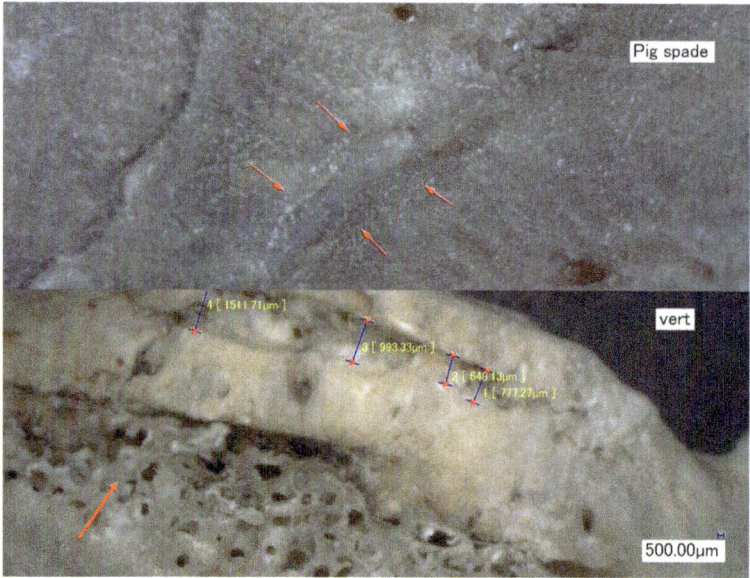

FIGURE 11.9 Sharp force injury (*corto-contundente*) resulting in blunt force fracture and similar morphology.

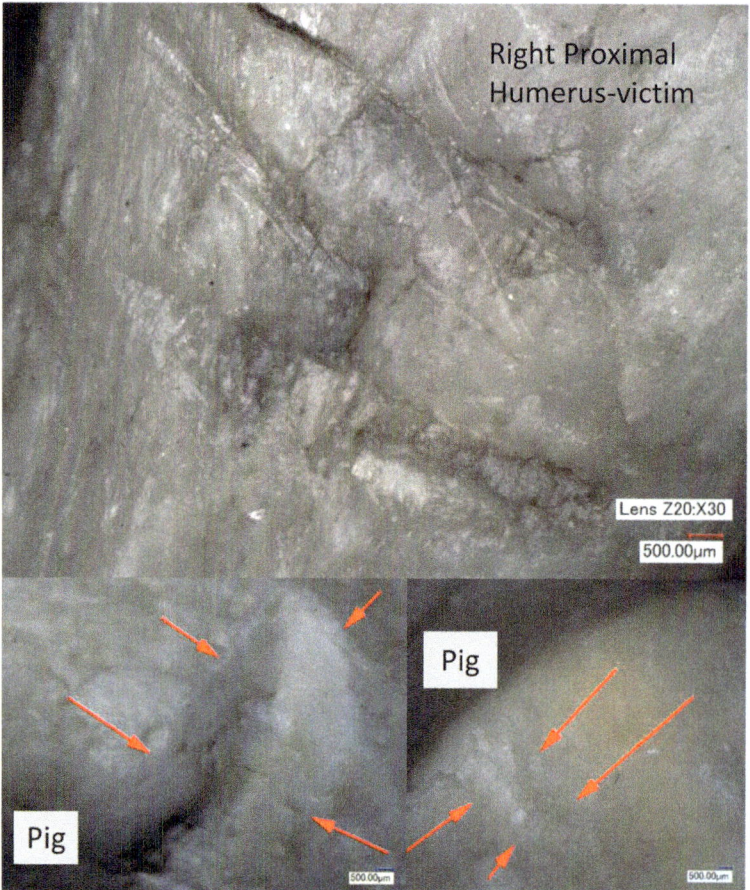

FIGURE 11.10 *Corto-contundente* trauma on long bones with similar morphology of test and witness marks.

The toddler's fragmentary remains showed evidence of multiple knife-incised (cut) wounds consistent with a slow loading (the amount of time the bone has to react to or deform before failure) instrument with a sharp, nonserrated edge with a heel that was sharp enough to incise the bone, such as a kitchen/chef's knife. In addition, there were multiple fractures on the cranial bones associated with blunt-force injury. On the inferomedial aspect of the occipital squama multiple impacts with associated linear fractures were evident, consistent with a diastatic fracture with plastic deformation. Microscopically the widest cut was approximately 1.5 mm or 1437.92 μm. These injuries were consistent with *corto-contundente* or incised-blunt injury with a weighted instrument with a sharp edge (Figs. 11.11−11.13).

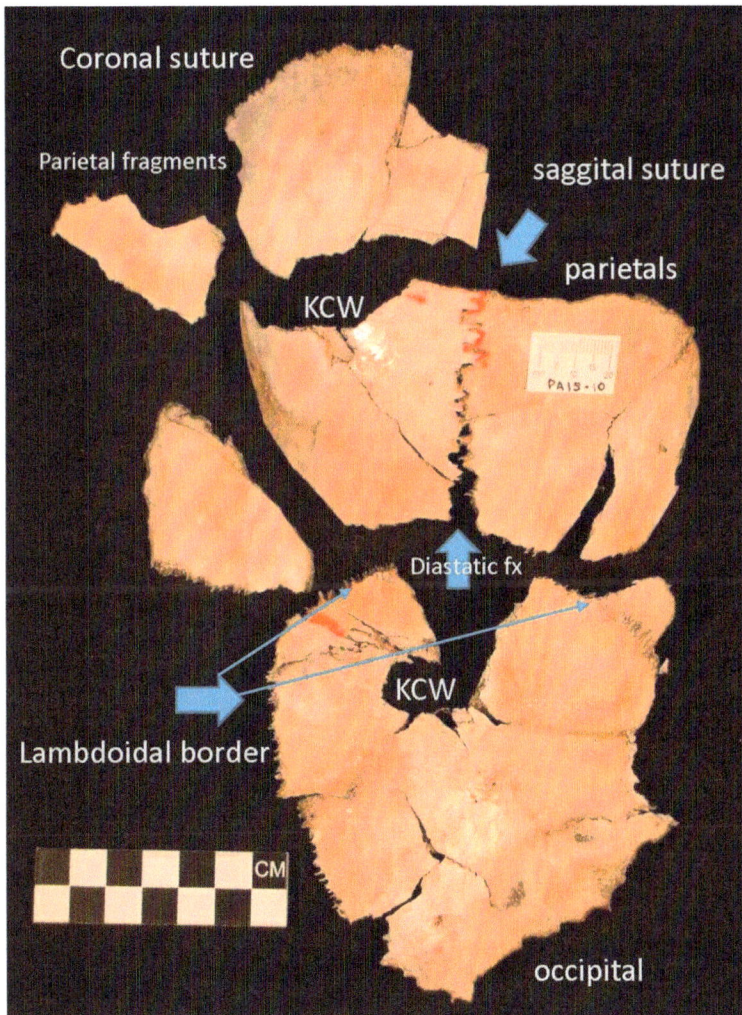

FIGURE 11.11   Infero-medial aspect of the occipital squama showing multiple impacts with associated linear fractures consistent with diastatic fracture and plastic deformation.

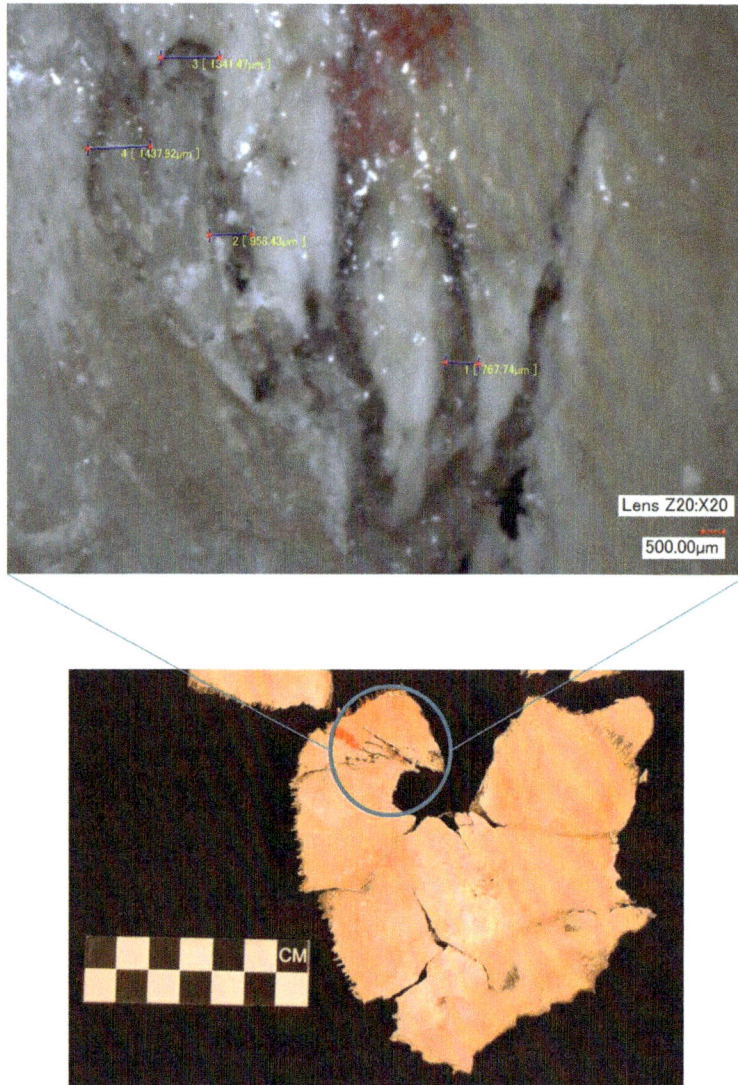

FIGURE 11.12   Microscopically the widest cut is approximately 1.5 mm.

GENERAL CONSIDERATIONS AND FUTURE DIRECTIONS

Adding to the scant availability of mutilation data, this chapter presents 11 cases of dismemberment occurring in North Carolina from 2006 to 2017 that are included in the meta-analysis (Chapter 12). Unfortunately, little information is available regarding the psychiatric evaluation of the perpetrators; however, detailed information is available regarding the mode and patterns of dismemberments. These cases are summarized in Table 11.1.

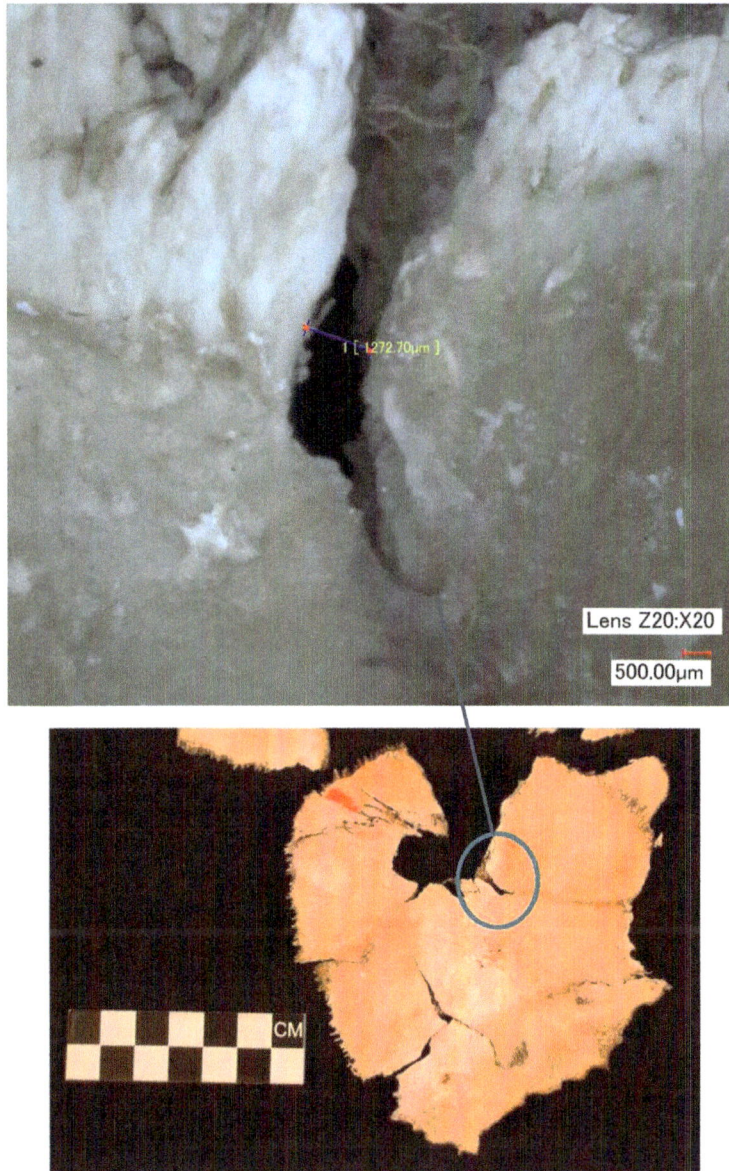

FIGURE 11.13   Microscopically this cut measured at 1.3 mm or 1272.70 micrometers.

As Thomson and Black (2017) stated, the interpretation and evaluation of toolmarks has a subjective element that needs to be controlled for by best practice in the laboratory (Baldwin et al., 2013). If a tool is submitted for comparison to the witness mark, the initial

TABLE 11.1 Summary of North Carolina Dismemberment/Mutilation Cases 2006–17

Case	Classification	Mode	Instrument	Body Area	Perpetrator Victim
1	Defensive, offensive, and maybe necromanic	Transection with sawing action	At least two different saw blades	Skull trisected, distal wrists, shoulder, distal femora, proximal and distal tibiae and fibulae, and feet at metatarsals	Person of interest in custody, trophies of hair mats and teeth found in home. No knowledge of anatomy. Crimes against prostitutes.
2	Defensive	Transection with sawing action	At least two types of knives and a saw	Cervical vertebrae, and right femoral neck and midshaft	Stepmother, no knowledge of anatomy. Child abuse.
3	Defensive	Transection with sawing action	Saw and knife for cutting soft tissue	Shaft left and right humerus, and shaft left and right femur	Hunter and cut marks show knowledge of skinning animal carcasses. Domestic violence.
4	Defensive	Transection with sawing action	Reciprocating saw	Cervical neck, shoulders, greater trochanter femur and femoral condyles, foot at metatarsal, torso severed in two	Ex, custody dispute, no knowledge of anatomy. Domestic violence.
5	Defensive	Transection with sawing action	Reciprocating saw	Severed into 9 pieces: neck, left and right proximal humerus, right distal humerus, left hand at distal radius and ulna, distal femora, and right foot at ankle	Live-in partner. Domestic violence. No knowledge of anatomy.
6	Aggressive, necromanic	Transection with chopping action	Unknown, *corto-contundente*, heavy object with sharp edge; COD was GSW	Proximal humeri, distal left humerus, proximal tibiae and fibulae	Overkill and possible trophy, symbol, fetish. Known Satan worshiper.
7	Defensive	Transection with chopping action	Unknown *corto-contundente*, serrated heavy object, COD GSW; body parts also burned in burn tank	Many parts not recovered. Left tibia and fibular fragments, long bone fragments, and phalanges were available.	Domestic violence from live-in girlfriend. Lesbian relationship.
8	Defensive	Transection with sawing action	Hand saw	Proximal femoral shafts	Domestic violence. Boyfriend charged.
9	Aggressive	Disarticulation	Straightedge shovel; *corto-contundente*	Disarticulation at shoulder joints and	Domestic violence, husband suffering from

(Continued)

TABLE 11.1 (Continued)

Case	Classification	Mode	Instrument	Body Area	Perpetrator Victim
		Transection with chopping action		almost complete decapitation	PTSD after returning from Afghanistan.
10	Defensive, aggressive	Transection with chopping action	Heavy object with sharp edge, *corto-contundente*	Fragmentary remains with evidence of burning.	Child abuse. Father charged with homicide and mother charged with abuse and accessory after the fact. Father sentenced to a minimum of 33 years.
11	Defensive	Disarticulation	Some type of straightedge knife	Multiple cut marks around joint surfaces; two victims	Dispute over money.

question of "did this tool produce the witness mark?" should be considered. Follow-up questions would include whether apparent differences in toolmarks rule out the specific tool, or could the differences be accounted for by how the tool was utilized? Any comparison is limited by the amount of detail and quality present on the witness mark that will affect the interpretation: elimination, inconclusive, or correspondence of the mark in question (Baldwin et al., 2013). The example in Case 1 shows excellent correspondence between the witness mark and the test mark, and would not be difficult to explain in court testimony. Unfortunately, these are still heavily dependent on the equipment available in the laboratory and the subjective nature of the practitioner's experience as there are insufficient data available concerning the commonality of tools to allow for a probabilistic expression (Baldwin et al., 2013). Based on the results by Love and colleagues (2013) and those observed in our own casework, the information recorded to elucidate class and subclass only includes kerf width as the singularly quantifiable measure at this time. However, kerf widths do not directly relate to blade thickness because saw blades taper and are wider at the teeth to prevent the blade from getting stuck. While kerf width can be useful in determining the type of saw used, it is not a unique variable, as many saws have similar widths (Rutty and Hainsworth, 2014). Other characteristics such as exit chipping, size of breakaway spur, harmonics, etc. have not been replicated in the laboratory and are most likely related to extrinsic factors, such as the way in which the tool is employed and the strength and dexterity of the user. In addition, characteristics such as the size of the breakaway spur and the number of false starts considered as criteria to differentiate between mechanical (electric) and hand saws have not been found to be reliable indicators as they appear to reflect how the operator wielded the instrument rather than power (i.e., manual versus electric).

Black and colleagues (2017) refer to the 2009 National Academy of Sciences (NAS) report that a major limitation of toolmark examination, including firearms, is lacking standard protocols for examination, and is heavily reliant on subjective experience-weighted testimony that has a limited scientific base. The NAS report states that the fundamental problem with toolmark examination is the absence of a "precisely defined process."While the report also states toolmark examination lacks the protocol specificity of DNA, it also states that it need not be as objective as DNA to be of probative value. Thus, this chapter is the first step in developing these precise and specific protocols for toolmark examinations/comparisons on bone.

The subjective component is not unique to toolmark analysis, but to many areas of patterned evidence analysis, including skeletal identifications via radiographic comparisons (Derrick et al., 2018; Stephan et al., 2011, 2018; Maxwell and Ross, 2014; Ross et al., 2015, 2016). An area that shows some promise is development of algorithms to automatically quantify geometric similarities of anatomical surfaces (Boyer et al., 2011). Stephan and colleagues (2018) perfectly summarized the complications encountered with automation and quantification of patterned evidence in general: "(t)he human involvement is required because computer algorithms cannot currently match the performance of the highly evolved human visual system that cannot only identify, differentiate, and interpret fine complexities embedded in biological images, but can perform under nonideal circumstances such as degraded image qualities" (Stephan et al., 2018: 278).Thus, at present, standardizing laboratory procedures of toolmark examinations is of critical concern.

References

Bachrach, B., Jain, A., Jung, S., Koons, R.D., 2010. A statistical validation of the individuality and repeatability of striated tool marks: screwdrivers and tongue and groove pliers. J. Forensic Sci. 55 (2), 348–357.

Bailey, J.A., Wang, Y., van de Goot, F.R.W., Gerretsen, R.R.R., 2011. Statistical analysis of kerf mark measurements in bone. Forensic Sci., Med., Pathol. 7, 53–62.

Baldwin, D., Birkett, J., Facey, O., Rabey, G., 2013. The Forensic Examination and Interpretation of Tool Marks, first ed. John Wiley & Sons, Ltd, Hoboken.

Black, S., Rutty, G., Hainsworth, S.V., 2017. Criminal Dismemberment: Forensic and Investigative Analysis. CRC Press, Boca Raton.

Boyer, D.M., Lipman St., Y., Clair, E., Puente, J., Patel, B.A., Funkhouser, T., et al., 2011. Algorithms to automatically quantify the geometric similarity of anatomical surfaces. Proc. Natl. Acad. Sci. USA. 108 (45), 18221–18226.

Capuani, C., Guilbeau-Frugier, C., Delisle, M.B., Rougé, D., Telmon, N., 2014. Epifluorescence analysis of hacksaw marks on bone: highlighting unique individual characteristics. Forensic Sci. Int. 241, 195–202.

Cerutti, E., Magli, F., Porta, D., Gibelli, D., Catteneo, C., 2014. Metrical assessment of cutmarks on bone: Is size important? Leg. Med. 16, 208–213.

Crowder, C., Rainwater, C.W., Fridie, J.S., 2013. Microscopic analysis of sharp force trauma in bone and cartilage: a validation study. J. Forensic Sci. 58 (5), 1119–1126.

Derrick, S.M., Hipp, J.A., Goel, P., 2018. The computer-assisted decedent identification method of computer-assisted radiographic identification. In: Latham, K.A., Bartelink, E., Finnegan, M. (Eds.), New Perspectives in Forensic Human Skeletal Identification. Academic Press, Cambridge, pp. 265–276.

Di Nunno, N., Costantinides, F., Vacca, M., Di Nunno, C., 2006. Dismemberment: a review of the literature and description of 3 Cases. Am. J. Forensic Med. Pathol. 27 (4), 307–312.

Di Maio, V.J., Dana, S.E., 2003. Manual de Patología Forense. EdicionesDíaz de Santos. EdicionesDíaz de Santos, Madrid, 2003.

Dogan, K.H., Demirci, S., Deniz, I., Erkol, Z., 2010. Decapitation and dismemberment of the corpse: a matricide case. J. Forensic Sci. 55 (2), 542–545.

Hainsworth, S.V., 2017. Identification marks—saws. In: Black, S., Rutty, G., Hainsworth, S.V. (Eds.), Criminal Dismemberment: Forensic and Investigative Analysis. CRC Press, Boca Raton, pp. 135–155.

Houck, M.M., 1998. Skeletal trauma and the individualization of knife marks in bones. In: Reichs, K.J. (Ed.), Forensic Osteology: Advances in the Identification of Human Remains, second ed. Charles C Thomas, Springfield, pp. 410–424.

Lossetti, O.A., Patito, J.A., 2000. Lesions of the brain trunk: study of electrocution and other ways of death. PrensaMedica Argentina 87 (9), 866–874.

Love, J.C., Derrick, S.M., Wiersema, J.M., 2013. Independent validation test of microscopic saw mark analysis. Doc No 241745, National Criminal Justice Reference Service. Available from: https://www.ncjrs.gov/pdffiles1/nij/grants/241745.pdf (accessed 09.01.2018.).

Maples, W.R., 1986. Trauma analysis by the forensic anthropologist. In: Reichs, K.J. (Ed.), Forensic Osteology: Advances in the Identification of Human Remains. Charles C Thomas, Springfield, pp. 218–228.

Maxwell, A.B., Ross, A.H., 2014. A radiographic study on the utility of cranial vault outlines for positive identifications. J. Forensic Sci. 59 (2), 314–318.

Nogueira, L., Quatrehomme, G., Rallon, C., Adalian, P., Alunni, V., 2016. Saw marks in bones: a study of 170 experimental false start lesions. Forensic Sci. Int. 268, 128–130.

Petraco, N., 2010. Color Atlas of Forensic Toolmark Identification. CRC Press, Boca Raton.

Puentes, K., Cardoso, H.F.V., 2013. Reliability of cut mark analysis in human costal cartilage: The effects of blade penetration angle and intra- and inter- individual differences. Forensic Sci. Int. 231, 244–248.

Quatrehomme, G., 2007. A strange case of dismemberment. In: Brickley, M., Ferllini, R. (Eds.), Forensic Anthropology: Case studies from Europe. Charles C Thomas, Springfield, pp. 99–119.

Quatrehomme, G., 2015. Traitéd'AnthropologieMédico-Légale. De Boeck, Paris.

Reichs, K.J., 1998. Postmortem dismemberment: recovery, analysis and interpretation. In: Reichs, K.J. (Ed.), Forensic Osteology—Advances in the Identification of Human Remains, second ed Charles C Thomas, Springfield, pp. 353–388.

Ross, A.H., Lanfear, A.K., Maxwell, A.B., 2016. Establishing standards for side-by-side radiographic comparisons. Am. J. Forensic Med. Pathol. 37 (2), 86–94.

Rutty, G.N., Hainsworth, S.V., 2014. The dismembered body. In: Rutty, G.N. (Ed.), Essentials of Autopsy Practice—Advances, Updates and Emerging Technologies. Springer, London, pp. 59–87.

Saville, P.A., Hainsworth, S.V., Rutty, G.N., 2007. Cutting crime: the analysis of the "uniqueness" of saw marks on bone. Int. J. Legal Med. 121, 349–357.

Spitz, W.U., 2006. Sharp force injury. In: Spitz, W.U., Spitz, D.J. (Eds.), Spitz and Fisher's Medicolegal Investigation of Death: Guidelines for the Application of Pathology to Crime Investigation, fourth ed. Charles C Thomas, Springfield, pp. 252–309.

Stephan, C.N., Winburn, A.P., Christensen, A.F., Tyrrell, A.J., 2011. Skeletal identification by radiographic comparison: blind tests of a morphoscopic method using antemortem chest radiographs. J. Forensic Sci. 56 (2), 320–332.

Stephan, C.N., D'Alonzo, S.S., Wilson, E.K., Guyomarc'h, P., Berg, G.E., Byrd, J.E., 2018. Skeletal identification by radiographic comparison of the cervicothoracic region on chest radiographs. In: Latham, K.A., Bartelink, E., Finnegan, M. (Eds.), New Perspectives in Forensic Human Skeletal Identification. Academic Press, Cambridge, pp. 277–292.

Symes, S.A., Berryman, H.E., Smith, O.C., Blake, C., 1992. Saw dismemberment of human bone: characteristics indicative of saw class and type. In: Proceedings of the Forty-Fourth Annual Meeting of the American Academy of Forensic Sciences, American Academy of Forensic Sciences, LA, vol. 166, Colorado Springs, CO, New Orleans.

Symes, S.A., Berryman, H.E., Smith, O.C., 1998. Saw marks in bone: introduction and examination of residual kerf contour. In: Reichs, K.J. (Ed.), Forensic Osteology: Advances in the Identification of Human Remains, second ed. Charles C. Thomas, Springfield, pp. 389–409.

Symes, S.A., Chapman, E.N., Rainwater, C.W., Cabo, L.L., Myster, S.M.T., 2010. Knife and saw toolmark analysis in bone: a manual designed for the examination of criminal mutilation and dismemberment. Doc No 232864, National Criminal Justice Reference Service. Available from: https://www.ncjrs.gov/pdffiles1/nij/grants/232227.pdf (accessed 09.01.2018.).

Thomson, G., Black, S., 2017. Principles of tool mark analysis and evidential best practice. In: Black, S., Rutty, G., Hainsworth, S.V. (Eds.), Criminal Dismemberment: Forensic and Investigative Analysis. CRC Press, Boca Raton, pp. 79–95.

Wang, J.Z., 2016. Real time examination of saw marks on/in bones produced by three common types of saws: a digital and quantitative method. Forensic Res. Criminol. Int. J. 2 (4), 00065.

Further Reading

Kimmerle, E., Baraybar, J.P., 2008. In: Skeletal Trauma: Identification of Injuries Resulting from Human Rights Abuse and Armed Conflict, CRC Press, Boca Raton.

The Pattern of Violence and Aggression

Ann H. Ross[1], Ashley Humphries[1] and Eugenia Cunha[2,3]

[1]Department of Biological Sciences, North Carolina State University, Raleigh, NC, United States [2]National Institute of Legal Medicine and Forensic Sciences, Lisbon, Portugal [3]Centre for Functional Ecology, Department of Life Sciences, University of Coimbra, Coimbra, Portugal

INTRODUCTION

Homicide cases involving mutilation evoke both morbid interest and repulsion as the act of dismemberment is thought to be relatively rare. However, Quatrehomme (2007) states they are rather common and Ross (see Chapter 11: Tool Mark Identification on Bone: Best Practice) states that dismemberments are underreported due to that current homicide reporting systems do not allow for accurate counts. Mutilation is "the act of depriving an individual of a limb, or other important part of the body; or deprival of an organ; or severe disfigurement, which also covers the term dismemberment" (Sea and Beauregard, 2016: 2). With increased attention on the strengthening of the forensic sciences (i.e., 2009 NAS report), cases of dismemberment and mutilation deserve more consideration as the interpretation of the context will be an important component in the progression of the investigation as well as for probative purposes. Three major intersections will be reviewed including the motive of the mutilation, and the interpretation of the tool marks and pattern of mutilation (mode) as these play an important role in the evaluation of the crime and ultimately the sentencing of the perpetrator. Further, a summary of trends including the perpetrator and victim profiles will also be reviewed in light of cultural variations. Finally, recommendations to clarify terminology and reporting of these unique cases will be presented.

Dismemberment can result from a number of instances. For example, it is not uncommon for dismemberment to occur in high velocity traffic accidents or suicides. Out of 3940 deaths occurring between 2000 and 2007, Dogan and colleagues (2010) identified seven dismemberment cases in Turkey, only one of which was related to criminal intent. Four of these incidents were the result of suicide via jumping in front of a train and two of them were due to traffic accidents. As a result, they conclude that most dismemberments in Turkey occur in accidents and suicides. This information is helpful in understanding dismemberment trends cross-culturally. However, we recommend distinguishing criminal dismemberment/mutilation from dismemberment/mutilation resulting from accidents or suicides as they have very different medicolegal processes and outcomes. Therefore, the remaining chapter will focus solely on criminal dismemberments.

CLASSIFICATION OF CRIMINAL DISMEMBERMENTS

In 1918, Ziemke defined defensive and offensive dismemberments in which a defensive dismemberment is performed following a homicide to transport, conceal, or hinder the identification of the victim (Konopka et al., 2007). This motivation can either be planned, such as in the case of a serial killer, or may occur without any foresight, such as in the case of a family dispute gone wrong (Rajs et al., 1998; Häkkänen-Nyholm et al., 2009; Dogan et al., 2010). However, at least in European contexts, defensive mutilations are more likely to be committed by a close family member or friend (Rajs et al., 1998; Konopka et al., 2007, 2016; see various chapters in this volume for examples).

An offensive mutilation is performed by a perpetrator who receives gratification through a sexually motivated homicide or through the dismemberment itself. Further divisions were proposed by Püschel and Koops (1987) to include aggressive and necromanic dismemberment. Aggressive dismemberments are those in which the homicide is brought on by a fit of rage where the dismemberment could be the continuation of an "overkill" or be the cause of death itself. Aggressive mutilations are commonly associated with impulsivity, multiple injuries, and the potential presence of defensive wounds (Rajs et al., 1998). For example, Dogan et al. (2010) report a matricide in which the victim's schizophrenic daughter murdered her mother. At least 71 incised and stab wounds were identified on the victim's head, five stab wounds were present in the right chest cavity, defensive cut marks were located on the hands, the right ear was severed from the head, and the victim was decapitated. In addition, the perpetrator removed the right arm at the location of the scapulohumeral joint and removed both hands at the level of the wrists. Due to the large number and superficial nature of the stab wounds on the head, Dogan et al. (2010) identified this dismemberment, at least in part, as an aggressive mutilation. However, due to the removal of the hands, an attempt to clean up the scene, and the fact that the perpetrator attempted to break the edges of the squat toilet to widen the opening for disposal of the elements, Dogan et al. (2010) agreed that the mutilation could also be considered defensive. Homicide by decapitation has also been identified as aggressive mutilation (as observed in several cases in this volume). Konopka et al. (2007, 2016) cited a case in which a mother chopped the necks of her two daughters with an ax, murdering them and nearly decapitating one.

Necromanic mutilation, the least common modern category, may be associated with necrophilia or carried out with the purpose of using a body part as a symbol, trophy, or fetish. The death of the corpse used in this instance may not necessarily result from homicide. A very clear example is described by Ehrlich et al. (2000) in which a male perpetrator committed at least 12 acts of necrophilia or paraphilia. He would specifically break into cemeteries to gain access to the corpses and admitted that he would often feel inclined to perform the acts after leaving his court mandated psychiatric appointments intended to help him with this inclination. In six of the instances the perpetrator either severed the breasts or skinned the trunk of the corpses and placed the skin on his naked body for sexual stimulation. In one instance he removed a limb. He also gained sexual gratification through covering himself in burial shrouds and/or lying in the coffins. To further clarify this category, Mellor (2016) uses the term necromutilophilia for individuals gaining pleasure from the mutilation of corpses and specifies the term necromutilomania for cases where mutilation of corpses is compulsive but not accompanied with homicide. According to Ehrlich et al. (2000), almost all necromaniac mutilations are committed by males. In their review of nine cases from German speaking countries, there was only one instance of a female perpetrator.

More recently, Persaud and Häkkänen-Nyholm (2012) included a fifth category, communication. Dismemberment as a means of communication includes those killings that are associated with organized crime in which the mutilation is a means of sending a message. Evidence of mutilation has been identified in the prehistoric and historic record. Motives for such dismemberments in these early contexts typically revolved around powerassertion and/or superstition (Klaus and Toyne, 2016). For example, public executions by "disruption" that were carried out by chaining each limb to four horses to be pulled apart in four directions (quartering) symbolized the power of the State. Such executions were reserved for enemies of the State serving as a symbol for others not to question their rule. As described by Klaus and Toyne (2016), dismemberment within Moche contexts involved combat, and capturing prisoners for public display and sacrifice. These behaviors were interpreted from mural and ceramic images, such as paintings depicting Moche warriors leading a line of nude prisoners with a rope tied to their necks, images depicting deep incisions on the penises and legs of prisoners suggesting torture, and images of male captives surrounded by severed heads and limbs (Klaus and Toyne, 2016). Cut marks examined by Klaus and Toyne (2016) on remains from Huaca de la Luna, Peru, are suggestive of mutilation around the eyes, nose, cheeks, lips, scalp, hands, and feet, and possible mutilation of the genitals. These patterns, held during a ritualistic display, would have likely had a bloody and intimidating effect on the victims and bystanders; and therefore, served to reinforce the State's power.

Recent modern-day examples include the dismemberments carried out during the armed conflict in Colombia in which dismemberment via machetes and axes was a widespread form of torture to instill fear in rural populations by paramilitary groups (see Chapter 2: Dismemberment of Victims in Colombia: A Perspective From Practice). In many of the cases, the dismemberment was the actual cause of death as no other evidence of trauma was evident and has been confirmed by numerous eyewitness accounts (Morcillo-Méndez and Campos, 2012). Dismemberment also served the purpose as a concealment mechanism allowing for the burial and nonburial disposal of a body (López and Umaña, 2007). Pachar Lucio (2015) has noted the increase in the number of mutilated and dismembered bodies in Mexico and Central American countries of Guatemala, Honduras, and El Salvador related to an increase in criminal activities of narcotrafficking, paramilitary groups, and other gang activities (see Chapters 3 and 4: Dismemberment in Brazil: From Early Colonization to

Present Days; Postmortem Criminal Mutilation in Panama). The motive behind these dismemberments is to either send a message (e.g., intimidation, settling of scores) to rival criminals or of a psychological, psychiatric, and symbolic etiology exhibiting mutilations of the tongue, genitals, decapitation, removal of the face, scalping, and signs of torture evidenced by placing these in public places or using them as trophies (Pachar Lucio, 2015; see Chapter 4: Postmortem Criminal Mutilation in Panama).

According to Rajs et al. (1998) and Konopka et al. (2016), the two most common forms of dismemberment are defensive and aggressive. These tend to be unplanned, disorganized, committed by someone known to the victim, and often influenced by alcohol and/ or substance abuse (Rajs et al., 1998; Konopka et al., 2016). Cases of criminal mutilation are not systematically reported; as such, there are few available for study and the case reviews that do exist are focused on developed countries. Therefore, these trends may be influenced by cultural factors not readily accounted for in the literature (Corzine et al., 1999; Salfati and Park, 2007).

MODES AND PATTERNS OF DISMEMBERMENT TRAUMA

Rainwater (2015) provides a recent review of the modes of dismemberment, summarizing dismemberment trauma into three categories. These include disarticulation around the joints, transection of bone via chopping, and transection of bone via sawing. Disarticulation around the joints is typically characterized by cut marks around major joints. This mode has been considered evidence of the perpetrator having some anatomical knowledge. An example of transection via sawing is discussed later in Chapter 11, Tool Mark Identification on Bone: Best Practice (see case example 1, Laura Ackerson), where a power saw was utilized. A unique example of a transection via chopping is described in Chapter 11, Tool Mark Identification on Bone: Best Practice of this volume (case example 2), in which a shovel was used to remove the head of the victim and arms at the shoulders. Transection of the bone via sawing was the most common mode of dismemberment observed among the 21 cases presented in this volume. Rainwater's classification, transection via chopping, may be more appropriately described with the term *corto-contundente* or incised-blunt injuries that are produced in chopping transections by a heavy weapon with a sharp cutting edge, such as axes, machetes, shovels, heavy knives, and boat propellers (Di Maio and Dana, 2003; Chapter 11: Tool Mark Identification on Bone: Best Practice).

Mutilation encompasses both disarticulation and any removal of body parts. Skin may also be removed in an attempt to remove tattoos, digits, genitalia, and breasts. The removal of tattoos and/or digits is consistent with defensive mutilation where the perpetrator is motivated by the desire to hinder identification. For example, in a historic 1935 double murder committed by Dr. Buck Ruxton, investigators reported that fingerprints and scars had been severed from the victims in an attempt to hinder identification (https://www.nlm.nih.gov/visibleproofs/galleries/cases/ruxton.html). Mutilation of the genitalia and/or breasts is consistent with offensive mutilations where lust/sexual desire may be a motivating factor (see Chapter 4: Postmortem Criminal Mutilation in Panama).

Aggressive mutilations are often accompanied by the presence of multiple injuries, defensive wounds, symbolic cuts to the face or particular body parts (Rajs et al., 1998).

PSYCHIATRIC ASPECTS

Defensive and aggressive dismemberments are typically disorganized, whereas offensive dismemberments are more commonly performed by an organized perpetrator. Rajs et al. (1998) found that defensive dismemberments were likely to be influenced by alcohol and/or substance abuse and most of the perpetrators had been under psychiatric care. Aggressive mutilations were found to be committed by individuals with psychotic tendencies, such as schizophrenia or affective disorders (Rajs et al., 1998). This is consistent with the matricide case reported by Dogan et al. (2010). Offensive mutilations are associated with a history of criminal activity including rape, arson, assault, battery, and cruelty to animals (Rajs et al., 1998).

Interestingly, one study found an increase in admittance of schizophrenic patients to psychiatric hospitals during the summer months with a peak occurring in June and July (Hare and Walter, 1978). Other studies have identified seasonal variation in other mental illnesses including bipolar disorder with manic/hypomanic symptoms peaking around the fall equinox and depressive symptoms peaking in months surrounding the winter solstice in bipolar I disorder (Akhter et al., 2013). Holmes (2017) identifies psychopathic personality as part of the suite of antisocial personality disorders that show traits of self-centeredness, absence of empathy, control over others, liability to brutal violence, and risk to others, which could predispose them to dismember without hesitation, revulsion, or remorse. Dismemberment by psychopaths is executed in a cold, dispassionate manner that differentiates them from those preceded by anger or rage (Holmes, 2017). These cases conducted by psychopathy and other personality disorders may not be associated to individuals labeled as mentally ill as these disorders do not disable the perpetrator, but instead those around them are the ones who suffer the consequences to their symptoms (Holmes, 2017). Another dimension in civilian contexts is that dismemberment/mutilation in homicide cases, the perpetrator is known to the victim while unknown in nonhomicide cases (Konopka et al., 2007, 2016; Holmes, 2017).

CULTURAL CONSIDERATIONS

Corzine et al. (1999) argue that aggression is a culturally encoded behavior and therefore, may lead to varying homicide patterns within different cultural contexts. Salfati and Park (2007) reviewed 70 cases in South Korea and found that compared with Western homicides, homicides in South Korea are less likely to involve an offender and a victim who have close ties. The authors hypothesize that this is due to a cultural value of interdependence and harmony with significant others. Therefore, we can hypothesize that dismemberment patterns may also vary cross-culturally.

Overall, necromaniac mutilations are considered rare (Rajs et al., 1998). However, this trend varies culturally. Labuschange (2004) and Steyn and Brits (see Chapter 5:

Dismemberment in South Africa: Case Studies) report on several South African cases in which human body parts were mixed with other ingredients or used alone to produce Muti. Muti, in the traditional belief system of the region, is considered "strong medicine" and human body parts are a highly regarded ingredient because it is believed they possess the essence of life and are very powerful. Steyn and Brits (see Chapter 5: Dismemberment in South Africa: Case Studies), suggest that the most likely cause of dismemberment in South Africa is the Muti trade. These dismemberments are primarily via decapitation, family members are often the victims, and the patterns suggest that there is preplanning involved (see Chapter 5: Dismemberment in South Africa: Case Studies). It should be noted that soft tissue, such as the breasts and genitalia are also used for Muti and will likely not leave evidence on bone.

Further, while defensive mutilations predominate in the European case reviews as well as in the North Carolina cases, mutilations committed by organized crime for the purpose of communication are more common in Latin America (see Chapters 2–4). Interestingly, Sweden showed the greatest frequency of offensive and aggressive mutilations.

META-ANALYSIS OF GEOGRAPHIC PATTERNS OF DISMEMBERMENTS USING PUBLISHED DATA

A meta-analysis to examine geographic patterns in dismemberments was conducted on combined data from the literature including Poland ($n = 23$, Konopka et al., 2007), Sweden ($n = 21$, Rajs et al., 1998), United Kingdom ($n = 80$, Black et al., 2017), and the United States ($n = 11$, Chapter 11: Tool Mark Identification on Bone: Best Practice). A Pearson Chi-square, which uses the observed and expected cell frequencies, was used to test whether motive of dismemberments differed among countries and to examine for variation in victim profiles, perpetrator relation to victim, and mode of dismemberment using the categorical response analysis platform in JMP 13.0 (SAS Institute Inc., 2016).

Results

The Pearson Chi-square results show that there are significant differences in motives among the different countries (Pearson Chi-square = 52.61, p-value = < 0.0001). Table 12.1 presents the frequency count of motive by country and shows that *defensive* dismemberments are by far the most common. However, Sweden had a greater frequency of *offensive* and *aggressive* dismemberments than any of the countries. Proportionally the United States has the greatest frequency of multiple motives of dismemberment per case. These country specific differences can be better visualized in the share chart (Fig. 12.1), which is calculated by dividing each count by the total number of responses and represents the frequency divided by response total (JMP 13 Consumer Research. Cary, NC: SAS Institute Inc, 2016).

Differences in frequency were also found regarding perpetrator profiles among the countries (Pearson Chi-square = 12.74, p-value = 0.05). By far, males were the most common perp (see Fig. 12.2 share chart). However, when we examined each individual

TABLE 12.1   Frequency Comparisons for Motive of Dismemberment

Frequency		Defensive	Offensive	Aggressive	Necromanic	Multiple	Total Responses
Reporting country	Poland	17	3	2	1	0	23
		73.9%	13.0%	8.7%	4.3%	0.0%	
Reporting country	Sweden	10	6	4	1	0	21
		47.6%	28.6%	19.0%	4.8%	0.0%	
Reporting country	UK	66	2	5	1	6	80
		82.5%	2.5%	6.3%	1.3%	7.5%	
Reporting country	USA	6	0	0	0	6	12
		50.0%	0.0%	0.0%	0.0%	50.0%	

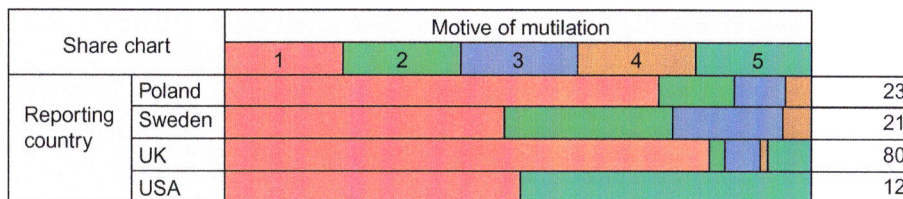

FIGURE 12.1   Frequency of mutilation type by country 1 = defensive, 2 = offensive, 3 = aggressive, 4 = necromanic, 5 = multiple types.

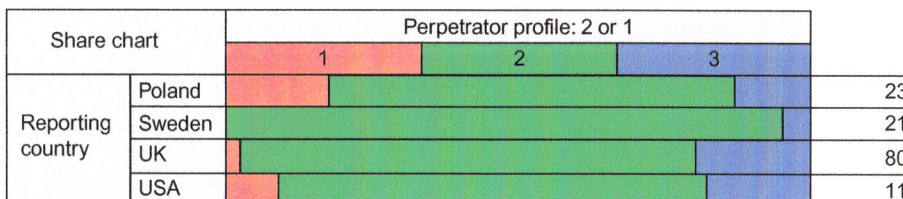

FIGURE 12.2   Frequency of perpetrator profile 1 = female, 2 = male, 3 = unknown.

sample, Poland differed significantly from both Sweden and the UK (p-value = 0.03, p-value = 0.05, respectively) having more female perpetrators. The relation of the perpetrator to the victim did not differ significantly among the countries with the perpetrator being known to the victim as the most common measure (Pearson Chi-square = 0.87, p-value = 0.853, see Table 12.2 for frequencies).

There was no significant difference in the victim profile (Pearson Chi-square = 10.35, p-value = 0.11) even though the United Kingdom has a greater frequency of male victims; however, this is most likely due to the larger sample size. (see Table 12.3).

TABLE 12.2   Frequencies of Relation of Perpetrator to Victim (1 = known, 2 = unknown), * = Alpha level 0.05, ** = Alpha level 0.1.

			Perpetrator Profile: Relation to Victim				
Frequency Share Comparisons			1	2	Total Responses	Compare	Compare Means
Reporting country	Poland	A	17	6	23		
			73.9% **	26.1% **			
	Sweden	B	15	6	21		
			71.4% **	28.6% **			
	UK	C	62	18	80		
			77.5% *	22.5% *			
	USA	D	8	4	12		
			66.7% **	33.3% **			

* = Alpha level 0.1, ** = Alpha level 0.05.

TABLE 12.3   Victim Profile (1 = Female, 2 = Male, 3 = Unknown)

			Victim Profile: 2 or 1				
Frequency Share			1	2	3	Total Responses	Compare
Reporting country	Poland	A	15	8	0	23	
			65.2%	34.8%	0.0%		
	Sweden	B	11	10	0	21	
			52.4%	47.6%	0.0%		
	UK	C	34	35	11	80	
			42.5%	43.8%	13.8%		
	USA	D	7	5	0	12	
			58.3%	41.7%	0.0%		

Interestingly, there was a significant difference in mode of dismemberment (e.g., transection or disarticulation) among the countries (Pearson Chi-square = 16.73, p-value = 0.01).The majority of the cases were dismemberment by transection with a smaller frequency of disarticulations. However, Poland had the highest frequency of disarticulations with 24% and in the United Kingdom100% were transections (see Table 12.4).

TABLE 12.4 Frequency in Mode of Dismemberment (1 = Transection, 2 = Disarticulation, 3 = Unknown)

Frequency Share Comparisons			Mode or Manner of Dismemberment					
			1	2	3	Total Responses	Compare	Compare Means
Reporting country	Poland	A	13	4	0	17		
			76.5% **	23.5% C**	0.0% **			
	Sweden	B	1	0	0	1		
			100.0% **	0.0% **	0.0% **			
	UK	C	48	1	0	49		
			98.0% A*	2.0% *	0.0% *			
	USA	D	10	0	1	11		
			90.9% **	0.0% **	9.1% **			

* = Alpha level 0.05, ** = Alpha level 0.1.

LESSONS LEARNED

The parallels observed in all of the chapters of diverse geographic origin is that every practitioner begins with a gross examination of the false starts (reported by everyone in this volume) and cross-sections. Auxiliary analyses were applied by almost everyone namely SEM and histology through which it was possible to find evidence of the offending implement as well the environment the victim occupied at some point. In Brazil, macroscopic analysis appears to be the only analyses performed on the skeleton and in Central American practice neither auxiliary analyses nor skeletal examinations were conducted. This may be a product of a lack of available resources and collaborative multidisciplinary opportunities.

Per contra, France, Italy, and the United States show more detailed ancillary analyses. As such, Delabarde and Ludes in Chapter 7, The Potential of Histological Analysis in Dismemberment Cases, provide best practice for histological methods, Ross and Radisch (see Chapter 11: Tool Mark Identification on Bone: Best Practice) and Adams and Rainwater (see Chapter 10: Intentional Body Dismemberment Following Nonhomicidal Deaths: A Retrospective Study of Body Packer Cases in New York City) for digital microscopy, and Amadasi and colleagues (see Chapter 8: Dismemberment and Tool Mark Analysis on Bone: A Microscopic Analysis of the Walls of Cut Marks) describe an experiment to achieve more reliable results proving that future research is necessary. The identification of the instrument used to mutilate the body has been demonstrated to be dependent upon the quality of crime scene protocols and on the recovery of suspect objects, which can later be compared with witness marks found on the victim. Multiple instruments are reported, such as heavy sharp edged tools, long, heavy tools (e.g., machetes), several types of knives, and saws. The majority of the lesions are a combination of sharp force and blunt force trauma leading Ross and Radisch to inclusively discuss the

Latin terminology *corto-contundente*, which they consider a more accurate descriptor of these types of lesions as opposed to the descriptor "transection via chopping" used by Rainwater (2015) and for which we are recommending inclusion in our standard trauma nomenclature.

Decapitation was a common element reported in approximately half of the cases presented in this volume, which is a significant finding especially if we take into account that it is the *modus operandi* of terrorists, such as Al Qaeda. Most of the decapitations were postmortem even if in some of the cases, the decapitation itself could have been the cause of death. Almost every chapter addresses the underlying motives for the dismemberment, which differ between the violent and less violent countries represented. Inconsistent with the meta-analyses presented above, males and females were proportionately the victim of dismemberment in the 21 cases presented throughout this volume. Adults were more frequently the victims of mutilation, where only two out of 21 victims were subadults.

Perpetrators are known generally when there is a conviction. Otherwise, they remain unknown, which precludes any inference to be made from the cases outlined in this volume where in only a few of the cases the perpetrator was caught. Moreover, it is more common that cases remain unsolved in violent countries where there are many more victims of homicide, limited resources, and where the government priorities are not directed toward the dead.

CONCLUDING REMARKS

As criminal mutilations are not systematically reported and most of the data available derive from developed countries, there is a gap in the data and a deficiency toward understanding global trends. For example, the meta-analysis included in this chapter is primarily comprised of European and one American data set. However, as demonstrated throughout the chapters in this volume, a slightly different trend is represented in the Americas (not including the United States), where the primary motivation for dismemberment is for the purpose of communication—the fifth type of dismemberment, identified by Persaud and Häkkänen-Nyholm (2012), that we recommend utilizing as it accurately describes a very specific motive observed in modern developing countries. Therefore, we recommend the development of best practices and encourage forensic practitioners to report cases of mutilation. Further, reporting of these cases varies considerably. For example, often information regarding the mode and tools utilized are not included, making global comparisons difficult if not impossible to make.

However, the 21 cases (not including the Australian context) presented in this volume allow us to make some general inferences. Are dismemberments a rare occurrence? As noted by Ross and Radisch in Chapter 2, Dismemberment of Victims in Colombia: A Perspective From Practice, there is a trend in the literature to claim that criminal dismemberment is a rare occurrence, and they cite that only Quatrehomme (2007) has stated that postmortem dismemberment was not an isolated event. The insights from the eight countries highlighted in this book unsurprisingly show that in the group of violent countries (e.g., Colombia, Brazil, Central America, and South Africa), dismemberments are common, whereas elsewhere they appear to be relatively rare events, although Ross and Radisch report 11 cases for a period of 7 years in North Carolina (2011–17). However, Ross and Radisch also suggest that the claim that criminal dismemberment is a rare occurrence may be related to how these types of cases are documented and reported. A common denominator appears to be an underestimation of these types of cases and unreliable statistics. For example, Sanabria reports that 7000 bodies were recovered between 2005 and 2017, but the percentage of dismemberments is unreported. Steyn and Brits state that Muti related killings happen with relatively high frequency in South Africa. Overall, these cases are underestimated and challenging to quantify. Finally, the practitioners in this volume demonstrate that Locard's exchange principle—that "every contact leaves a trace"—still holds true today.

References

Akhter, A., Fiedorowicz, J.G., Zhang, T., Potash, J.B., Cavanaugh, J., Solomon, D.A., et al., 2013. Seasonal variation of manic depressive symptoms in bipolar disorder. Bipolar Disorder 15 (4), 377–384.

Black, S., Rutty, G., Hainsworth, S., Thomson, G., 2017. Appendix II. In: Black, S., Rutty, G., Hainsworth, S., Thomson, G. (Eds.), Criminal Dismemberment. Forensic and Investigative Analysis. CRC Press, Boca Raton, pp. 200–202.

Corzine, J., Huff-Corzine, L., Whitt, H.P., 1999. Cultural and subcultural theories of homicide. In: Smith, M.D., Zahn, M.A. (Eds.), Homicide: A Sourcebook of Social Research. SAGE Publications, Thousand Oaks, pp. 58–71.

Di Maio, V., Dana, S., 2003. Manual de patologíaforense. Ediciones Diaz de Santos S.A, pp. 108–109.

Dogan, K.H., Demirci, S., Deniz, I., Erkol, Z., 2010. Decapitation and dismemberment of the corpse: a matricide case. J. Forensic Sci. 55 (2), 542–545.

Ehrlich, E., Rothschild, M.A., Pluisch, F., Schneider, V., 2000. An extreme case of necrophilia. Legal Med. 2 (4), 224–226.

Klaus, H.D., Toyne, J.M., 2016. Ritual of violence in ancient Andes. In: Klaus, H.D., Toyne, J.M. (Eds.), Ritual Violence in the Ancient Andes: Reconstructing Sacrifice on the North Coast of Peru. University of Texas Press, Austin, pp. 29–63.

Häkkänen-Nyholm, H., Weizmann-Henelius, G., Salenius, S., Lindberg, N., Repo-Tiihonen, E., 2009. Homicides with mutilation of the victim's body. J. Forensic Sci. 54 (4), 933–937.

Hare, E.H., Walter, S.D., 1978. Seasonal variation in admission of pyschatric patients and its relation to seasonal variation in their births. J. Epidemiol. Commun. Health 32, 47–52.

Holmes, D., 2017. Psychology and dismemberment. In: Black, S., Rutty, G., Hainsworth, S., Thomson, F. (Eds.), Criminal Dismemberment. Forensic and Investigation Analysis. CRC Press, Boca Raton, pp. 27–39.

JMP, 1989–2016. Version 13.0. SAS Institute Inc, Cary, NC.

Konopka, T., Bolechała, F., Strona, M., Kopacz, P., 2016. Homicides with corpse dismemberment in the material collected by the Department of Forensic Medicine, Krakow, Poland. ArchiwumMedycynySadowej I Kryminologii 66 (4), 220–234.

Konopka, T., Strona, M., Bolechała, F., Kunz, J., 2007. Corpse dismemberment in the material collected by the department of forensic medicine, Cracow, Poland. Legal Med. 9, 1–13.

Labuschange, G., 2004. Features and investigative implications of muti murder in South Africa. J. Invest. Psychol. Offend. Profil. 1, 191–206.

López, A.M.G., Umaña, A.P., 2007. Who is missing? Problems in the application of forensic archaeology and anthropology in Colombia's conflict. In: Ferllini (Ed.), Forensic Archaeology and Human Rights Violations. Charles C Thomas, Springfield, pp. 170–204.

Mellor, L., 2016. Mincing words: refining the language and interpretation of mutilation. In: Mellor, L., Aggrawal, A., Hickey, E.W. (Eds.), UnderstandingNecrophilia: A Global Multidisciplinary Perspective. Cognella, San Diego, CA, pp. 25–39.

Morcillo-Méndez, M.D., Campos, I.Y., 2012. Dismemberment: cause of death in the Colombian armed conflict. Torture 22 (Suppl. 1), 5–13.

National Academy of Science Committee on Identifying the Needs of the Forensic Sciences Community, National Research Council, 2009. Strengthening Forensic Science in the United States: A Path Forward. National Academies Press, Washington, D.C.

Pachar Lucio, J.V., 2015. La investigaciónpericialforense de los cuerposmutilados. Revista Ciencias Forenses de Honduras 1 (2), 20–33.

Persaud, R., Häkkänen-Nyholm H., 2012. The psychology of corpse dismemberment. The motivation behind the most grotesque crimes. The Blog. Huffington Post. Available from: http://www.huffingtonpost.co.uk/dr-raj-persaud/the-psychology-of-corpse-dismemberment_b_1577919.html (accessed 17/02/2018.).

Püschel, K., Koops, E., 1987. Dismemberment and mutilation. Archiv fur Kriminologie 180 (1–2), 28–40.

Quatrehomme, G., 2007. A strange case of dismemberment. In: Brickley, M.B., Ferllini, R. (Eds.), Forensic Anthropology: Case Studies From Europe. Charles C Thomas, Springfield, pp. 99–119.

Rainwater, C.W., 2015. Three modes of dismemberment: disarticulation around the joints, transection bone via chopping, and transection of bone via sawing. In: Passalacqua, N.V., Rainwater, C.W. (Eds.), Skeletal Trauma Analysis: Case Studies in Context, first ed. John Wiley & Sons, pp. 222–245.

Rajs, J., Lundström, M., Broberg, M., Lidberg, L., Lindquist, O., 1998. Criminal mutilation of the human body in Sweden—A thirty-year medico-legal and forensic psychiatric study. J. Forensic Sci. 43 (3), 563–580.

Salfati, C.G., Park, J., 2007. An analysis of Korean homicide crime-scene actions. J. Inter. Viol. 22 (11), 1448–1470.

Sea, J., Beauregard, E., 2016. Mutilation in Korean homicide: an exploratory study. J. Inter. Viol. 1–15.

Ziemke, E., 1918. Ueber die kriminelleZerstückelung von Leichen und die SicherstellungihrerIdentität. VjsschrgeruchtlMed 56, 270–318.

Index

Note: Page numbers followed by "f" and "t" refer to figures and tables, respectively.

CPI Antony Rowe
Eastbourne, UK
May 27, 2020